Echoes of Coinherence

Echoes of Coinherence

Trinitarian Theology and Science Together

W. ROSS HASTINGS

CASCADE Books • Eugene, Oregon

ECHOES OF COINHERENCE
Trinitarian Theology and Science Together

Copyright © 2017 W. Ross Hastings. All rights reserved. Except for brief quotations in critical publications or reviews, no part of this book may be reproduced in any manner without prior written permission from the publisher. Write: Permissions, Wipf and Stock Publishers, 199 W. 8th Ave., Suite 3, Eugene, OR 97401.

Cascade Books
An Imprint of Wipf and Stock Publishers
199 W. 8th Ave., Suite 3
Eugene, OR 97401

www.wipfandstock.com

PAPERBACK ISBN: 978-1-5326-1684-6
HARDCOVER ISBN: 978-1-4982-4080-2
EBOOK ISBN: 978-1-4982-4079-6

Cataloguing-in-Publication data:

Names: Hastings, Ross, 1956–

Title: Echoes of coinherence : trinitarian theology and science together / W. Ross Hastings.

Description: Eugene, OR: Cascade Books, 2017 | Includes bibliographical references and index.

Identifiers: ISBN 978-1-5326-1684-6 (paperback) | ISBN 978-1-4982-4080-2 (hardcover) | ISBN 978-1-4982-4079-6 (ebook)

Subjects: LCSH: Religion and science | Trinity—Criticism, interpretation, etc.

Classification: BL240.3 H367 2017 (paperback) | BL240.3 (ebook)

Manufactured in the U.S.A.   09/15/17

Dedicated to my father-in-law, Everett Bligh,
My most faithful reader and encourager

Contents

Acknowledgments | ix

Introducing the Relationship between Theology and Science | 1

Chapter 1
Communicating Coinherence: Aims, Meaning, and Scope | 16

Chapter 2
Coinherence in the Theology/Science Tradition | 37

Chapter 3
The Coinherent *History* of Ideas | 60

Chapter 4
The Coinherent *Epistemologies* of Theology and Science | 95

Chapter 5
The Coinherent *Ontologies* of Theology and Science: The Being of God and the Being of Creation, Part One | 122

Chapter 6
The Coinherent *Ontologies* of Theology and Science: The Being of God and the Being of Creation, Part Two | 142

Chapter 7
The Coinherent *Ontologies* of Theology and Science: Humanity in the Image of God as *Intelligent, Personal and Relational, and Vocationally Significant* | 169

Chapter 8
Trinitarian Theology as the "Theory of Everything" and Its Practice: *Bringing Epistemology and Ontology Together* | 203

Bibliography | 225
Name/Subject Index | 241

Acknowledgments

I AM DEEPLY GRATEFUL for the community with whom I have interacted in the making of this book. In some ways the journey towards this book began during my first career in chemistry research and teaching. I am grateful to my undergraduate professors of chemistry at the University of Zimbabwe (organic chemist Dr. Williams, in particular) and the University of the Witwatersrand in Johannesburg (Drs. Michael, Staskun, Colville, Gerrans, Howard, Orchard, Moelwyn-Hughes), for imparting to me the rigors of the scientific process as well as the love of chemistry. The inspiration of classmate, the now Professor Helder Marques was considerable also. I am grateful also to Professor M. C. Baird, my PhD supervisor in the Queen's University, Kingston, Ontario, who sharpened these critical and analytical skills by giving me the opportunity to carry out research in the area of organometallic chemistry and catalysis. The journey theologically speaking has been led and inspired by Professor Alan Torrance at St Andrews, most recently through numerous chats and hospitality extended by his wife Margaret during our sabbatical at St Andrews in the fall of 2016. Conversations with Professors Tom Wright in St Andrews, who gave generously of his time, were also hugely helpful, as were times spent with Professors Malcolm Jeeves, Andrew Torrance, Steve Holmes, and Oliver Crisp, as well as seminars in the Templeton funded science / analytic theology seminars at St. Mary's. The formative influence of the community of scholars at Regent College across the disciplines has been significant for me. I am particularly indebted for inspiration and insights gained in this particular project from Iain Provan, Bruce Hindmarsh, Craig Gay, Edwin Hui, Iwan Russell-Jones, Paul Spilsbury, Yonghua Ge, and Jens Zimmermann. The inspiration of Professor Emeritus James Houston has been significant also, as well as that of our president, Jeff Greenman. The contribution made to my knowledge by our brilliant students at Regent has been inestimable also, and in particular in the theology and science classes. My colleague in the Templeton Grant, Ashley Moyse, has stimulated my thinking in significant ways also.

I am deeply grateful for the generosity of Jimmy and Janet Chee and their family in their endowment of the Chair of Theology and Pastoral Theology which I occupy at Regent and for their personal encouragement in this project. I am equally grateful for the generous grant of the John Templeton Foundation which has contributed to my funding for this project. Research funds from Regent College also facilitated my sabbatical in my native Scotland where the book was written. This reminds me that there were many people in that sabbatical experience whose kindness and hospitality made it so memorable. David and Michelle and Lucy (especially) Redfern were so hospitable, as was our landlord, Chris Wood. The Great British Bake-Off on Wednesday nights was the relief and refreshment needed in an intense writing program! Margie McKerrow, Donnacha and Shallini, George and Marion Paton, Willie and Ina Stewart were so kind to Tammy and me. Which brings me to an expression of thanks which is always inadequate, to my dear wife, Tammy, for all her prayers, emotional support, and rich and joyful companionship on numerous walks and bus rides around the beautiful countryside of Fife. I am thankful also to my children and their spouses and grandchildren who made sacrifices to allow us to be away for so long.

I am grateful for the excellent work of the editorial team at Wipf and Stock, Karl Coppock, Robin Parry, Ian Creeger, and Jim Tedrick. The editorial assistance of Jordan Fannin at an earlier stage of the manuscript is also appreciated. Last, but not least, I am very grateful to my research assistants at Regent, Meredith Cochran and Gillian Chu who have worked diligently and sacrificially in their research and in their formatting and proofreading of this book.

This publication was made possible through the support of a grant from the John Templeton Foundation. The opinions expressed in this publication are those of the author and do not necessarily reflect the views of the John Templeton Foundation.

Introducing the Relationship between Theology and Science

I HAVE FOUND OVER the years of playing the occasional golf game with people I don't know, that it is best to try to keep my vocation as a pastor or professor of theology a secret. On one occasion on Burnaby Mountain, in the Vancouver area, one chap I was joined with swore like a trooper all the way through the first nine holes, which he played abominably. A blue hue followed him everywhere he played a shot. At the tenth, he found himself under a tree, swung with full abandon and wrapped his shaft around a branch. After swears and cusses at the highest level yet, he turned to me, and I kid you not, in his next breath asked me, "So what do you do for a living?" On revealing that I was a pastor, he said, "No wonder my golf game is so bad! I've been cursed for swearing in front of a pastor!" I told him that I played a lot of rugby and was used to this kind of language, and that it was really a matter between him and God anyway. He was not much put at ease. When I told him that I have a PhD in chemistry, and that my first career was in science teaching, he looked utterly bewildered, and he said what is almost always said to me in this situation, "How do you put those two things together?" That is the question I want to try to answer in this book.

The importance of the topic of the relationship between Christianity and science cannot be overestimated. Contemporary theologians have borne witness to this, claiming that "the major challenges for Christian theology in the twenty-first century remain in two areas: in the engagement with the sciences and in the encounter between religions,"[1] and again, "a wise constructive rapprochement between faith and science is one of the world's urgent needs, and this need will only intensify as the global era raises a host of ethical issues."[2] It is my hope that this book will be a further voice toward

---

1. Amos Yong, in his evaluation of the work of John Polkinghorne in "From Quantum Mechanics."

2. Giberson and Collins, *Language*, front cover tribute to the BioLogos Foundation

overcoming the warfare model and that it will make a contribution toward just such a constructive rapprochement.

The fact that great progress has been made toward the integration of Christianity and modern science by people such as John Polkinghorne, T. F. Torrance, Francis Collins, and a host of others has not reached the realm of the church for the most part, let alone the wider culture. If they are even vaguely aware of this work, Christians can sometimes simply take comfort that smart minds have found solutions and are content to rest there. However, the attendant risk is that this attitude can be coupled with an apathy toward the discovery of the riches of God's good creation as it is being discovered through science. This falls short of the curiosity and wonder about creation, and then its stewardship, that are what make human persons human. The plague of apathy runs deeper, for even people who possess science expertise and are employed in science careers can neglect this curiosity and wonder. I must confess that this is sadly true of certain stages of my own studies and career in the sciences. It easily became just a job, or a driven pursuit of success measured by publications. By contrast, my father, who had scant knowledge of science, having left school at fourteen years of age in Scotland because there was no money to pursue further education, showed greater curiosity and wonder as he poured over his monthly *National Geographic* than I did in my pursuit of science degrees. What prevents the inquisitive pursuit of the knowledge of creation in adulthood, something naturally present in children, is perhaps the lack of a framework within which to house the knowledge areas of science and theology—one that is wide and profound enough to truly be inclusive of the richness of the disciplines of theology and science.

The framework offering the greatest promise, I argue, would be a framework for the integration of the knowledge and practice of theology and science based in the theological doctrine of coinherence. Much more will be explained in the chapters ahead concerning what may appear to be an obscure concept. By way of introduction, we are speaking specifically of a coinherence model grounded in the coinherence of the created human and the Divine nature of the one person of Jesus Christ (that is, the incarnation), which, along with the doctrine of creation through Christ, is the very basis for the link between God (theology) and creation (science). We are speaking also of the coinherence of the three persons in the one God (that is, the Trinity). In its theological context, the doctrine of coinherence denotes the mutual indwelling of two or more entities with preservation of the identity of each entity. Each holds the other, each donates their being to the other.

---

by Os Guinness.

Introducing the Relationship between Theology and Science 3

Each is in the other as far as their *being* is concerned, and with respect to *doing*, each participates in the acts of the other. Each is therefore mutually internal to the other, such that each is being enriched by the other, while at the same time, each maintains its own irreducible identity.

Coinherence of the Divine and human natures in the one person of the Son of God, Jesus Christ, means that each of the natures is in the other, though in this case, there is an asymmetry by which the Divine nature assumed the human nature. Coinherence of the persons of the Trinity—the three *hypostases* (persons) in the one *ousia* (essence of the Godhead)—is the only fully true case of coinherence, whereby it is only in the Divine mystery of the Trinity that each person is truly a person by means of the relations of each to the other, that is, each is mutually internal to the other, and yet each has irreducible identity as Father, Son, and Holy Spirit. Persons in the Trinity are generally spoken of as "persons-in-relation" in the Trinity on the Eastern account of the Trinity and as "relations-as-persons" in the Western account;[3] however, in both accounts, there is a fundamental relationality that defines the Godhead. Coinherence can also be extended by way of analogy to include human persons, as persons-in-relation made in the *image* of the triune God. There are dangers inherent in analogies made in too facile a manner, and the question of "*how* one moves from talking about the Triune being of God to human being is decisively important,"[4] as Alistair McFadyen has pointed out. Protecting the transcendence of God is all important, clearly. Though what is meant by "persons" in the Trinity is not exactly the same as what we mean by the term "persons" for humans (thus we say the meanings are not univocal), there is evidence in the Christian theological tradition, that the term "person" used of humans has its heritage in the patristic christological and Trinitarian dialogues,[5] and therefore

---

3. Miroslav Volf observes this distinction between the descriptions of Western theologian, the then Cardinal Ratzinger, and Eastern Orthodox theologian John Zizioulas, in Volf, *After Our Likeness*.

4. McFadyen, "Trinity," 10–18, emphasis added. See also McFadyen, *Call to Personhood*.

5. For instance, see O'Donovan, *Resurrection*, 238. "Christian thinkers of the patristic period, in the course of their debates about the Trinity and the person of Christ, brought the term 'person' into theological, and eventually into philosophical, currency in order to escape from an impasse created by classical patterns of thought about human individuality. They had inherited from the ancient world the conception that individuality resided in 'reason' (*nous*) or 'soul' (*psyche*). But when these genetic categories were applied to the individuality of Christ, they led to a range of unthinkable options: either Christ, by virtue of being both God and man, was two individuals; or, being one individual, he did not have all the attributes of humanity and divinity; or (closest to the classical world) the highest attributes in man were anyway divine. Their solution to the impasse was to draw the sharp distinction between the concepts of 'person' and 'nature'

carries meaning from this source. This analogy is ultimately grounded in the personhood of the human-divine person of Christ.[6] A fuller discussion of this "analogy of relations" (*analogia relationis*) will come in a later chapter. I will also offer evidence that the concept of coinherence can by analogy also be used of creation as *trace* rather than image, with its particularity-in-relationality. I will contend that coinherence can and must also be used of the human world of ideas, and specifically therefore of how theology and science relate. Each is in the other and yet each is its own entity, its own discipline, with its own appropriate guild and set of criteria. With reference to the incarnation, I will suggest that theology and science are in an asymmetrically coinherent relationship.

---

famously maintained in the Chalcedonian definition. In speaking of Christ as 'one person in two natures' the Council of Chalcedon used the term 'person' (*hypostasis*) to represent the non-generic principle of individual existence, and 'nature' to represent the complex of attributes, divine or human, which constitute the generic distinctness of divinity and humanity. Through the influence of Boethius' Fifth Tractate upon philosophers this conception became generalized from the unique person of Christ to all persons. Thus the human individual was conceived not merely as a concretization of his human attributes, but as a bearer of them: he is not merely a 'chip off the old block' of total humanity, but *someone who is* human. This perception has its roots in the biblical understanding of individual vocation. Prior to those events which bring our humanity to being, we are called by God: 'Before I formed you in the womb I knew you' (Jer 1:5)."

6. Alan Torrance emphasizes this also when he refers to the "radical and dynamic continuity between the divine and the human that is the event of Christ" (*Persons in Communion*, 209). A key argument for the validity of the modeling of human personhood on Divine personhood is the historical legacy of the term "person" and its meaning. The true legacy of the term "person" is not Western, Cartesian individualism ("I think, therefore, I am"), but the fourth-century trinitarian debates ("I am because you are"), in which it became clear that by sheer Divine grace, human personhood was analogous to Divine trinitarian personhood. Alan Torrance affirms John Zizioulas's inversion of the Western category of substance, with its individualistic connotations, when applied to the concept of the person. Whereas Boethius famously argued, "*persona est substantia individua rationabilis naturae*" (the person is an individual substance with a rational nature), Torrance states that "Zizioulas translates the Latin *substantia* into the Greek *hypostasis* and then introduces a wordplay to make his point." And this is Zizioulas's point: The person is a unique kind of being which has his or her *hypostasis* in *ekstasis*, that is, precisely in its noncircumscribability. The person is a uniquely Christian category, and the West has lost this vision characteristic of patristic (Cappadocian) thought.

Torrance, at the most fundamental level, suggests *person* is to be conceived in such a way that relations are fundamental to their being. When they are conceived in terms of the monadic individualistic categories characteristic of much Western Christianity, the most fundamental feature of their being is lost. Wolfhart Pannenberg has also indicated that the meaning of the term "person" for a human person gained its meaning in Western culture in the context of the articulation of "persons" in God (see Pannenberg, *Basic Questions*, 228–32). We owe this debt actually to the Eastern Fathers, the Cappadocians, whose discoveries were inherited by the West.

It is important to clarify my relative aims in this project on coinherence. I am first seeking to *describe* coinherence *as* a feature of the Divine life, acknowledged widely in the tradition of the church, both in the incarnation and within the Trinity. Second, I am seeking to *support* the further claim that coinherence *can* be seen to have echoes in creation, by way of image in humanity, and trace in the rest of creation. And third, I wish to *propose* that we *may*, because of the first two, predicate coinherence of the disciplines of theology and science. That is, I affirm that coinherence *is* part of the Divine life (an ontological statement), *can* be said to have echoes in creation (a metaphysical statement), and *may* be predicated further as a way to frame these two great disciplines of human knowledge (an epistemological statement). Much more of that later.

It is also important to clarify that a proposal of coinherence between theology and science is not a "mixing" of the disciplines, just as the human and Divine natures of the incarnate Christ are not confused or mixed. Each has its own irreducibly distinct entity as a discipline. It is also crucial to clarify that the proposal of coinherence between theology and science is not to be confused with a concordist view of these disciplines, in which biblical passages are artificially made to be in concord with a particular scientific theory. When theories grow more sophisticated in science and change, this leaves the biblical position adopted to account for the theories in serious jeopardy, further damaging the credibility of Christianity. Rather, a coinherent relationship has a dynamic nature, leaving room for growth in understanding in each. It simply asserts that there is a place for each discipline in the other. The proposal of coinherence between theology and science envisions the inter-animation and enhancement of each discipline, gained from insights in each. The assertion that they will coinhere and not contradict *ultimately* is an assertion of faith, though as such, for reasons which will follow, warranted faith.

The need for conciliation between Christianity and science arises first out of perceived differences in how we *know* what we know in each case. The challenges for many people in Western culture with its cherished Enlightenment dualisms is that these disciplines are assumed to operate in different realms of knowing. Science is sometimes deemed to be the realm of objective thinking based on hard evidence, while religion is assumed to be the subjective realm, along with values and the arts. On this account, only science, for it deals in facts, can be present in the public square. Religion, because it deals with feelings and values and wishes, belongs in the private realm. These unfortunate assumptions have bifurcated and impoverished the intellectual life of Western humanity, thereby de-humanizing it.

British scientist and novelist C. P. Snow exposed this problem for Modernity as far back as 1959, when in his Cambridge Senate House address (now published as *The Two Cultures and the Scientific Revolution*) he declared that Western intellectual life was split into the titular two cultures of the sciences and the humanities and that this was a serious obstacle to solving the world's problems. The burden of his address then seems to have been the lack of *scientific* knowledge within a British culture which at that point favored the arts. Applying this to the contemporary Christian church in the West has some real traction. The scandal of the Evangelical mind has been well reported in general, and specifically with respect to knowledge of science.[7] Though it was aimed at the many arts-oriented folk of his time, Snow's rebuke might justly be applied to those contemporary evangelical Christians alarmed by the findings of astronomical and biological science in particular. The people of Britain in Snow's time could not give definitions of "the Second Law of Thermodynamics," let alone "mass, or acceleration, which is the scientific equivalent of saying, *Can you read?*" The "great edifice of modern physics" was going up, said Snow, "and the majority of the cleverest people in the western world" had "about as much insight into it as their neolithic ancestors would have had."[8]

But if the primary barrel of the gun of Snow's diatribe had to do with a scientific deficit, in today's very technological Western societies, it is possible that it is the second barrel of the arts and theology that needs to be fired more urgently in our times. The brilliant work of Iain McGilchrist[9] provides the critique of modern Western culture that it is demonstrating symptoms on a large scale that result from the dominance of the left hemisphere of the brain such that the right hemisphere is underdeveloped and underused. The right hemisphere, the "Master" which governs metaphor, music, imagination, poetry and *faith*, is intended to take the lead, while the left hemisphere, which crunches the numbers and facilitates the details, is designed to back it up (hence, the "Emissary"). The result of left brain or Emissary dominance over the right brain Master in Western technological culture, according to McGilchrist, has the same effect in a culture as when the bean counters take over in business. For McGilchrist, the larger purpose of being human—living into the good, the true, and the beautiful—is thus sacrificed for bean counting.

---

7. For a helpful interrogation of this scandal, see Noll, *Scandal*, 177–210.

8. Snow, *Two Cultures*, 15.

9. As both a neuro-scientist and a literary critic, McGilchrist has bridged the two-culture divide. See McGilchrist, *Master*.

If McGilchrist is to be believed, then what is at stake in the science-theology divide is the very question of what it means to be human. In Western society the dualism of reason and faith, or fact and value, has served to distance science and Christian theology. This robs science and scientists of the wider context and meaning of their discoveries. One example is the loss of awareness of the particular context of the social and global arena of science. This is the theological context of the doctrine of creation and the cultural mandate of the early chapters of Genesis, involving the stewardship and care of creation. Given that knowledge and care of creation is one of the important dimensions of what it means to be made in the image of God, and therefore to be human, the loss of this perspective is regrettable, diminishing something of the richness of the vocational significance of being a scientist. A loss of the awareness of a God who is both large enough and small enough (the specifically triune God who is both transcendent and immanent) to create and sustain the cosmos while granting to creation and humans a freedom to be derived, in his freedom, and to participate in its own creation, also robs the scientist of a doxological and priestly orientation. The ability of scientists to perceive more than facts, but also the beauty of the creation, from molecule to galaxy, and to create what is beautiful, is also robbed of its wider context.

For the general population, assumptions that science has disproved God or that science is incompatible with Christian faith or the Bible, has no doubt been one factor preventing persons from pursuing relationship with God. This makes this one of the most significant missional issues of our time, one that urges a reasoned yet humble apologetic. Within the church, defenses against the findings of science have not always been helpful, from the time of Copernicus and on into the present, as the chapter on history will show. The imagination has sometimes been stunted, leading to a lack of openness to the grand scale of the universe in terms of time, size and grandeur. This has been to the detriment of the humanity of Christian persons, who could, with a greater openness to science, live more effectively as image-bearing, creation-caring humans.

Beyond denying empirically demonstrated realities in science, the defenses against these have reflected a way of reading Scripture which does not reflect either the science of hermeneutics or the art of nuanced reading that gives attention to genre (like poetry) and historical context. Modern apologetics that reflect a lofty view of reason, as if it can be isolated from faith or interpretive assumptions, are in fact *of* modernity[10] and fail to acknowledge the fullness of human knowledge, which, as we will see, is tacit and

10. Smith, *Introducing Radical Orthodoxy*, 44.

personal. Such an epistemology, which neglects the empirical, runs counter to how knowledge is gained in both theology and science—through critical realism. The assumption of critical realism is that epistemology (knowing) actually reflects something that is really there, that is, being or ontology.

Intrinsic to this approach is the unfortunate attribution of scientific findings to biblical passages that were not written to be scientific textbooks, and went well beyond the intent of the biblical authors. This did not help in overcoming the conflict model of theology and science. The consequence is that followers of the *science* pathway in the bifurcated society Snow referred to could be impoverished in other aspects of their being by a minimum of exposure to the arts and Christian faith. The *arts* deficit in society may also have affected the way in which Scripture was read in the more conservative quarters of the church. Unnuanced readings of the Bible that pay no attention to the literary genre of texts and their historical context led not only to the rejection of evolutionary science, but they diminished the integrated humanity of the reader.

A faith/reason dualism has persisted not just with Christians, but also for those for whom science has become supreme, that is, the followers of natural*ism* and scient*ism* and evolution*ism*—views that simply perpetuate the old dualisms. Less charitable than even acknowledging different realms, for those for whom science is all we *can* know, and is indeed the only way to see the world, religion is viewed to be either just harmless nonsense, or even less charitably, to be oppressive and repressive dogma that must be stamped out. This kind of scientist-ic fundamentalism turns out to be simply a cousin of religious fundamentalism.

The origins of the "two culture split" of Snow, and the dichotomy between the sides of the brain in McGilchrist, can be traced to the movement of the seventeenth to nineteenth centuries known as deism, with seeds in the older but more insidious ancient Epicureanism of the Greeks. Deism is the idea that God created the cosmos, wound it up like a large clock, and is letting it wind down. God is at a distance from creation, transcendent over it but not immanent to it. Many early scientists, even though confessionally Christian, were Deists, including the scientifically brilliant Isaac Newton (1642–1726/7),[11] who rejected the doctrine of the Trinity, thereby robbing him of a way to put the transcendence and immanence of God together. Deism was, however, simply a fresh manifestation of "its older and more rigorous cousin Epicureanism, an elite philosophy in the ancient world which taught that even if the gods exist they are a long way away and never concern themselves with our world, and that our world simply makes itself as it goes

---

11. McGrath, *Science and Religion*, 26–32.

along, evolving under its own steam."[12] N. T. Wright, pointing in the direction of this culprit for the dualism of Modernity, notes how "ancient Epicureanism was a protest against ancient paganism; fifteenth-century Epicureanism was a protest against western mediaeval theology; Enlightenment Epicureanism was a protest against the perceived errors of the ongoing western church."[13]

He alerts us to the fact that this latter Epicurean revival served serious political agendas, including the French Revolution. He comments that even more insidiously, "by kicking God upstairs and insisting that the downstairs world of 'facts' could get on by itself, it paved the way for massive exploitation both of natural resources and of the conquered lands and peoples of the European empires." Wright then asserts unequivocally that the "*split between science and religion is one aspect of a larger split between God and the world, affecting equally the question of faith and public life.*" The roots of the science/theology split can only be understood, he insists, if we "map it on to the much larger split and take into account the other areas where the same problem has taken hold, particularly in the political sphere."[14] It is for this reason that the rhetoric of the new atheists like Peter Atkins and Richard Dawkins regarding science and faith is directed toward keeping "the church out of public life."[15] The scientism of Dawkins really is a fundamentalism grounded in Epicurean deism!

The conflict model pertaining to religion and science continues to be culturally prominent, even though modernism has also been somewhat deconstructed by postmodernism. It has been exacerbated by both these dogmatic atheist scientists, on the one hand, and by fundamentalist Christians and Muslims, who consider science to be a threat to their faith, the Christians in particular seeing the theory of evolution as being in contradiction with their literalistic reading of Genesis 1 and 2. But although this warfare model is culturally influential, as theologian scientist Alister McGrath correctly observes, it is "not seen by historians of science as being particularly reliable or defensible."[16]

Despite this, the need for a more adequate framework for the relationship between Christian theology and science becomes ever more evident. The idea that Christian theology and science might possibly be coinherent is probably counterintuitive within contemporary culture, including that of the church. That they might hold each other, enhance each other, animate

12. Wright, "Wouldn't You Love to Know," 5.
13. Ibid.
14. Ibid.
15. Ibid.
16. McGrath, *Science and Religion*, 1.

each other, and guide each other, seems like wishful thinking on behalf of a few optimistic and fideistic theologians. But this is precisely what I wish to propose, rather than impose, in this book. This is, I realize, a bold and radical proposal. It goes a little beyond what Jonathan Sacks has suggested—that religion and science ought to be a "great partnership," in which "science takes things apart to see how they work, while religion puts things together to see what they mean."[17] It certainly includes both the clear identity of the two disciplines preserved in this statement, as well as the collaborative union implied. But a coinherent view of theology and science goes further. While preserving the irreducible identity of the guilds, we suggest interpenetration and inter-animation of the disciplines, and an underlying and overarching union and telos grounded in the specifically triune God who is *both* one in essence and communion, *and* three in irreducible person. It is a differentiated union grounded in the God who is both Creator and Redeemer, and in the narrative of creation that moves through redemption on to the new creation, and it is grounded in the crucial matter of what it means to be human.

The proposal for a new framework for the relationship between theology and science is offered within the larger, and recent, resurgence of dialogue between the two disciplines. Other scholars have recognized the need for such a framework, noting first that "neither science nor religion can claim to give a total account of reality"—and this despite claims by Dawkins to the notion of "universal Darwinism."[18] New stimuli include (i) awareness that "science and religion are perhaps better thought of as operating at different levels, often reflecting on similar questions, yet answering them in different ways";[19] (ii) awareness that both disciplines are concerned with "making sense of things,"[20] and that in this there are differentiated roles, science tending to answer the "how question" or clarifying mechanism, while theology answers the "why" question or offering meaning";[21] and (iii) awareness in the scientific research community of that community's inability to answer questions concerning broader issues raised by research—primarily those of an ethical nature.[22] These stimuli have, however, provided motivation for a framework in which these dichotomies are not as rigid as suggested here.

---

17. Sacks, *Great Partnership*, 21.

18. McGrath, *Science and Religion*, 2.

19. Ibid. This accords with the mutuality thesis of Alan Padgett as explained in *Science and the Study of God*, xii, 8–12.

20. McGrath, *Science and Religion*, 3.

21. Ibid.

22. Ibid., 3–4.

The coinherence model provides just such a model.[23] It acknowledges that there are distinctions to be made between the disciplines, based on their subject material, for example, and the validity of the guilds,[24] but it presses also for mutuality in the knowledge gained and with respect to meaning, given that *both* come under the rubric of theology, and both involve the work of God as Creator and Redeemer.

The modest aims of my project are to explore this coinherent relationship between the disciplines of science and theology, with attention to how knowledge is obtained, and with respect to resonances that relate to being, or ontology. By claiming epistemological resonances between theology and science (that knowledge is gained in the same way in each), I open up the possibility of exploring further claims, and particularly that a surprising number of features of the modern scientific account of reality fit well with the being of the Creator God of Christian theology—not a monadic God and not the deistic God who has wound up the clock as the great Divine Clockmaker, and sits disinterested above its concerns—but the specifically triune God. The God who is both transcendent and immanent, in the two "hands" of the Trinity[25] which Irenaeus of Lyons, that third-century church father, spoke of: the Son and the Spirit.[26] This is the same God of grace who has revealed himself supremely in the Son who became incarnate and was discovered to be so empirically, through sight and touch and hearing (1 John 1:1); the God of wisdom who in the Word and by the Spirit reveals himself in the written Word and in the creation intelligibly, by image and

23. T. F. Torrance, for example, has rejected a too rigid dichotomy precisely in light of the coinherence of the disciplines. See Torrance, *Christian Frame of Mind*, 24–25.

24. Oliver Crisp's distinction between methodological naturalism and metaphysical naturalism is helpful in differentiation of the two fields of study. He states that it is "not that the scientist should set aside methodological naturalism, only metaphysical naturalism. One can adopt methodological naturalism and still hold metaphysical supernaturalism, as is the case with most scientists who are persons of religious faith. But metaphysical naturalism is inconsistent with orthodox Christian faith; [since] it entails the denial of supernaturalism." Oliver Crisp, "On Original Sin," 254.

25. Irenaeus, *Against Heresies*, IV.20.1; V.6.1.

26. For Wolfhart Pannenberg, for example, the resolution of the tension between the transcendence and immanence of God was found precisely in his triune nature. The Trinity is that which is seen to "clarify the unity and tension between transcendence and immanence." Olson, "Wolfhart Pannenberg," 203. God is the transcendent Father who is present by perichoresis in the Son and the Spirit in the economy. Thus, God's acts in the economy reveal his inner life in the immanent Trinity. As Grenz and Olson have noted, commenting on Pannenberg's work, "His [God's] immanence is obvious . . . the immanent Spirit is what animates creatures in raising them beyond themselves to participate in some measure in the divine life" . . . yet "God is more than the chain of the finite parts of time and space. And the divine life is more than the sum of the lives of finite creatures." Grenz and Olson, *20th-Century*, 194.

by trace; the God of freedom who created contingently, out of love, not necessity, through the agency of the always-going-to-be incarnate Son, so giving rise to a contingent creation that can't be known in advance, but only empirically, only *a posteriori*; the God of freedom who by the agency of the Spirit, provides a gentle providence over creation, yet grants to it its own freedom to be itself and even participate in its own creation; the personal and relational God who has created image-bearing persons-in-relation, as well as relational electrons and a relational cosmos; the God who in his triune harmonious being is beauty, has created a beautiful universe, and has given his image bearers the capacity to experience that beauty.

WHAT IS AT STAKE FOR THEOLOGIANS AND FOR SCIENTISTS

From the perspective of Christian theologians, given that the triune nature of God is crucial and central to Christian theology, it would be somewhat disconcerting if there were no signs of the Trinity in creation, and in science. There is, of course, a need for discernment here. The approach to seeing vestiges of the Trinity in humanity and creation needs to be nuanced in two important ways. First, the search must begin with the revealed God, and not with the vestiges. It should be grounded in a knowledge of the Trinity as revealed in the personal and biblical revelation of God in Christ, by the Spirit. Augustine provides justification for our approach in his quest for the Trinitarian image of God in humanity in the second half of *De Trinitate*, only because it is clear that he first had a knowledge of the Trinity from Scripture.[27] Bonaventure also adds credibility to this approach. He looks for phenomenal categories in God's "book of creation" with categories defined by who we know God to be by revelation from the book of Scripture, categories like greatness, magnitude, beauty, activity, plenitude and order, in order to explain how these basic phenomenological categories reveal God, both subjectively in the act of our knowing them and objectively in their self-manifestation" which, significantly for our project, Michael Hanby calls "itself a sort of *vestigia trinitatis*."[28] Second, the signs of the Trinity or "intimations of divinity" will not be expected to be obvious, as if there are facile vestiges everywhere. Rather they will be a "pale reflection of the nature of the Creator," to use the words of John Polkinghorne, quantum physicist and priest, who will be one of our primary conversation partners. He states, "Just

---

27. Augustine, *De Trinitate*, I.4. Karl Barth acknowledges a number of theologians in the tradition who followed Augustine's example in this regard (*CD* I/1, 340).

28. Hanby, *No God, No Science*, 89.

as God does not write messages on the clouds for all to read, so the universe will not be found to be full of items stamped 'Made by God.' Divine revelation is more subtle than that." He goes on to say, "What might be expected is that there are certain aspects to the history and nature of the universe as known to science, but not explained by it, which seem too remarkable to be treated simply as inexplicable brute facts and which can become satisfyingly intelligible when viewed in the light of theological insight."[29] In chapter 1, we will visit the work of a number of theologian scientists who have noticed the need to bring together the coinherence of the Trinity and science.

The legitimacy and value of a Trinitarian coinherence model for holding theology and science together will be supported also by key theologian of science T. F. Torrance,[30] whose work we will consider in depth. Torrance, though not a scientist by training, spent twenty years studying science, won the Templeton prize in theology and science, and not only was (remarkably) awarded an honorary doctorate at Heriot-Watt University in Edinburgh, but compared by the awarding principal to Einstein.[31] He observed the scientific method of Einstein closely and noted the methodology of science as well as the levels and layers of meaning in science.[32] Sir Bernard Lovell, the works of Maxwell, and Michael Polanyi also had a significant impact on his thought and method. It is most interesting that the American physicist Jim Neidhardt approvingly notices the coinherent approach in Torrance's work. In *Ground and Grammar of Theology*, Torrance speaks of how the Divine and human natures of the incarnate Christ "interpenetrate each other without the integrity of either being damaged by the other."[33] Neidhardt, in response to these words, applies this to the disciplines of theology and science, giving what I believe to be the most articulate definition of coinherence I have seen: "The word indicates a sort of dynamic, mutual containing, or mutual involution, of realities which is often spoken of as a *coinherence* (the root *chora* is also present in choreography, which describes the orchestration of dancers, indicating the root's dynamic aspects). Such a dynamic

---

29. Polkinghorne, "Trinity and Scientific Reality," in *Blackwell Companion*, 523.

30. The relationship between coinherence or perichoresis in the incarnation, then by extension to persons of the Trinity, and then on to concepts in science (modern particle theory and quantum theory), as well as the relationship between the disciplines, is implicit in Torrance's *Ground and Grammar*, 174–78. Physicist Jim Neidhardt, who writes the introduction to *The Christian Frame of Mind*, makes the connection explicit with respect to the coinherence of the disciplines of theology and science in Torrance. Neidhardt, *Christian Frame*, xl.

31. For details of this event, see Myk Habets, *Theology in Transposition*, 22.

32. T. F. Torrance, "Stratification of Truth," in *Reality and Scientific Theology*, 131–59.

33. T. F. Torrance, *Ground and Grammar*, 172.

coinherence between theology and science would preserve the integrity of both disciplines while healing the breach that has opened up between them."[34] For a very "confused culture" that accepts "the legitimacy of both astrology and the findings of satellite-based astronomy," Neidhardt believes that a "deeper, clarified understanding of the *perichoresis* between theology and natural science could have a substantial healing impact upon our scientific-technological society, for," he states, "such a refined understanding would restore the sense of purpose and moral guidance our civilization lacks."[35] This does not understate what is at stake in this matter.

Having introduced the preliminary ideas for a framework for holding together theology and science in a coinherent way, and what is at stake in this, we now shift to looking at this from the perspective of science.

From the perspective of the scientist there is an awareness that the thirst for a comprehensive understanding of the universe cannot be quenched by science alone. There is present also in scientists the deep desire to gain understanding, accompanied by an acknowledgment of the limits of scientific inquiry. Contemporary science is actually in our time "opening up religious questions, rather than closing them down, or declaring them to be meaningless."[36] As Polkinghorne has indicated, it is being increasingly recognized that natural science can "throw up questions that point beyond itself and transcend its power to answer."[37] The questions of contemporary science are in fact the same as those of ancient religious thinkers, a reality that has been recognized by astronomer Robert Jastrow:

> It seems as though science will never be able to raise the curtain on the mystery of creation. For the scientist who has lived by his faith in the power of reason, the story ends like a bad dream. He has scaled the mountains of ignorance; he is about to conquer the highest peaks; as he pulls himself over the final rock, he is greeted by a band of theologians who have been sitting there for centuries.[38]

Throughout this book, therefore, the desire of scientists and philosophers of science for a greater sense of integration and holism will be kept uppermost as we search for evidences of coinherence in reality and in how it is perceived by us. This book represents years of theological reflection

---

34. Neidhardt, introduction to *Christian Frame of Mind*, xl.
35. Ibid.
36. McGrath, *Science and Religion*, 1.
37. Polkinghorne, *Science and Creation*, 23.
38. Jastrow, *God and the Astronomers*, 115–16.

back on the science I was once fully engaged in, and was in some measure formed by, with a desire to bring together what God has already joined. My study of God as Trinity in essence and Trinitarian in his works of creating and reconciling the universe have, together, cried out for a more satisfyingly interdisciplinary account of its resonances in creation and how human beings understand it. The account that follows will speak to and learn from previous reflections, but will suggest that the presence of coinherent correspondences provide a provocative and holistic point of departure that promises to invigorate this persisting and much-needed discussion.

Two caveats may be in order. First, to reiterate what has already been stated, this study will not encourage an overly facile form of vigilant Trinitarianism that looks for images of the Trinity everywhere, in three-leaf clovers, in water as liquid, ice or steam, in Russian dolls that fit the one within the other, and so on. All analogies for the Trinity are inadequate and in some cases they are either modalist or tritheistic, and therefore, heretical. However, I will suggest that there are *conceptual* resonances of the Trinity in creation, mediated by the incarnation. If the creation bears the marks of its Creator (and its incarnate Redeemer), this will not be a surprising claim. However, this study exists to focus our attention on what kind of claim this is, and what the resonances of this claim are for the study undertaken *both* by scientists and theologians.

The second caveat guiding this study and those who read it must be one of scope: this book is not and cannot hope to be an exhaustive account of the interface between Christian theology and science—a subject of ever-growing import as well as ever-expanding reach. Even to speak of science as one discipline, interacting with theology, seems a bold proposition given the diversity of sciences and how each of these can be thought of as having a second-order theology associated with it. Each of the sciences has its own theology and theological interaction to do. Rather, my modest aim is to provide a theological framework for science as we know it, including the best theories we have. Accordingly, I hope to offer a framework big enough to hold both disciplines—one that accounts for epistemological and ontological resonances between God, his creation, and science, and in such a way that preserves the primacy of theology as the "queen of sciences" (a metaphor used since medieval times to describe theology as the overarching discipline which held together and governed all knowledge in all other fields of study), but also proposes the coinherence of theology and science without violating the integrity of either discipline.

My rather audacious hope is that this work may help scientists to value their work and to contextualize their science within a broader creative and even doxological framework, thus helping them and all humans to pursue their vocations in more satisfying and humanizing ways.

Chapter 1

Communicating Coinherence
Aims, Meaning, and Scope

THE AIMS: COMMUNICATING COINHERENCE

THERE ARE THREE PRIMARY goals in our study. The *first* is to *describe* and offer explanation of the coinherence concept from the incarnation and the Trinity. The *second* is to *support* and clarify claims of the legitimacy (and limits) of the application of coinherence, by way of analogy, to humanity and creation. Scripture and the tradition speak of humans as the *image* of God, and the tradition, building on biblical inferences, speaks of the nonhuman creation as containing *traces* of the triune God. This will lead us to demonstrate various resonances between the nature of God as Trinity, Trinitarian theology, and various aspects of creation as discovered by science. The *third* goal of the book builds on these resonances between Trinitarian theology and science by suggesting that they may *as disciplines* be considered to be coinherent.

The methodology shaping the second and third objectives borrows from Mark Achtemeier's suggestion that an appropriate way to study theology and science is to consider first the history of ideas in the two disciplines, then epistemology (how we know) and then ontology (being).[1] Thus we will first look in chapter 3 at the surprisingly intertwined nature of the history of the development of science within the history of Christian theology. Then

---

1. Achtemeier, "Natural Science and Christian Faith," 269–302.

we will briefly explain resonances arising from this comparison that relate to knowing (epistemological) and then to being (ontological), that is, how the being and acts of the triune God are reflected in an analogous way as "image" and "trace" in created humanity and created nonhuman reality. We will also suggest that even the disciplines of theology and science are—by their historical, epistemological and ontological coinherence—themselves a trace of the Trinity.

Under the heading of *knowing*, we will explore the epistemological coinherence of Christian theology and science, showing marked similarities between how knowledge is arrived at in each field, an unsurprising phenomenon considering, hopefully, that both scientists and theologians are human! The basis for this commonality, I will argue, is the model of *critical realism* as the way of doing knowledge. Briefly, the way of knowing in both disciplines is more *a posteriori* than *a priori*. That is, knowing in both science and theology is a consequence of an empirical process in which the results may be predicted on the basis of what is already known, but never known with any degree of certainty until the experimental data are in. It is the idea of warranted belief, as opposed to that of logical positivism, the philosophical school of thought whose central thesis is verificationism—a theory of knowledge which insists that only statements that are verifiable through empirical observation are cognitively meaningful. Critical realism takes the empirical very seriously but is not as enamoured with the degree of certainty, the objectivity of the knower, and the power of human reason, expressed in positivism. Critical realism expresses more modest aims in a more humble manner. It is cognizant of the subjectivity of the knower; it answers questions like, what best explains the data and what is internally consistent; and it includes categories for knowing that transcend reason, while not contradicting it, such as tacit or personal knowledge. And it does not privilege scientific knowledge above other forms of knowledge, such as Christian theology.

On this account, in both theology and science, the only way we can know follows the Augustinian dictum, "faith seeking understanding" and crucially, the knowing of human persons as the knowing of loving persons. It may be easier for some readers to see how knowing in science can be described by critical realism, but not so much theology. After all, theological tenets such as the resurrection of Jesus from the dead cannot be experimented with and are not therefore reproducible. However, this does not negate the reality that Christianity is a historical faith, one in which good historical research may verify the real history contained in the Bible and especially that concerning the life and death and resurrection of Jesus of Nazareth, as attested by many witnesses and a community over many centuries. Polkinghorne suggests that there are reasons that "the defence of critical realism is a more subtle matter in theology than in science" but nevertheless affirms "there to be a cousinly relationship between the way in which theology and science each pursue truth within the proper domains of their interpreted experience. Critical realism is a concept applicable to both, not because there is some kind of entailment from method in one to method in the other—for the differences in their subject material preclude so simple a connection—but because the idea is deep enough to encompass the character of both these forms of the human search for truthful understanding."[2] In chapter 4, as we develop this theme of coinherent epistemology, while encroaching at the same time into ontology, we will also consider the *intelligibility* of God through the *Logos* and his revelation of himself in creation, and the intelligence of his image bearers who have the capacity by grace to receive it. We will also consider the *beauty* in the triune God, the Supreme Harmony of All, and this beauty as portrayed in his act of creation, as well as the human capacity by grace, first to perceive it—all the way from sunsets to organic molecules—and then, second, to express beauty through science and the arts. The source of this human capacity to discover truth and to know God, as it is understood within different traditions (the *analogia entis* and the *analogia adventus/fidei*) will be discussed also. We will then, in chapters 5–7, explore, under the heading of being, the ontological aspects of the Trinity and creation and science. That is we will investigate resonances between God and creation related to the various aspects of the life and attributes of God as triune. We will explore the profound *relationality* of the Trinity (persons in relation) and therefore of creation, from humans (persons in relation) to atoms to quantum particles; we will explore the *freedom* of God, and that of humans and creation in participation with him; we will explore the *goodness* in both God and in his creation which is related to *intelligibility* (revisited from an ontological perspective) which permits the ordered study of science; we will explore the *immensity-with-immanence* of God, or the vastness and yet particularity, of the triune God and his creation; we will explore the reality of *agency* in the Trinity, in humans, and in every particle of creation; we will explore the *fecundity* or fruitfulness in God and therefore in his creation with its capacity for complexification; and we will explore the mutuality and particularity in God and creation. All of these resonances we have spoken of create an ethos for the mutuality of theology and creation and have profound implications for human vocation and also for worship, which we will also explore in chapter 7.

---

2. Polkinghorne, *Quantum Physics and Theology*, 14, 15.

The *third* goal of the book will thus be accomplished by building on these resonances between Trinitarian theology and science by suggesting that they may *as disciplines* be considered to be coinherent. This idea will crystallize in chapters 5–7 and be brought to a head in chapter 8. Coinherence suggests profound overlap, while giving freedom for each to conduct its business in ways that are distinctive and particular to each discipline. While preserving the idea of the supremacy of first-order creedal theology (God as Creator), science contributes by enriching our *understanding* of first-order theology. The final authority in theology is always that of the Word of God as properly interpreted. The tradition of the church, reason and experience also play a role in the discovery of truth, and it is in the latter two that the philosophy of science and science play a role. Another way to see this, beyond this Wesleyan quadrilateral, is to say that science contributes to the development of a second-order theology (for example, the issue of *how* God creates), thus making theology encyclopedic, in the sense that *theology overall must consider and respond to all reality* as it may be found in every realm of human scholarship. This posture toward science rests in the providence of God, and in the warranted belief that his revelation in Scripture and what is discovered through interaction with creation (science) cannot contradict. The postulate concerning the coinherence of theology and science is made reasonable in light of the understanding that the one God is the author of both, in Christ, by the Spirit, and in light of the oneness of his two primary means of revelation—God's two books, the Bible and the creation.

Thus one can see that by way of coinherence, Snow's two-culture divide may be healed, and the brain compartmental dominance of McGilchrist's Emissary made subservient once again to the Master. A classic expression of this dissonance is heard in Julian Huxley's view that with the discovery of evolution, "there is neither need or room for the supernatural."[3] This is unacceptable today even to postmodern philosophers without any religious faith. His proposal of a secular religion, one without revelation, is problematic, because in the history of Jesus Christ there simply is . . . empirically attested revelation. In the remainder of this chapter, the context within which coinherence is proposed is described. That is, coinherence will be considered over against various other ways in which theology and science have typically been envisioned. The concept of coinherence will then be introduced, by a preliminary consideration of its *meaning and scope*.

---

3. Huxley, "Evolutionary Vision," 252–53.

A WINDOW OF COINHERENCE: ITS CONTEXT

The claim to a relationship between theology and science that is one of coinherence moves well beyond any of the four classical models which have typically been proposed. These are conflict, independence, dialogue, and integration.[4] Coinherence will, of course, obviously stand in contradiction of the conflict model and even of that of the more respectful biologist Stephen Jay Gould, who advocated that science and faith should occupy separate "non-overlapping magisteria." There is at least in Gould an acknowledgment of theology as a magisterium. He rightly gives freedom to each discipline in its *modus operandi*. He is worth quoting at some length here:

> To say it for all my colleagues and for the umpteenth million time (from college bull sessions to learned treatises): science simply cannot (by its legitimate methods) adjudicate the issue of God's possible superintendence of nature. We neither affirm nor deny it; we simply can't comment on it as scientists. If some of our crowd have made untoward statements claiming that Darwinism disproves God, then I will find Mrs. McInerney and have their knuckles rapped for it (as long as she can equally treat those members of our crowd who have argued that Darwinism must be God's method of action). Science can work only with naturalistic explanations; it can neither affirm nor deny other types of actors (like God) in other spheres (the moral realm, for example).

This is, on Gould's part, a clear demarcation of the boundaries between science and theology, something a coinherent view would also affirm. However, it denies any possibility of mutuality of content, or of the ways of knowing that content. In the same vein, Gould appeals to the empirics of theist and atheist adherents to the particular science of evolution:

> Forget philosophy for a moment; the simple empirics of the past hundred years should suffice. . . . Move on another 50 years to the two greatest evolutionists of our generation: G. G. Simpson was a humanist agnostic. Theodosius Dobzhansky a believing Russian Orthodox. Either half my colleagues are enormously stupid, or else the science of Darwinism is fully compatible with conventional religious beliefs—and equally compatible with atheism, thus proving that the two great realms of nature's factuality and the source of human morality do not strongly overlap.[5]

---

4. Barbour, *Religion in an Age of Science*.
5. Gould, "Impeaching a Self-Appointed Judge," 118.

While acknowledging the magisterial nature of Christian theology, Gould in fact expresses sentiments that betray his compliance to the "science as fact and theology as faith" dichotomy we have spoken of. This removes the possibility of any overlapping of the disciplines. It affirms particularity of the guilds but denies any mutuality. Though it seems like a peaceful route to take, I am not quite as content as he to avoid the overlapping. There are overlapping realities and methodologies and limits to knowledge, within good theology and good science. In a way that counters the conflict and the non-overlapping approach, this book hopes to offer a reasoned defense for the mutuality between Christian theology and science, while preserving their irreducible identity as disciplines. This defense is undertaken with a view toward integration of the Christian mind, and the human person. Coinherence gives color to integration, however, and it subverts the assumption that theology and science are not already one. This may also assist toward restoring the credibility of thoughtful Christianity in the public square. This, it is hoped, may inspire more Christians toward pursuing careers in science, and to do so with fresh and fearless engagement. It will perhaps serve also as integrative for scientists who are Christian but have lived with a dualism between what they do on Sunday and what they do Monday to Friday. It will be an encouragement to see their work, in light of the mandate given by the Creator in Genesis 1–2 to humans to care for creation and steward it for him, to see their work as priestly and as a valuable living out of what it means to be human image bearers.

The somewhat ironic reality is that in many of the greatest forbears of the especially Reformed wing of evangelical Christianity, the vast chasm between Christian theology and science was not present. Even as recently as in the nineteenth century, Charles Hodge spoke of theology and science as "twin daughters of heaven."[6] Under Hodge, 20 percent of the content of the *Princeton Review* was of a scientific nature. B. B. Warfield, another of the Princeton greats, known for his masterful defense of the authority and inspiration of the Scriptures,[7] believed not only that the earth was very old, and in the theory of evolution, but that these were compatible with proper interpretation of Scripture.[8] Close analysis of evangelicalism by scholars

---

6. Hodge, "Princeton College and the General Assembly," 137–38.

7. Warfield, *Inspiration and Authority*.

8. On the age of the earth, see Yarchin, *History of Biblical Interpretation*, 67n71; on evolution, see Livingstone and Noll, "Biblical Inerrantist," 283–304, and Noll, *Princeton Theology*, 293–98. In a class lecture in 1888, Warfield states, "I do not think that there is any general statement in the Bible or any part of the account of creation, either as given in Genesis 1 and 2 or elsewhere alluded to, that need be opposed to evolution." Alexander, *Rebuilding*, 177.

such as James Smith[9] and Mark Noll[10] have led to the conclusion that it was not science itself that caused the rift, but the theology of fundamentalism, which was and is, decidedly modern.

In recent times, the breach has begun to be healed by people like T. F. Torrance and John Polkinghorne, and Francis Collins, the American physician-geneticist noted for his leadership of the Human Genome Project. It was Collins in fact who coined the term "Bio-Logos," which reflects a move toward a relationship between the magisteria of science and theology that Douglas E. Coe describes as "not merely compatible but complementary."[11] Moving even further than this, I wish to affirm the yet bolder claim that the disciplines of Christian theology and science are more than complementary and are, in fact, coinherent. Science and theology are not non-overlapping: they are compatible and complementary because coinherent, and they are coinherent because theycohere in the same Person, who in turn is a coinherent Person within the triune Godhead.

I even suggest that although Divine and created reality are metaphysically distinct, that by virtue of the mediacy of the Son of God who has entered forever into a human body by means of the hypostatic union, that there is coinherence between Divine and created reality, the latter being the stuff of scientific inquiry! Jesus Christ is not just *homoousios*, that is of one substance with the Father and the Spirit in the Godhead, he is *homoousios* with us, of one substance with us in our humanity, and therefore with creation. The incarnation will be a central reality in the bringing together of these disciplines. This is inferred by the great Pauline affirmation of Colossians 1: "The Son is the image of the invisible God, the firstborn over all creation. For *in him* all things were created . . . *through him* to reconcile to himself all things . . ." (Col 1:15–20).

This coinherence model I am proposing has some similarities with the "mutuality model" of theology and science in the aforementioned work of Alan Padgett, though he does not, like Torrance, go as far as to view theology as a science.[12] He classifies his own view as somewhere between the "dialogue" and "full integration" models Barbour outlines, as noted above. It may therefore be thought of as a fifth model. His "collegial metaphor" between the practitioners of science and theology, is agreeable, but his "mutuality model" between the disciplines fall short of what I am proposing,

---

9. Smith, *Introducing Radical Orthodoxy*, 37, 64–76.
10. Noll, *Scandal*, 177–210.
11. On the cover of Collins, *Language*.
12. Padgett, *Science and the Study of God*. Padgett does not consider theology to be empirical, an assumption I do make and explain here.

which may be considered a sixth model. Coinherence moves beyond the mutuality model by suggesting that theology and science are not merely interdependent, but mutually internal to each other. Admittedly this is a model grounded in faith, rooted in a theological, and particularly Trinitarian, reality. But I believe the coinherent model to be inherently integrative. My model and that of Padgett share in the belief that the mutuality of theology and science practiced within the rubric of image-bearing and stewardship has some crucial implications for how science can function in ways that contribute to the shalom of humanity and the flourishing of the planet.

I recognize that both the mutuality and the coinherence model are far from the lived reality of the contemporary church. I recognize that many Christians struggle to bring science and theology together, that often Christians who are scientists struggle with dissonance as they attend church on Sunday, and that their Monday to Friday experience is one of practical atheism. And if scientists unwittingly model a practical atheism, many Western Christians model a practical dualism—a division of things material and things spiritual that goes back beyond the Enlightenment and the vestiges of Gnostic Christianity to early Greek Platonic thought. For these Christians, as for many contemporary Evangelicals, the God of creation and the God of redemption are far apart. The Christ of creation and the Christ of reconciliation are distant for them. They assume that by salvation God will take us out of creation, when the biblical truth is that we are saved as whole beings, for creation, and at the consummation we will be new creations, embodied persons, not disembodied spirits (1 Cor 15:35–44; 1 Thess 5:23). The point of the resurrection of Jesus in a body seems to escape them!

Rather daringly, what is meant by a coinherent relationship between theology and science is that—in contrast to the warfare model of theology and science, or the non-overlapping magisterial model, or even the compatible model—the relationship of theology and science is *analogous* to that enjoyed by the persons of the Holy Trinity. That is, I propose that the two fields are distinct yet mutually related, and each is in the other, even though one (theology) has functional precedence. I will offer the concept of asymmetric compatibilism (meaning they are compatible) discerned in Barth's consideration of the incarnation, and in his consideration of Divine and human freedom, as a helpful analogy for the relationship between conciliar theology and science. Understood in this way, these two great disciplines can be seen as being in a mutuality that suggests profound overlap in substantial ways, yet giving freedom for each to conduct its business in ways that are distinctive and particular to each discipline.

Nothing about such a model need threaten either the fearless pursuit of reality in the sciences or the supremacy of the queen of sciences, theology, as infallible, first-order conciliar theology. I use the term "conciliar" (or creedal) carefully, in distinction from the term "confessional." The confessions of some denominations no doubt include commitment to a literalistic interpretation of Genesis and young earth creationism, but these are secondary matters that have never been deliberated on in the great tradition, or been part of a discussion at an ecumenical church council or part of the creed. *That* God created all things in heaven and on earth is conciliar. *How* he did so is not! However, the need for the dynamic shaping of a broader scientific theology, and more broadly still, an encyclopedic theology, will also be encouraged, in the sense that the regal science[13] must take up into itself reality found in every realm of human scholarship. The exact "dogmatic rank and the epistemic status of scientific judgments" is a matter for ongoing study and debate, but it is not at the level of the conciliar. It needs to be clarified, however, that this does not lead me to affirm the complete ignoring of science on the part of some young earth theologians. The neglect of both science and the science of hermeneutics is in evidence, for example, in some recent statements of Hans Madueme. He makes a judgment that ancient Near Eastern readings of Genesis 1–2 have led to the loss of the dogmatic status of a literal Adam and Eve and so have fundamentally altered the "shape of the story." He expresses the opinion that a literal Adam and Eve "are integral to the redemptive-historical narrative, grounded in biblical exegesis, and widely affirmed by earlier Christians who did not have our blind spots. We rank them high dogmatically, humbly recognizing that some theological realities by their very nature are more secure than the best of what we know, or can know, from scientific investigation."[14] Leaving for a moment the vexed question of a literal Adam and Eve, such a statement borders on antirealism, making science epistemically nigh on worthless.

A WINDOW OF COINHERENCE: ITS MEANING AND SCOPE

Having introduced the objectives of our study and the context within which our proposal of a coinherent relationship between theology and science is presented, I now want to press a little more deeply into the meaning of

---

13. The treatment of theology as the regal or Divine science goes back to Thomas Aquinas. This is in fact how his *Summa Theologica* begins (see the prologue, and question 1, articles 1–10), Aquinas, *Summa*, 1–7. This is taken up by the Protestant theologian scientist T. F. Torrance who speaks of theology as theological science and as the queen of the sciences (see Torrance, *Theological Science*, 283).

14. Madueme, "Adam and Eve," 182.

coinherence and its history. The challenge with Barbour's four categories, useful though they may be is, as Philip Hefner has suggested, that they "are predicated on the separateness of religion from science."[15] The problem with this, suggests Hefner, is that "by emphasizing exclusively their discrete and different methods and identities we disguise the ways in which religion and science interpenetrate each other." In a way that adds support to our proposal, he concludes that it "may be preferable to speak of the co-inherence of religion and science. We need to recognize the ways in which religion and science are not separate."[16] The window that coinherence provides for investigating the relationship between these two great disciplines, assumes that under the one triune creating and redeeming God, they are not separated in the first place. They are distinct but they are also mutually interrelated in all kinds of ways. The best way to account for the nature of these interrelationships, I am proposing, is by viewing them as echoes of the coinherent relationship between the persons of the Holy Trinity, as revealed by the incarnate Son through the Holy Spirit, each being completely mutual to and yet distinct from the other. I hope to show, for example, that the cradle for science, historically speaking, was Christian theology; that there is a profound similarity about the ways in which *knowing* (through empiricism, and critical realism) is arrived at in science and in theology; that theology is in fact theological science; that theology has been enriched by a scientific approach, and that science is enriched by the sense of vocation and meaning which theology brings to it; that there are echoes of the coinherence in the Divine being which may be heard within creation, and which may be uncovered by science; and that the two arenas of human thought, though rightfully distinct guilds, by virtue of their different subject matters, are nev-

---

15. Hefner, "Religion and Science," 781–84. Hefner cites Gilkey to illustrate a coinherent relationship between theology and science. Gilkey believed that "divine presence and everyday life are fused" and that daily life, which includes the formative influences of scientific understandings, is (quoting Gilkey) "saturated, so to speak, with the ultimate and the sacred." Hefner suggests that for "any culture to be totally secular, in which no sense of the sacred is expressed, is, he thought, a human and historical possibility" (Gilkey, *Naming the Whirlwind*, 781–82). He suggests that the "outlines of ultimacy" are present, if studied, in the "fundamental dynamics of any culture" (782). Hefner states that "for both Szerszynski and Gilkey ultimacy and the sacred are not encountered in some otherworldly realm apart from everyday existence, on the contrary they engage us whenever and wherever we experience that our lives are rooted in the imponderables of mystery—mystery that both threatens us and offers us hope." He adds that from such a viewpoint, "the richness of reflection on religion and science lies in the ways in which they co-inhere" (Szerszynski, *Nature, Technology and the Sacred*, 782). What is missing in this account of coinherence is any reference to the Trinity as the ground of coinherence, or to the incarnation as the source of the groundedness spoken of.

16. Hefner, "Religion and Science," 781.

ertheless most delightfully understood as coinherent dance partners. Just as the Father who is irreducibly distinct from the Son, though he shares the same Divine essence (John 10:30), and is fully in the Son as the Son is in him (John 10:38), delights in the Son (John 5:20; 2 Pet 1:17) and the Son in him (John 8:29).

The term "coinherence" has been used in the tradition as a synonym for the "perichoresis," or interpenetration, first of the Divine and human natures of Christ, and then of the persons of the Trinity. In both the incarnation and the Trinity, the idea is that irreducibly distinct natures (in the one person of the incarnate Son) or persons (in the one triune God) are mutually internal to one another, and that they inter-animate one another, while retaining their own identity.[17] Given that this coinherent Son has come into this union with humanity, and given that the tripersonal God is the Creator, then it can reasonably be expected that the creation might show echoes of coinherence in its essence and functioning. It might also reasonably be expected that realms of knowledge concerning the Creator and the creation may show at minimum, a compatibility, and mostly likely, a mutual dependence and intertwining that echoes coinherence.

Naturally, one is extremely cautious about drawing an analogy between what is true of the transcendent God and the mysteries of his inner life, and the life and thought of finite humans, and the nature and life of creation. The relationship between concepts and terms used for God and for humans, or between who God is and what creation is, is not a univocal one, as suggested. That is, there isn't a direct or exact equivalence of coinherence in the triune God, and the coinherence of a mother and her newborn child, or of a man and a woman joined together in matrimony, or matter at its deepest quantum levels, or the coinherence of all fields of knowledge including theology and science. Yet the Bible speaks of human persons as the *image* of God, and the Bible (Ps 19) and tradition speaks of *traces* of God in creation. These realities are coinherent in an *analogous* way and always in an incomplete manner. By turning first to a theological account of coinherence, we may then profitably return to this crucial nuance.

---

17. The verb *perichoreō* is found in the writings of one of the Cappadocian Fathers who were influential at the Council of Nicaea when the doctrine of the Trinity was recognized by the church. This was Gregory of Nazianzus (d. 389/90), who used it to describe the relationship between the Divine and human natures of Christ (Prestige, *God in Patristic Thought*, 291). John of Damascus (d. 749) also used it in this christological way, but he also extended its use to include the "interpenetration" of the persons of the Trinity (Cross and Livingstone, "Circumincession," 357, and Ott, *Manual de Teología*, 131). Maximus the Confessor (d. 662) used the term perichoresis as the technical term for this mutually internal nature of the three persons (Prestige, *God in Patristic Thought*, 291).

The Theological History of Coinherence

It needs to be said that coinherence has a long theological history, one that has been traced in an exemplary way by patristic scholar G. L. Prestige.[18] The essence of what coinherence means is present in the pages of the New Testament, and then, as with many of the doctrines of the faith, it is developed in the face of various heresies: *modalism*, in which the oneness of God is stressed at the expense of the irreducible identity of the persons, on the one hand, and *tritheism*, on the other—in which the persons are emphasized at the expense of co-essential and communal oneness, resulting in a creed of three gods, not one. Athanasius (ca. 296–98–May 2, 373)—one of the most important influences in the development of the doctrines of the full divinity and full humanity of Christ, of the incarnate Christ, and of the Trinity—though he does not use either the term coinherence or perichoresis, expresses the substance of this concept in order to defend the identity of the one Divine *ousia*. This term described the substance or essence of God in the time of the church fathers leading up to the Council of Nicaea (AD 325) where the doctrine of the Trinity began to be clarified. The standard expression after Nicaea was to speak of God as one in essence (one *ousia*) and three in person (three *hypostases*). Yet the question persisted: *how* could God be one in essence and yet three in person?

Athanasius expressed the importance of the essence of God, or *ousia*, which should be considered to be as real or concrete as the persons. It is the "psychological centre" of the Godhead for Athanasius.[19] How he reconciles that oneness with the threeness of the persons is to use what we may in retrospect call a perichoresis of essence—that is, a sharing of each of the persons in the essence of the Godhead. For example, Athanasius speaks of the Son being omnipresent, because he is in the Father and the Father is in him. Yet he preserves the distinctiveness of the persons in this. When speaking of the Spirit being in the Son and in the Father and therefore belonging to the *ousia*, Athanasius nevertheless states, "He is not called the Son, yet he is not outside the Son."[20] What Athanasius seems to be saying is that the

---

18. Prestige, "Co-inherence," 282–301, recalls this history. Charles Williams called Prestige's account "the clearest exposition I know of the theological definition of the Divine Life [of the Trinity] in this sense" (Williams, *Figure of Beatrice*, 92n1). Williams adds that "humanly, the word stands for the idea of 'in-othering' and 'in-Godding' of men which appears in Dante." For other accounts of the history of perichoresis, see Leithart, *Traces of the Trinity*; Twombly, *Perichoresis and Personhood*.

19. This is Prestige's assessment; see Prestige, "Co-inherence," 284.

20. Athanasius, *Ad. Serap.* 3.4, cited in Prestige, "Co-inherence," 284.

perichoresis of the sharing of the Divine *essence* cannot be separated from the perichoresis of the eternally existent *persons* in one another.

There is also no question but that the Cappadocian Fathers (a group of Greek theologians from Cappadocia that include Basil the Great [AD 330–79], Gregory of Nyssa [ca. AD 332–95], and Gregory of Nazianzus [AD 329–89 AD]) expressed the concept, again without using the terms. Gregory of Nazianzus actually uses a verb form (*perichoreuō*)[21] of the word that later becomes, in nominal form, the standard word for coinherence, perichoresis. He uses it only with respect to the relations between the Divine and human natures of Christ. Gregory of Nyssa most definitely uses language that is synonymous with coinherence in his influential work on the Trinity.[22] Nyssa's defense against tritheism is, in fact, perichoresis. He emphasized "the fact that the Father is in the Son and the Father and the Spirit in both."[23]

Offering support for this work's proposal that coinherence (a description of the Divine) may be echoed in creation and may, by way of extension, be predicated of human thought disciplines, was the use made by Hilary of Poitiers (AD 310–67), sometimes called the "hammer of the Arians" or the "Athanasius of the West," "of the conception that the several Persons mutually contain one another." This is highlighted by Prestige, who comments that this is "strikingly developed by Gregory of Nyssa" (*Adv. Ar. Et Sab. 12*). The word χωρειν (contain) had for centuries been accepted as a technical expression for the pervasion of all created things by God. It originally meant either "to be extended and fill space, or, transitively, to 'hold' an imperial pint. God as all-pervasive Spirit, is omnipresent in all space and 'holds' all extended matter; He 'contains' the universe. It was by a most valuable extension of this concept that it now came to be applied to the mutual relations of the Divine Persons."[24]

The theological development of the concept of coinherence comes in the sixth century along with the use of the term perichoresis, which begins to be formalized with reference to the doctrine of the Trinity. It does so in response to the full resurgence of the heresy of tritheism. This came about as theology began to be in its abstract or more philosophical phase. He states that "the three hypostases were the only elements in the conception of the Trinity that were anchored safely in concrete objects," and as a result, a

---

21. Gregory of Nazianzus, "To Cledonius."

22. See, e.g., Gregory of Nyssa, "On 'Not Three Gods,'" 331–36.

23. However, as Prestige notes, "the language in which the faith was expressed did not progress far beyond the actual phrases of Scripture" with very little theological development. Prestige, "Co-inherence," 289.

24. Ibid.

"real outbreak of tritheism occurred."[25] John Philoponus (AD 490–570) of Alexandria, who in other regards, and especially with respect to science, is helpful, was the main culprit in this assertion of tritheism. The general idea of the *ousia* (substance) seemed to him to be an abstraction with no real existence. He could only think of *physis* (nature) in a concrete sense, and associated it with the concrete *hypostaseis*. The three *hypostaseis* were thus three *physes*, that is God was three Gods, not one. With respect to Christ, he could not make sense of his two natures as two *physes*, as this would mean two *hypostaseis*, which was absurd, and so, in what is called the Monophysite heresy, he spoke of Christ as being of "one nature incarnate of God the Word," rather than two natures, that of God and humanity, in one person. The Divine nature in the Son was not for Philoponus the common Divine nature of the Godhead, as a single, particular embodiment of the *physis* of the Trinity, but a concrete *hypostasis*. Pseudo-Cyril of Jerusalem,[26] an unknown author of the eighth century whose work is quoted extensively in the *Orthodox Faith* of John of Damascus,[27] was the theologian who articulated a response to Philoponus. He did so precisely by drawing attention to the reality that the concrete *physis* Philiponus looked for was in fact the *ousia* of the common triune Godhead. He did so by bringing theology back to "the true and concrete doctrine of identical *ousia*, but he gave it a term to express the co-inherence of three Persons in one another. This term was perichoresis, or in the Latin, *circumincessio*."[28] In other words, the concreteness of the *ousia* was derived in the concreteness of the *hypostaseis*, and vice versa. Or to say it another way, the coinherence of the persons, that is, that each is completely in the other, serves as an aid to understanding the oneness of the Godhead, without sacrificing the irreducible identity of the persons.

The specific concept of perichoresis begins to be in theological use for the Trinity after pseudo-Cyril, and finds its fullest development in Maximus the Confessor of Constantinople (ca. 580–August 13, 662), who uses the noun commonly. John of Damascus popularized the doctrine of perichoresis also. He did so by "laying stress (*fid. orth.* 1.14) on the 'mansion and session' . . . of the *hypostaseis* in one another."[29] However, there was little to add to it, in light of what pseudo-Cyril had already expressed, namely, "the

25. Ibid., 282.

26. Pseudo-Cyril is so named because his writings come under the pen name of "the holy Apa Cyril," that is, Cyril of Jerusalem, a theologian of the early church (ca. AD 313–386). See Broek, *Pseudo-Cyril*.

27. John of Damascus, *Exposition*.

28. Prestige, "Co-inherence," 282–83.

29. Ibid., 299.

formula of the perichoresis or *circumincessio* of three co-inherent persons in a single substance."[30]

In more recent Trinitarian theology, the concept of perichoresis lives on, in both the Eastern and Western traditions, though it may be nuanced in slightly different ways. For those favoring the Eastern (Orthodox) tradition, the "threeness" of the Trinity, or the irreducible reality of personhood, is emphasized. However, this is the case largely because of an equal, balancing emphasis on the complementary reality that the persons are one in the Father's essence by the perichoresis of the persons (e.g., John Zizioulas), or one in the perichoretic communion of the three (e.g., T. F. Torrance, following Athanasius). Followers of the Western tradition, which typically has emphasized the oneness of the Godhead, have tended to speak of a coinherence of essence, or of a coinherence of the natural attributes of God (memory, intellect, and will or love), derived in a psychological analogy of the Trinity (Jonathan Edwards).

Coinherence in Charles Williams

An author worthy of special notice for his writing about coinherence as a ubiquitous phenomenon in creation and history, and as an extrapolation of coinherence in God, is Charles Williams, one of the "Inklings." His works are notoriously difficult to follow. Lecturing on *Descent of the Dove*, for example, once a set work for a "Christian Thought and Culture" course for some years at Regent College, J. I. Packer referred to it as "clotted glory." It requires serious wading, but it does indeed yield moments of gloriously rich insight. This book contains the term coinherence/-ent twenty-seven times, and its meaning and usage do indeed reflect the glory of a coinherent God and his communicated glory in the sacred space that is creation and the history of humanity. The Co-inherence[31] at the center of the universe becomes not just "the centerpiece to all Williams' theology."[32] It is in fact a worldview for seeing the universe in coinherent ways, particularly because that coinherent God had not only created the cosmos, but had become one with creation and humanity though the incarnation of the Son. Not surprisingly, Williams viewed the incarnate union of God and humanity in Jesus to be precisely a case of coinherence. The ordering of Williams's thought

---

30. Ibid., 297.

31. Williams spells this as co-inherence, though I have chosen not to use the hyphen. Synonymous terms which Williams used for coinherence were "Exchange," "Substitution" or "Substituted Love," and "Romantic Theology."

32. Williams, "Concept of Co-inherence."

is expressed by the outworking of coinherence from God, to humanity, to creation. It moves from the coinherence in the inner being of the Trinity, to the revelation of the coinherence of the Divine and human natures of the Son in the incarnation ("The Incarnation, or rather the Motherhood of the Incarnation, is the function for which we were created . . ."),[33] to echoes in the community of human persons, echoes in all forms of love between human persons, in the workings of the state, in a woman's physically bearing a child to the point of birth, but echoes *especially* in the manner by which humans participate in the history of Jesus Christ, his death and resurrection, for their salvation, and then in the presence of Christ in the Eucharist.[34]

Drawing the strands of Williams's work together, as he extended it from the Godhead outward, might lead to a definition of coinherence something like this: it describes entities that exist in essential relationship with another, as innate components of the other, yet distinct in their identity. In light of his work and that of others, in summation of what we have learned so far, coinherence is grounded in the essential nature of God as Trinity. Yet, cognizant of the transcendence of Almighty God, and therefore of the uniqueness and fullness of the perichoretic reality in his inner life, we are nevertheless also cognizant by way of scriptural revelation that we can *know* that God by his revelation which is also coinherent. The Father has revealed himself to us in the Son incarnate because he is in the Son, and he has done so by the Spirit, who is the Spirit of the Father and of the Son. That work of revelation and, indeed, *all* the works of God have been coinherent. "Each is on the other" in the economy of God's working in creation, the incarnation and the reconciliation of humanity and creation. These notions have biblical justification. While here on earth, Jesus said, with respect to his *being*, that he was one with the Father (John 10:30), that he was in the Father, and that the Father was in him (John 14:10, 11, 20). But he also insisted that even his *doing*, his work here on earth, indeed, all that he did, he only did coinherently with the Father, that is, as he saw the Father doing it (John 5:19). The perichoresis of God's *being* has in the Latin tradition been called *circuminsessio* while the perichoresis of God's acts or *doing* was called *circumincessio*.[35] The wonder of the Christian gospel is that we as human persons can participate in his perichoretic life, by the Son and through the Spirit. The heart of the gospel is not just forensics but it is first filial, that is, we are brought into union with Christ to become members of the family

---

33. Williams, *Figure of Beatrice*, 92.

34. For a fuller consideration of these themes in Williams, see Ridler, *Image*, and Hefling, *Charles Williams*.

35. Burgundio of Pisa (d. 1193) is attributed with first translating the Greek perichoresis into Latin *circumincessio*. Cross and Livingstone, "Circumincession," 357.

of God, and are participants in the Divine nature, and our justification is a logical consequence of that union. Being in union with God, we therefore model the perichoretic life in our communal reality as persons-in-relation. Thus by way of *image* we would expect humans to reflect that coinherent life in the communion of the church (*communio*) and in general communal life. Even in their pre-fall days, the first human persons who reflected the image of God only did so, according John Calvin, because they were in union with or in participation with the preincarnate Christ.[36]

The Legitimacy of Coinherence beyond the Trinity?

But further, given that this triune God whose three-in-one existence is explained by perichoresis, is the Creator of all things, by Christ and through the Spirit, we might expect *traces* of that "being-in-relationality" in all aspects of creation. If the reality at the heart of the universe is a coinherent being, and if the preeminent revelation he has given us of himself in the incarnation is the coinherent interpenetration of the Divine and human natures, that is, the interpenetration of God with creation (in Christ's body), and if the anthropology of image-bearing involves humanity's participation in Christ, and models coinherence in analogous ways, and if all creation participates in the person of the Son by the Spirit in a relational rather than substantial way, and if the center of the worship of the church, which is God's community, is the Eucharist which in *some* sense (depending on one's tradition) involves the coinherence of Christ in bread and wine, *might we not expect*, by way of analogy, that coinherence might characterize the creation, and that disciplines of study might be coinherent?

It is important to emphasize that creation does not only reflect coinherence in its Creator by way of *modeling* the Creator. It is not just that creation is *like* God, in that sense. Rather, the tradition has always insisted that in one way or another, creation participates in the life of God. As I have stressed elsewhere, this participation is not a sharing of the Divine essence with creation in some form of Platonic *methexis* which compromises the distinctness of God and creation. Rather, by way of the agency of the person of the Son and the Spirit, God is in a relational way participating in creation, so much so, that without this κοινωνία participation, the universe would not exist. As Julie Canlis expresses it, "Creation is not self-enclosed but is only itself when participating in God (and as we know, Calvin never sees this as

---

36. *Calvin's Commentaries*, Col 1:15–16. See a discussion of the participation of creation and humanity in the preincarnate Christ in Wen, "Monergistic Theme."

God *simpliciter*, but as in Christ, by the Spirit),"[37] and again, "*Communion* [κοινωνία] is the underpinning of all creation."[38] Signs of coinherence in creation are the consequence of its being a sacred space that is made sacred by its being *like* God because it is in communion with God. Creation is *in* God, in particular in Christ, in this *relational* sense.

This is consistent with the content of the great Christ hymn of Colossians 1:15–17, which twice refers to the in-ness of creation in Christ: "The Son is the image of the invisible God, the firstborn over all creation. For *in him* all things were created: things in heaven and on earth, visible and invisible, whether thrones or powers or rulers or authorities; all things have been created through him and for him. He is before all things, and *in him* all things hold together." One might call this a modified form of panentheism (the notion present in the thought of Jürgen Moltmann, for example, that creation is in God, that God has opened up space within himself for the creation), but it should be understood in a strictly relational participational sense, not a sharing in the essence of God. The boundaries between God and creation are kept clear. Coinherence precisely describes this communion or participation between God and creation in which the union between God and creation is one which is unmixed and unconfused, just as in the case of the two natures of Christ, who is the sole mediator between God and creation, first in an ontological way by the incarnation through which he was brought into union with it, and second, in a salvific way by the work of reconciliation which his incarnation, vicarious life and death accomplished. What about creation prior to the incarnation, we may ask? Of course, creation was in Christ and belonged to Christ prior to the incarnation because as our Colossians text asserts, "all things were created in him." As such he seems to have always been that person within the triune being and councils of God who from all eternity was assigned to be God's agent in creation, and therefore who had an orientation toward creation and its redemption, precisely as the Son destined for incarnation (Barth refers to this as the *Logos incarnandus*, a Word that will be incarnated).[39] That he has always been the mediator between God and creation ontically is evident from texts in the New Testament that speak of the death of Christ as being according to

---

37. Canlis, *Calvin's Ladder*, 83.

38. Ibid., 82, emphasis mine. Canlis adds, "In the mediation of creation, we find Calvin constantly funneling all reality toward and into the Son, in order to establish its reality."

39. Karl Barth, *CD* IV/2, 683. He is *incarnandus* in the OT and *incarnates* in the NT. Barth in this regard is preserving the notion of the correspondence between the economic Trinity and who God is in his immanent being.

"God's deliberate plan and foreknowledge" (Acts 2:23), as in fact being the Lamb "slain from the creation of the world" (Rev 13:8).

If creation shows signs of coinherence, and especially in the image of God, that is, in humans, we might expect also that all that humans in the life of God encounter and come to know, would be fully integrated. The pursuit of knowledge in creation through science would therefore come within the realm of knowledge of God as Creator and Redeemer, which is to say, that theology and science would be coinherent, not conflicted. And that as persons in communion with the triune God by his sheer grace expressed in creation and in redemption, they might have a doxological orientation toward this God expressed in vocation toward the continued shalom and flourishing of his reconciled and being redeemed new creation.

In sum, then, coinherence may be thought of as the language of "in-ness"[40] without merger. With regard to justifying the extension of this concept of coinherence to what is in creation as discovered in science, or to the relation between theology and science, caution must be exercised, as we have indicated. We acknowledge freely that coinherence can only be true in the fullest sense in the Trinity. Nevertheless, it is important to note, as we have above, that the concept was actually used first for the incarnation or the hypostatic union of the two natures of Christ. God has in fact, therefore, not only created a cosmos, but has participated in it by the incarnation. The incarnation is a vital bridging concept or reality between God and the world. In considering the way in which God participates or becomes involved perichoretically in the creation, it is true to say that there are levels of the echo of coinherence. The perichoretic relation becomes increasingly asymmetric as we move from Godself, to God's relationship to humanity in Christ, to God's relationship to humanity in the church, to God's relation to humanity in general, and finally to God's relation to the animate and non-animate creation. God's coinherence within Godself, thus participates in these other relationships in more and more asymmetric ways.

Take for example, the incarnation. Even though historically perichoresis, in verb form, was spoken of in the hypostatic union before it was applied specifically to the Trinity, Prestige records the difficulty of speaking about the union of the Divine and human natures as symmetrical. The perichoretic reality was actually only truly symmetrical in the Trinity. In his discussion of Maximus' articulation of the hypostatic union, Prestige notes how Maximus retreats from saying that the human and Divine natures actually mutually interpenetrate, and Prestige is somewhat scathing in his explanation of this:

---

40. A term used by Julie Canlis, in private correspondence, but also found at Dictionary.com.

"because no one ever had the hardihood to suggest that the human nature is capable of interpenetrating the divine . . . ."[41] There may be interchange and there may be reciprocity, but not true perichoretic interpenetration. It is for this reason that Cyril of Alexandria among the Fathers, and Karl Barth in modern times, spoke of this relationship as asymmetric. It was the Divine nature that assumed the human. One does see a profound echo of coinherence in this union, and it must not be forgotten that humanity has been forever taken into the Divine being in the now ascended, human-Divine Son. Yet this is a mediated case of coinherence. This is an important and mediating example of the participation of God in humanity, and more will be said later of the hypostatic union when it is employed as a model for how God relates to or participates by Son and Spirit in the creation. With these cautions stated, we can nevertheless affirm the way in which general character of coinherence in the Godhead might be applied in all his relations, moving down the levels. At the God-human level, that is, anthropology, we will explore how humanity images the coinherent God both by participation and therefore by model. Similarly, we will also emphasize that it is by both participation *and* by model that coinherence is seen as trace in the cosmos and in the human disciplines of the study of science and of God.

There have no doubt been abuses and misuses of the term perichoresis, as some recent theologians have noted.[42] We assert, nevertheless, that there remains a legitimate place in the tradition for appropriate use of the concept unequivocally in the Godhead and in the incarnation. Then with care, we *support* the notion suggested in Scripture and in the tradition, that by way of image and trace, there are echoes of coinherence in humanity and creation, and therefore in science, by way of modeling God and as a result of participation in the life of God. This leads us to *propose* the possibility that theology and science as disciplines are coinherent in the coinherent God. These successive moves are not steps of anthropomorphic reductionism, but rather they are consequences of an approach to humanity and creation that come "from above," have biblical precedent (Gen 1:26; Ps 8; Ps 19:1–6), and are critical to a proper understanding of anthropology and other fields of knowledge in science. A final word of support for this theological direction comes from the work of Gabriel Fackre, who stated that as a result of being in God's image, human persons have "a derivative freedom for partnership," with an underlying propensity for partnership with God which "derives

---

41. Prestige, "Co-inherence," 292–93.
42. See Otto, "Use and Abuse," 366–84; Crisp, "Problems with Perichoresis," 119–40.

from the harmonies of the divine perichoresis." Significantly, he adds that humankind's partnership [with] God is then "stamped on all creation."[43]

---

43. Fackre, *Doctrine of Revelation*, 39.

Chapter 2

Coinherence in the Theology/Science Tradition

ONE MIGHT WELL ASK, is this proposal regarding coinherence in God, and in humanity and in the nonhuman creation, and between theology and science, an original proposal on my part, with no precedent in the Christian tradition or scholarship? If this were so, we might be on rather thin ice. In this chapter I want to introduce some theologian scientists and scientist theologians (recognizing that in most cases both titles may be appropriate) who have noticed the coinherent nature of Trinitarian theology and science. In introducing some of these scholars and retrieving the evidence of coinherence in their work, we will enhance our understanding of the coinherent nature of theology and science. This will prepare the way for discussion in subsequent chapters of how this coinherence is evident in the history, epistemology and ontology of the two disciplines. Just by way of reminder, our aims are to *describe* with as much clarity as possible, the reality of coinherence in the Divine life, to *support* the claim that it is possible to extrapolate this by way of analogy, by image and trace, to human and created life and matter, and thereby to *propose* the possibility of viewing theology and science as coinherent disciplines.

THEOLOGIAN SCIENTISTS AND SCIENTIST THEOLOGIANS WHO HAVE NOTICED THE COINHERENCE

Primary Conversation Partners

Among the most important contributors to a coinherent view of theology and science are Thomas F. Torrance, *theologian* scientist, and John Polkinghorne, *scientist* theologian. Works on theology and science, irrespective of tradition, that neglect these contributors are the poorer for it. They will be our primary interlocutors, along with Michael Hanby, who has offered a robust Trinitarian doctrine of creation and also a convincing exposé of the fact that science cannot be done without metaphysical and theological assumptions. Torrance's approach to the theology of the incarnation and the Trinity, and science, is in fact one of coinherence. This is implicit throughout his work in this area, and explicit in certain instances. John Polkinghorne, whose work as a quantum physicist, alongside his Trinitarian theology, led him to speak of the latter as the "Theory of Everything."[1] The works of Alexei Nesteruk, Wolfhart Pannenberg, Jürgen Moltmann, Colin Gunton, Alister McGrath, Amos Yong (with his particular emphasis on the Spirit in creation and science), and Thomas Jay Oord, in the theology science field, have all been significant, some explicitly Trinitarian in their integration, but all implicitly so. Most will receive mention in this project.

Our immediate purpose is not to make a systematic study of the work of each of these and other contemporary, thoughtful theologian scientists / scientist theologians (Mark Noll, Chris Southgate, Alan Torrance, Loren Wilkinson, Jennifer Wiseman, Francis Collins, David Livingstone, John Lennox, Denis Alexander, Ronald Numbers, Jeff Schloss, etc.) or biblical scholars engaged in this area (Peter Enns, V. Philips Long, Tremper Longman, Iain Provan, Bruce Waltke, John Walton, N. T. Wright, etc.) who have contended helpfully in this last generation for the union (re-union, really) of these disciplines. Rather, we will seek to retrieve the findings of scholars most relevant to this project, with a view to finding support for a constructive proposal regarding coinherence as an appropriate analogy and framework for the manner in which science and Christian theology are related. We will do so by considering the work of theologian scientists and scientist theologians from across the traditions who represent the state of the art in the study of Trinitarian theology and science. The theologian scientists are: Langdon Gilkey (1919–2004, ecumenical Protestant), Lazar Puhalo

---

1. Polkinghorne, *Science and the Trinity*, 6, 61.

(b. 1941, Eastern Orthodox), Michael Hanby (b. 1966, Roman Catholic Thomist), T. F. Torrance (1913–2007, Protestant Barthian Reformed) and Graham Buxton (b. 1945, Protestant) who represents the voice of Jürgen Moltmann (b. 1926, German Reformed) and Colin Gunton (1941–2003, United Reformed); and the scientist theologians are: José M. Romero-Baró (b. 1953, Roman Catholic), Curtis L. Thompson (b. 1946, Lutheran) and Joyce M. Cuff (b. 1945, Lutheran), and John Polkinghorne (b. 1930, Protestant Anglican).

Theologian Scientists

We begin with ecumenical Protestant theologian Langdon Gilkey,[2] who is explicit about there being a coinherent relationship between Christian theology and science. Gilkey's foundational belief that "divine presence and everyday life are fused" and that daily life, which includes the formative influences of scientific understanding, is "saturated, so to speak, with the ultimate and the sacred."[3] Drawing on Gilkey's work, Philip Hefner suggests that for "any culture to be totally secular, in which no sense of the sacred is expressed, is, he thought, a human and historical possibility."[4] Hefner states that "for both Bronislaw Szerszynski[5] and Gilkey, ultimacy and the sacred are not encountered in some otherworldly realm apart from everyday existence, on the contrary they engage us whenever and wherever we experience that our lives are rooted in the imponderables of mystery—mystery that both threatens us and offers us hope." He adds that from such a viewpoint, "the richness of reflection on religion and science lies in the ways in which they co-inhere."[6]

Moving now to the Eastern Orthodox tradition, we consider the work of Lazar Puhalo. Without doubt, he provides an example of how Trinitarian theology and science have been brought together, principally through awareness of God as Trinity. In addition to describing some of the tenets of Puhalo's Trinitarian approach to theology and science that support the coinherence proposal, we will also critically engage some of his assumptions. Puhalo believes that a primary reason for the conflict model has not so much been modern science, as if it were some kind of "international

---

2. See Gilkey, *Naming the Whirlwind*. Gilkey was formed largely by the theology of Reinhold Niebuhr and Paul Tillich.
3. See Hefner, "Religion and Science," 781–84.
4. Ibid., 781–82.
5. Szerszynski, *Nature*.
6. Hefner, "Religion and Science," 782.

plot" to overthrow Christianity, but rather what he considers to be the "bad" Scholastic theology of the West in both the Catholic and Protestant traditions, and a fundamentalism present especially within the latter. These Western traditions, he asserts, were shaped uncritically by the influence of Greek philosophy, specifically that of Aristotle which came through Islamic philosophers, and Neoplatonism through Augustine. Puhalo states that "Aristotle had written on the essence of natural mechanisms, but he favoured the search for truth in philosophical processes rather than experimental ones. It was Aristotelianism that formed the dogmatized canon of 'scientific fact,' or at least the canon of acceptable thought."[7] He insists that under scholasticism, philosophy sat over both science and theology, the former being determined by presuppositions about the unchangeable and static nature of the cosmos, and misreadings of Scripture, and the latter by its idolatrous reductionisms concerning God, robbing humanity of its relationship with creation, and depriving persons of their formation through the empirical discoveries of creation through science. Puhalo concedes that the systematic reasoning process of the Scholastic West was important in the development of scientific process ultimately, but he maintains that it was the empiricism (deriving truth through experiment, or encountering reality, including historical reality; discovering things *a posteriori*, not determining them *a priori*) and apophaticism (knowledge obtained through negation)[8] of the East that enabled science to prosper. This tradition discouraged making positive comments about the *essence* of God because he is invisible and incomprehensible and beyond the scope of human intellect, and instead en-

---

7. Puhalo, *Evidence*, 36n39.

8. Apophatic theology also known as negative theology, the *via negativa*, is a type of theological thinking that attempts to describe God and the Divine essence, by negation, that is, to speak only about what may not be said about the perfect goodness that is God. For example, the fourth-century Cappadocian Fathers affirmed belief in the existence of God, but spoke of God's existence as being unlike that of everything else, since it was uncreated and transcendent. The essence of God is completely unknowable, therefore, whereas he is known through his energies. Clement of Alexandria, as well as Gregory of Nyssa, John Chrysostom, and Basil the Great, emphasized the importance of negative theology to an orthodox conception of God. John of Damascus employed it when he wrote that positive statements about God reveal "not the nature, but the things around the nature." Pseudo-Dionysius the Areopagite contributed influentially to apophatic theology. Maximus the Confessor also was a devotee. It continues to be prominent in Eastern Christianity via Gregory Palamas through Orthodox theologians such as Vladimir Lossky, John Meyendorff, John S. Romanides, and Georges Florovsky. Cataphatic theology, by contrast, makes positive statements about the nature of God, based on revelation. It is more prominent in Western theology. However, theologians like Meister Eckhart and St. John of the Cross exemplify some aspects of or tendencies toward the apophatic tradition in the West. The medieval works *The Cloud of Unknowing* and *St. John's Dark Night of the Soul* are particularly well known in the West.

couraged the direct experience of the love or the *energies* of God as the way to knowing him. It is this latter empirical approach to faith which Puhalo saw as being a factor compatible with the development of science. Puhalo also spoke, controversially, of the importance of the nominalism (the belief that general ideas or universals have no reality, whereas only particular objects exist, thus emphasizing the particularity of things) of William of Occam and the particularism of Duns Scotus (a focus on the "thisness" or particularity of things)[9] in the birthing of science.

Puhalo notes that the dynamic interplay of science and theology is certainly missing in the fundamentalist quarter of the church today, and it has failed to learn from the sad chapter concerning the relationship between the findings of Copernicus, Giordano Bruno, and Galileo and the church's response. During the medieval period when Scholastic theology emerged, both theology and science were, as Puhalo says, "essentially, departments of Aristotelian (and eventually also Platonistic) philosophy." It was in this context that scientists became the victim of "the breach of this harmony."[10] Puhalo gives graphic illustration of this:

> Thus, when Bruno, the brilliant, if erratic disciple of William of Ockham and Erasmus, dared to venture toward authentic science, and strive for a more accurate knowledge of the solar system, he paid the supreme price. When Galileo made irrefutable discoveries about the solar system that conflicted with the Biblical interpretations of scholastic fundamentalism and upset the artificial tandem of a much repressed and suppressed science, he was quickly reminded of Bruno's fate and forced to renounce truth in deference to dogmatized ignorance. The question of truth was of no consequence; what mattered was the maintenance of the pseudo-harmony.[11]

An important point for our project is the case that is made by Puhalo, convincingly in my opinion, that new or quantum physics is compatible with Trinitarian theology, and especially the apophatic theology of the Trinity of his Orthodox tradition. That which is clearly revealed concerning the Trinity does shed some light on humanity and creation, as will be our contention throughout this project. However, that which eludes our finitude, the things which we can only define by negation, also, according to Puhalo, has an interesting parallel in quantum science. Careful nuancing regarding

---

9. Puhalo, *Evidence*, passim.
10. Ibid., 33–34.
11. Ibid., 34.

the correspondences between quantum science and apophatic Trinitarian theology is required, with respect to both the science and the theology.

On the science side, the danger of what "one might call quantum hype—the invocation of the peculiar character of quantum thinking as if it were sufficient licence for lazy indulgence in playing with paradox in other disciplines,"[12] has been signaled by John Polkinghorne. Even so, on the basis of a phenomenon like entanglement in which quantum particles, however distant from each other they may be, undergo the same changes simultaneously, a phenomena which implies a cosmos that seems to work on principles that defy common sense, and on the basis of string theory which adds seven dimensions to the four we are familiar with, Puhalo and others are right to acknowledge a mystery in the core essence of matter that has *analogy* with the mystery of the Trinity. I hasten to add, however, that this is not to say that scientists must cease probing to unveil the quantum mysteries. Ultimately, on the basis of a doctrine of creation the Christian assumes that these mysteries will prove to be amenable to human reason and mathematics. Science, which in essence is the understanding of being, gained by empirical evidence, need hold no fear for the Christian. It is our friend. It keeps humanity grounded in the created given-ness of concrete reality. It is an incarnational pursuit, compatible with a faith defined by the incarnation. And, in fact, its method is the same as that by which the inscrutability of the Trinity was unveiled in the person of Jesus Christ, and the empirical historical encounter of the church with him.

On the theological front, one can affirm with the Orthodox tradition the ineffable and mysterious nature of the Trinity, and be cognizant of the dangers of probing beyond mystery, given the transcendence of God. With Puhalo, I *do* think that the nature of matter at the quantum level *does* provide an *analogy* of the mystery of the Godhead, and that there *is* an apophatic *dimension* to the knowledge of God. The New Testament suggests this when it speaks of a glory which we may not approach (see John 1:18, "*No one has ever seen God*"; 1 Tim 6:15–16, "*God, the blessed and only Ruler, the King of kings and Lord of lords, who alone is immortal and who lives in unapproachable light, whom no one has seen or can see*"). The *via negativa* which is the apophatic way "attests to an *intrinsic* conception of limit and the different way that theology and philosophy (one might say, science) copes with this infinite difference"[13] between God and the world, as Michael Hanby affirms. The challenge, however, is to know what the borders of that mystery are, and what to do with the mystery. For there are realities that *have* been *revealed*

---

12. Polkinghorne, *Quantum,* ix.
13. Hanby, *No God,* 28.

to us in the Christ event, that is, the economic Trinity, and in the Scriptures which describe it, and these must not be overlooked. We have come to know the economic Trinity in empirical ways in the history of Jesus Christ and the church, and the economic Trinity is our foundation for knowing what we can of the immanent Trinity. If the real God is something different to or back of the revealed God, we are, as Barth insisted, back on our quest looking for God. This empirical approach in theology mirrors the empirical methodology of science, a point to which we will return. One must surely assert then that we must be as positive or as "cataphatic" as Scripture and historical, personal revelation allows, and we must be as "apophatic" as the silence of Scripture, and as the transcendence of God demands. Apophaticism in science is applicable, not as a means to stop research, or to justify a "God of the gaps" approach. Rather it is an appropriate response to the fact that even when we know what we know in our most sophisticated scientific models, we must assume that these accurately represent a reality we often cannot fully know. This discussion anticipates the discussion of how we know what we know in a later chapter, the basic thesis of which is that critical realism is the way in which we approach knowledge in both disciplines, and that in this epistemological way, theology and science are coinherent. That is, they have a mutuality with respect to knowing, and yet there is a distinctiveness in how critical realism is applied in each.

We next consider the contribution of Michael Hanby to the relationship between Trinitarian theology and science. Coming from the Catholic and Thomist tradition, he has in his monograph *No God, No Science?* argued that the Christian doctrine of creation is essential to the intelligibility of the world and therefore to science. He also argues convincingly, in my opinion, that the universe is itself a fundamentally metaphysical and theological concept, and that therefore, metaphysics and theology (of the transcendent God)[14] are not options in the realm of science. Contrary to the views of "atheistic" scientists, or even those of the magisterial non-overlapping viewpoint, a very important methodological point is made by Michael Hanby that "there is an irreducibly metaphysical and theological dimension to scientific inquiry, that is not obviated by retreat to the putative neutrality of

---

14. It is important to clarify what exactly Aquinas (and Hanby) meant by theology and philosophy. Theology is the theology belonging to metaphysics, and concerns the transcendence of God. It treats God "as an inexorable aspect of its treatment of the world, regarding God not as he is revealed to be in Christ but as a principle from which the world takes its departure precisely as world." Hanby, *No God*, 10. In other words, it is the Scholastic theology of reason to which Puhalo objected. Despite reflecting their traditions, these theologians ultimately reach very similar conclusions with respect to the importance of the Trinity and the incarnation to the coinherent relationship between theology and science.

scientific method," that there are metaphysical reasons why this is the case, and that in fact, "a putatively neutral method conceals a questionable metaphysics and theology."[15] He pointedly remarks that once this is established, the question of the relationship between science and theology becomes "not so much *whether* theology, but *which*."[16] In other words, an "extrincist" view of the relation between theology and science is untenable, and the view that science can proceed indifferent or without reference to metaphysics and theology, is naïve. The extrincist viewpoint is undergirded by a positivist view of the world. This view "takes the world as unproblematically—and uninterestingly—given," which as Hanby points out "is a standpoint no less metaphysical than the metaphysics it deplores."[17] Science, in other words, is a science, not because its essence excludes metaphysics or theology. Yet, the prevalent and naïve assumption is, as Hanby has so eloquently expressed this, that "natural science . . . is first philosophy which ultimately pulls itself up from the 'empirically given' by its own intellectual bootstraps."[18]

Inherent in the naïve assertions of scientism that science can avoid metaphysics are two underlying assumptions. The first is that science involves premises that are self-justifying, or that they are *a posteriori* without any *a priori* input. On this account, scientific inquiry does not depend on any form of rationality "higher" than itself but is in fact the final basis of all other forms of rationality, "including one's own metaphysical assumptions."[19] This combination of evolutionary biology and pragmatic philosophy is what has led to the "'Darwinization of everything,' without need of submitting the Darwinian 'algorithm' of natural selection to anything more comprehensive or fundamental than itself."[20] This is what makes the dialogue between Darwinistic absolutists like Dawkins and their religious opponents unlikely to produce much light. The second assumption which undergirds the idea that "science is capable of grounding itself and justifying its own metaphysical hypothesis," is that "the empirical and experimental methods of scientific analysis are ontologically neutral precisely as *method*, and therefore stand *outside* of metaphysics and theology."[21] On this account even scientism is disparaged in favor of "pure science" and a rapprochement of a kind is put

---

15. Hanby, *No God*, 9.
16. Ibid.
17. Ibid., 10.
18. Ibid.
19. Ibid.
20. Ibid.
21. Ibid., 11.

forward of the non-overlapping magisterial type, each "minding its own business."[22]

Hanby goes back to the Greeks to illustrate his point. It was not just the differentially inferior nature of matter in the view of the Greeks that led to their impotency with respect to science. Empiricism is, of course, not possible when touch and tinkering with the created order is beneath one's intellectual dignity. It was also the fact, ironically, that the Greeks could not adequately differentiate between matter and God. That is, the demiurge and even the emanations of the *pleroma* were part god and part creation. Hanby, in demonstrating the impossibility of doing science without having some sort of a theology, speaks of the Greek notion of the unity of the cosmos as "irreducibly metaphysical and theological." However, he comments that "the Greeks were never able to arrive at an adequately comprehensive conception of this unity because they were never able to arrive at an adequate conception of the difference between God and the world, and this, in turn, introduced limitations into their conceptions of being that would prove fatal to these cosmological ambitions."[23]

It took the Christian doctrine of creation *ex nihilo* to provide the unity the Greeks sought for, along with the doctrine of the incarnation of the Son, in that this revealed the God who is "at once nearer and more remote than was conceivable within the confines of the Greek imagination, disclosing the paradigmatic form of the God-world relation and disclosing within the structure of worldly being a gratuity and novelty beyond Greek conception." Hanby thereby demonstrates that the doctrine of creation *ex nihilo* "is not a freestanding cosmology," but a "function of the doctrine of God and the modifications forced upon that doctrine by the Incarnation, which impregnated a metaphysical revolution that would take up the Greek inheritance and fulfil it from beyond its own resources."[24] This provides further evidence of the importance of the Trinity and in particular, the incarnation of the Son, in the development of science, and of the coinherence of science within theology. Hanby's point in a nutshell is that science cannot avoid being metaphysical and theological. Or to restate this in light of the thesis of this book, theology and science are coinherent. Unavoidably. Inevitably.

This means, each cannot be done without invoking the other. However, and Hanby is clear in this regard, this does not mean that each does not have its own distinct identity and its own "order of theory" and its own languages. But this is merely to acknowledge the Trinitarian analogy with

22. Ibid.
23. Ibid., 3.
24. Ibid.

respect to perichoresis or coinherence. Each of the Divine persons is *in* the other, both with respect to being and act, but equally, and mysteriously, each is *not* the other. Each has irreducible identity, or a differentiation with respect to their relations (the Son is generated by the Father, the Father is filiated by the Son, the Spirit proceeds from the Father and the Spirit spirates the Father) and their acts in the economy. Similarly, the different subject matter of theology and science leads to some distinctions in the fields of study. But, as Hanby states, "the metaphysical concern for the structure of being and the unity and interiority of living things mediates and unites in a new way these different theoretical orders and their incommensurable assumptions and problems." It is to the incarnation that Hanby turns for the grounding of this union, for it discloses the paradigmatic form of the God-world relationship, which means that this form extends by analogy to everything else."[25] Hanby's last word concerning the God-world relation is the ontological principle which arises first in Christology, and then moves by way of analogy to the relation between theology and science. He sums it up in this way: "The radical difference between God and the world, and thus between the theological and scientific orders, intimates a new and more intimate unity between them that simultaneously preserves and deepens their distinction."[26]

In light of this, Hanby is quick to reassure the scientist that he has no interest in "theology *supplanting* science, or in *fusing* science and theology into some sort of hybrid (theistic evolution)."[27] The proposal of this distinct but unified model, which is in keeping with a coinherent model of theology and science, is grounded in the incarnation as a unity-in-distinction in which, at times, the distinction sounds more emphatic. He sums up his thoughts in this regard:

> Just as God's interior presence *to* the world in the Incarnation and in creation is a function of God's infinite transcendence *of* the world, and just as the world's positive difference from God is a function of this interior and immediate presence, so too I wish to distinguish *more radically* than usual between theology, metaphysics, and science but in a way that simultaneously brings theology and metaphysics more immediately and interiorly to bear on science while underscoring their abiding difference from it.[28]

25. Ibid., 4–5.
26. Ibid., 5.
27. Ibid., emphases added.
28. Ibid.

It is the self-conscious invocation of the doctrine of God "in its Trinitarian and Christological development"[29] that makes Hanby's reconstruction of the doctrine of creation *ex nihilo* relevant to our project. The doctrine of creation is considered first in what Aquinas called its "active" sense, as a revelation of the doctrine of the triune God in Christ, and "not as a freestanding cosmology or a 'mechanical' explanation of how the world came to be but as a . . . ." This revelation of the God who created through the agency of the Word who entered creation is "contrasted both with the tacit theology of Greek metaphysics and with the tacit theology of modern science generally and Darwinian science particularly."[30] It is the failure to grasp this doctrine of God as determined by the doctrine of the Trinity, and the doctrines of creation and incarnation, along with the failure to discern the theology implicit in his theories that led to the distortion in Darwin's understanding of the meaning of creation. Hanby avers that the Christian doctrine of creation refuses to answer the questions of the "forms of causation." It is not, he insists, a doctrine concerned with *temporal* origins and the question of *how* the world is understood in a scientific way. It is a doctrine concerning *ontological* origins, telling us "*what the world is* at every moment of its existence." This anticipates the second, passive sense of creation Hanby (and Aquinas) speaks of. Creation imparts an ontological structure to the world and "an ontological identity, indivisible unity, and the incommunicable interiority of things that were evacuated in modern science's conflation of nature and art and in Darwinism's perfection of this logic in its attempted conflation of being and history."[31] Creation, rather than being in opposition to evolution, "is necessary to preserve the organism as the subject of its own being and as the subject matter of evolution. The theology of creation is thus necessary to save the scientific character of Darwinism because it saves the objects and the subjects of evolutionary science from Darwin's own universal acid."[32] His book goes on to argue that science is not only compatible with creation, but that indeed, "science needs creation in order finally to be science and to avoid falsifying itself and its objects." This, because "theology performs for the sciences a service which they cannot perform for themselves. Theology 'saves the appearances' for science by saving the being that is the condition of possibility for the truth *of* appearance."[33]

---

29. Ibid.
30. Ibid.
31. Ibid.
32. Ibid., 5–6.
33. Ibid., 6.

The heart of Hanby's thesis and what makes his work of interest to our project is his insistence that the foundational theological insight which allowed the church to unite and yet differentiate between God and the world, and to establish the meaning of created things, came from Trinitarian realities discovered by the Fathers. First there was the novel patristic distinction made between the one essence (*ousia*) and three *hypostases* or *persona* of the Trinity at Nicaea, which expressed the "coincidence of unity and distinction within the Godhead."[34] This led, second, to the christological distinction made at Chalcedon, in which the second person of the Trinity was described as having two natures (*natura*) in one *hypostasis*, or two natures in the one person. This hypostatic union was seen to be paradigmatic of the God-world union. Balthasar, as Hanby has commented, used the analogy of the church as sleepwalker, in the sense that "the Church coins a formula that only later on reveals all the dimensions of its meaning."[35] Specifically with respect to the definition of the mystery of the incarnate Christ in the formulations of Chalcedon, the mystery is not so much defined. Rather it has "negative boundaries"[36] placed around it. The history of the terms like *hypostasis* is not at all straightforward. This term was co-opted to support monophysitism (Christ had only one nature) and monotheletism (Christ has only one will). However, true to Balthasar's comment, after many centuries and the "great syntheses of Maximus the Confessor and Thomas Aquinas, among others," the "transformation of Greek ontological categories" was completed and the "ontological import of the Christian achievement" emerged with "full clarity."[37] This history of ideas was in essence the "passage from individual to person" which "contains the whole span of the transition from antiquity to Christianity, from Platonism to faith."[38] What is the reason for this? Hanby answers that it was because "the distinction between *persona*, or hypostasis, and *natura* provided a positive, ontological basis for distinguishing a 'who' from a 'what,' for distinguishing between *natura* and the *bearer* of that nature."[39]

Balthasar stated that a *hypostasis* is "the ontological subject of the ascription of an essence."[40] Hanby reminds us that Aristotle had also "identified substance as the underlying subject of predication, but since he

---

34. Ibid., 305.
35. Balthasar, *Cosmic Liturgy*, 211.
36. Hanby, *No God*, 305.
37. Ibid.
38. Ratzinger, *Introduction*, 160.
39. Hanby, *No God*, 305.
40. Ratzinger, *Introduction*, 223.

identified substance with form, and things as substances insofar as they are identical with form, he lacked a *positive* ontological principle for the distinction between a thing's being and its form." By contrast, the "notion of the person . . . represents a certain primacy of the subject of a nature over the nature itself, a primacy which nevertheless protects the 'rights of nature' in its very distinction from its bearer."[41] John Zizioulas from the Eastern Orthodox tradition, has expressed similar sentiments, though he is more confident that this was already present in the Cappadocians of the fourth century. That is, the notion of the elevation of the concept of hypostasis, the supremacy of *hypostasis* as an ontological category, was, as he describes it, the "great innovation in philosophical thought, brought about by Cappadocian Trinitarian theology," which, in turn "carries with it decisively a new way of conceiving human existence."[42] Zizioulas states that this caused the Cappadocians to underline "the idea that personhood can be known and identified through its absolute uniqueness and irreplaceability, something that has not ceased to be of existential relevance in philosophy."[43] The personhood of each of the persons in the Godhead in their appropriate irreducible differentiation is conveyed as Divine eternal persons in communion. The Cappadocians were also able to reconcile incommunicability with relationship. This was accomplished, as Zizioulas indicates by their "freeing divine existence from the servitude of personhood to substance, a servitude which applies only to created existence." In that they are uncreated, the three persons were "not faced with a given substance, but exist freely." "Being is," therefore, "simultaneously relational and hypostatic."[44]

The distinction between persona/hypostasis and nature was what permitted the definition that the second person of the Trinity had both a Divine and a human nature, without compromising the divinity, or "mixing"[45] the two natures. Hanby expresses what are for him the limits of the definition of the hypostatic union reached when reaching the point of seeking to understand "how" the Divine *logos* possesses a human nature.[46] Once again, only negative parameters can be set around this. The most helpful light that has been shed on this issue in the tradition, in my opinion, is that offered by

---

41. Hanby, *No God*, 305.

42. Zizioulas, "Doctrine of the Holy Trinity," 49.

43. Ibid., 50.

44. Ibid.

45. Cyril of Alexandria used the terms, without confusion, mixture or blending. See Hanby, *No God*, 307.

46. Hanby, *No God*, 305.

Cyril of Alexandria and then expounded by Karl Barth.[47] The essence of the matter is that the Son of God was Lord even in the manner in which he assumed humanity, so that the participation and coinherence is asymmetric. This is tightly expressed (for Barth) in this manner:

> The indispensable closer definition of this mutual participation must be this. The Son of God is the acting Subject who takes the initiative in this event, and not either His divine or His human essence ... He himself grasps and has and maintains the leadership in what His divine essence is and means for His human, and His human for His divine, in their mutual participation.[48]

This provides a model or precedence for considering theology and science as coinherent and yet asymmetrically so when understood from the faith perspective of the doctrine of creation.

Similarly, the term *hypostasis*, because it is not *ens* or essence, also defies exact definition. Socrates had recognized this, but as Hanby notes, the difference between how Socrates understood this, and the way in which Maximus viewed it was "no longer due to a dearth in intelligibility and actuality or to the limitation of form by matter or act by potency." Rather, with the concept of *hypostasis* as formulated by Maximus, "the outlines of a positive view of existence began to appear," as Balthasar has stated.[49] Balthasar asserted that "*hypostasis* can only be described by approaching it from two directions, which mutually complement each other: From that of nature and its ever-more narrowly circumscribing qualities that is, from the viewpoint of the being which the hypostasis 'has' and from that of the act of coming to possess this nature."[50] Although it did take centuries to clarify the metaphysical implications of this principles, nevertheless, even from its Chalcedonian roots, there was a "real distinction between essence and existence." What is crucial for the doctrine of creation and science is that this distinction which was implicit at the "high point" of the union of divinity and creation in the incarnation, was "sufficient to preserve and

---

47. Barth explains that "the participation of His divine in His human essence is not the same as that of His human in the divine.... The determination of His divine essence is *to* His human, and the determination of His human essence *from* His divine.... This means that the word mutual ... cannot be understood in the sense of interchangeable.... The relationship between the two is not reversible" (CD IV/2, 70–71). See Neder, *Participation*, 64–65.

48. Barth, CD IV/2, 70.

49. Balthasar, *Cosmic Liturgy*, 65.

50. Ibid., 225.

in fact deepen the difference between God and the world."[51] Here I quote Hanby at length to explain this distinction:

> The difference was preserved from God's side, because the distinction meant that the divine hypostasis could "become" human and assume a human nature without this imputing any change to his divinity, thus making it possible to conceive of a union that was at once "indivisible" and "unconfused," and thus truly a union. From the side of the world, the nonidentity of essence and existence implied in this distinction actually secures the relative autonomy of *natura*, and thus "the man Jesus' own active doing and willing," with respect to the *hypostasis*. This is half the point in formulating the distinction in the first place. *Natura* even enjoys a certain primacy, inasmuch as it precedes, in the order of development, its own free taking over of itself. This, surely, is part of the significance of insisting that Mary is *Theotokos*, and that the Son, eternally begotten of the Father, was born of the Virgin Mary. The formulation of an orthodox Christology thus becomes central to formulating the distinction between God and the world required by creation.[52]

There are some significant consequences from this incarnational definition. The first is that the union of the Divine and the human does not only preserve the divinity unmixed. It also preserves the identity of the humanity as humanity. Thus, Balthasar emphasizes the point that it was only when Christ appeared that it "became irrefutably clear that the creature is not simply pure negation with respect to God, and thus, cannot be saved simply through mystical absorption in God." Rather, no matter how elevated humanity is by its sharing in the Divine being, "the creature is saved only in the express preservation and perfection of his nature."[53]

Furthermore, it is apparent from the incarnational union that God can be immanent to the creation and, as Hanby states, "can assume a human nature without detriment either to his divinity or his humanity precisely *because* he infinitely transcends it." That is, "God can enter into intimate union *with* the world . . . because of his infinite difference *from* it." Hanby draws out the implications of this with respect to the ontological constitution of the world. The inseparability of God and the being and identity of things becomes apparent. Science is thus dependent upon the nature of God as Trinity. Science indeed, I would propose, building on Hanby's conclusions,

---

51. Hanby, *No God*, 306.
52. Ibid.
53. Balthasar, *Cosmic Liturgy*, 208.

is coinherent within theology. Mutual to it, without merger. Mutual and mutually enriching, yet retaining its own irreducible identity, as distinct from theology as creation is from God. Mutual in an asymmetric way that gives primacy to the God who created its objects of study and gives them their identity and meaning.

The manner in which Hanby views the disciplines of theology and *philosophy* does illustrate this coinherent relationship, and this may be applied to science. Reflecting Aquinas again, Hanby speaks of theology as being "constitutively incapable of exhausting the God-world relationship from God's side," and philosophy as being "incapable of exhausting it from the side of the world."[54] Theology and philosophy are, in Thomistic fashion, spoken of by Hanby significantly, for our purposes, as *each subsisting in the other*.[55] Philosophy "resides in the heart of theology," he states, "because God, presiding over his own appearance, can only appear to us from within the world in which theology is conducted," and theology "resides in the heart of philosophy because an intuition of the whole resides in every part, because it harbors a legitimate aspiration to ultimacy, and because some form of the God-world relation is inherent in however it understands its subject."[56] In sum, Hanby in fact offers a view of theology and science which fits well within the coinherence category. They are, on the basis of the doctrine of creation, and the incarnation, on the one hand, inseparable, and, at the same time, distinct.

By way of further precedent for the proposal of a coinherent relationship between theology and science, we consider briefly the work of T. F. Torrance, a theologian of the twentieth century in the Reformed Protestant tradition. "Magisterial and highly original,"[57] is Mark T. Achtemeier's assessment of the contribution of T. F. Torrance to the dialogue between theology and science. It still rings true, even if science has continued to advance.[58] Alister McGrath, impressed by the *scientific* acumen of Torrance,[59] referred

---

54. Hanby, *No God*, 28.

55. Ibid., emphasis added.

56. Ibid.

57. Achtemeier, "Natural Science," 269.

58. Ibid., 269–302.

59. Elmer Colyer records the fact that Torrance's early interest in theology and science was stimulated by the influence of his wife's cousin, the eminent physicist and radio astronomer Sir Bernard Lovell (1913–2012). Torrance felt that before he could even talk to Lovell about the relations between science and theology, he need to learn much more about science and so spent twenty years studying science, especially physics and the philosophy of science. This contributed to Torrance's acumen and reputation as a theologian of science. Colyer, *How to Read T. F. Torrance*, 40–41.

Coinherence in the Theology/Science Tradition 53

to his work in this area as "serious, informed and important . . . quite simply, of landmark significance."⁶⁰ It is my own considered opinion that if one has not come to terms with Torrance's *theology* as it was affected by science, and the discipline of *science* as it has been considered by Torrance's theology, one will not have an adequate grasp of either of these magisterial realms of knowledge. Myk Habets, in his summation, has commented that "Torrance's academic career was almost entirely absorbed by concerns over methodology . . . a clearing of the epistemological ground for a starting point in theological discourse."⁶¹ This search for an explicitly Christian epistemology took him in the direction of interaction with the natural sciences to the extent that he articulated theology as indeed the science of theology, as is reflected in his *Theological Science* (1969).

This association of the scientific and the theological, "created significant misunderstanding (and misgiving) about Torrance's theological and methodological vision for many," as Elmer Colyer has indicated. However, once it is clarified that this did not imply a "preconceived idea of *science as a universally applicable method (scientia universalis)* . . . with presuppositions and/or procedures to which all (*scientia speciales*), including theology, must conform if they are to be scientific," fears of practitioners in both science and theology are allayed. Rather, "each science has to be developed *kata physin* [according to the nature of the object], in strict conformity to the nature of the object"⁶² being studied, including theology, which because of the nature of its object has its own particular requirements and procedures. More will be said to clarify the concerns for both vocations. Suffice it to say that Torrance acknowledges both the irreducible distinctiveness of science (and the various sciences and their different hierarchical levels of knowledge) and theology *and* their formal similarities and mutually enriching nature, both with respect to epistemology and ontology.

Torrance's writing in this integrative field, more than any other scholar, have influenced my own conviction that the relationship between theology and science is *not* one of "conflict," or even non-overlapping magisteria ("independence"), nor yet mere "dialogue" or bridge-building, but one of *coinherence*. It may from the perspective of protagonists in both fields still require much "integration,"⁶³ but rather, based on the interwoven history of ideas, Torrance viewed it with the eye of "faith seeking understanding," to be

60. McGrath, *T. F. Torrance*, xii.
61. Habets, *Theology*, 21.
62. Colyer, "Scientific Theological Method," 206–7.

63. The terms, conflict, independence, dialogue and integration, reflect Ian Barbour's typology for the various ways in which theology and science are related. See Barbour, vol. 1, ch. 1.

one of coinherent mutuality-yet-distinctiveness of the two disciplines. In a manner analogous to the persons of the Holy Trinity, theology and science have their own irreducible identity as disciplines and yet have profound mutuality such that each is in the other and each animates the other.

The Christian theologian's counter to the warfare model or the polarization between science and theology in modernity,[64] is to insist that they are complementary and even coinherent. It is to say that each of these great traditions of thought have, as Torrance himself insisted, "deep mutual relations," and are the richer for the reality of the other. I find myself in profound resonance with Torrance on this matter. He argued for a "hidden traffic between theological and scientific ideas of the most far-reaching significance for both theology and science. It is in that situation where theology and science are found to have deep mutual relations, and increasingly cry out for each other."[65] Torrance was above all convinced that "both result from *a posteriori* reflection on an independent reality which they attempt to describe in their respective manners."[66] This is to say that our way of knowing involves "faith seeking understanding," and that critical realism applies to both. This is not a reductionistic move however, for as Achtemeier states, "grounded in the narration of a complex, interdependent history in which ideas from the disciplines tend to cross-fertilize with one other, Torrance's work resists neat categorization to any single typological category."[67]

The proposal of the coinherence of theology and science which is either implicit or explicit in the theologians we have considered is affirmed also in the work of Graham Buxton, who has boldly stated that "God's

---

64. The influence of chemist and philosopher of science Michael Polanyi on Torrance's pursuit of a Christian epistemology was significant. The fiduciary component of human knowledge was one of the emphases which Polanyi emphasized. Over against logical positivism, he argued for a "post-critical philosophy" which he believed to be consistent with the great tradition since Augustine, who stated, "Unless you believe, ye shall not understand" (cited in *Personal Knowledge*, 266). From the Enlightenment and John Locke's introduction of the dualism of knowledge and faith, what had been joined together was put asunder. As Polanyi wrote, "All belief was reduced to the status of subjectivity: to that of an imperfection by which knowledge fell short of universality" (*Personal Knowledge*, 266). His rebuttal of this is heard in the following statement: "We must now recognize belief once more as the source of all knowledge. Tacit assent and intellectual passions, the sharing of an idiom and of a cultural heritage, affiliation to a like-minded community: such are the impulses which shape our vision of the nature of things on which we rely for our mastery of things. No intelligence, however critical or original, can operate outside such a fiduciary framework" (*Personal Knowledge*, 266–67). This Augustinian-Anselmian-Barthian conviction shaped Torrance profoundly.

65. T. F. Torrance, *Reality*, x.

66. McGrath, *Science and Religion*, 226.

67. Achtemeier, "Natural Science," 270.

relationship with the natural world is likewise the province of trinitarian theology, as Colin Gunton and Thomas Torrance, amongst others, have consistently argued."[68] In fact, it is Gunton and Jürgen Moltmann, in particular, who influence Buxton's thought in this regard, and his work provides a good summation of these Trinitarian theologians and their contribution to the theology science conversation. One aspect of a world "charged with the glory of God" (Gerard Manley Hopkins) which Buxton emphasizes, is its relationality, which is a trace in creation of the relationality of the inner-trinitarian life of God expressed in the doctrine of perichoresis.

Gunton's doctrine of creation, which in many ways reflects that of Karl Barth, has been a significant bridge between theology and science. As created by the love of God, "the world is not impersonal process, a machine or a self-developing organism—a cosmic collective into which the particular simply disappears—but that which itself has a destiny along with the human."[69] The creation is, according to Gunton, a "perichoresis of related systems."[70] In physics, Buxton comments on the new awareness that "everything in the universe is bound up with everything else"—indeed, that "all things are what they are because they are related to everything else."[71] One could add from the chemist's perspective that there is also a remarkable common constituency to all matter, whether terrestrial or extra-terrestrial, and a tendency for elements to bond in accordance with electron affinities—more on that later. Here Buxton references Moltmann, who referred to this interrelatedness of the universe as the "creation-community," a community consisting of both creatures and environments contributing to a "web of life" on earth. This concept in Moltmann is perichoretic as a consequence of the fact Moltmann's vision of the Trinity is not only open, through the incarnation, for human relations, but also to the non-personal creation, in fact, so wide open that the whole world can find room and rest and eternal life within it."[72] Buxton also notes that what Moltmann expressed by way of the interconnectedness of all creation in a perichoretic God finds consonance with a growing awareness through developments in quantum theory, chaos theory and self-organizing systems that the universe is best understood in holistic rather than reductionistic terms. In other words, as theoretical chemist Guiseppe Del Re has noted, "The concept of system" for the universes is more than a "collection of loosely coupled subsystems or particles";

68. Buxton, *Trinity*, 125.
69. Gunton, *Promise*, 13.
70. Gunton, "Relation," 108.
71. Buxton, *Trinity*, 195.
72. Moltmann, "Perichoresis," 117.

rather it is more like "a tightly integrated whole, such as an organism."[73] Buxton relates how this has been most evident in quantum mechanics, a theme to which space will be devoted in a later chapter on relationality in the non-personal world. The correspondence between the phenomenon of entanglement and perichoresis will be of particular interest.

Scientist Theologians

Having considered the work of various theologian scientists who have noted the analogies between the Trinity and creation, and introduced the possibility of a coinherent relationship between theology and science, we now consider some scientist theologians who have gestured in the same direction. We begin with an example of a chemist whose integrative work has been centered in the theology of the Trinity. This is Spanish author José M. Romero-Baró, a scientist theologian in the Western and specifically Catholic tradition. This author is relevant for his work on the theme of the second objective of our study, the presence by way of analogy of signs of the coinherent Trinity in his creation. He makes a distinction between two ways in which the triune God has left his mark on creation, that of image, and that of trace (a phrase that comes from John of the Cross). Humanity is the *image* of God, but there are *traces* or *vestiges* of a creative, triune God in the rest of the creation also. Romero-Baró's paper begins "with a discussion of some representative texts on this teaching (by Saint Augustine, Saint Thomas Aquinas and Saint John of the Cross), providing a distinction between trace and image." Unlike Puhalo who works with the social model of the Trinity, in keeping with his Western tradition, Romero-Baró employs the Augustinian, psychological model of the Trinity. He suggests that "the image of God in human beings is recognized in memory, intellect and will, while mode, species and order reflect the trace of God in the rest of Nature, since each appears to explain the way of being of each object, the form in which it appears or its complete movement. The Augustinian *ordo amoris* (the order or law of love) is developed as a theological and physical foundation that may give meaning to the ultimate purpose of every natural movement."[74] Thus, the Holy Spirit is spoken of as the active agent in the vivifying and unifying of creation, on this model.

Romero-Baró, gives examples of the order of love in creation from the fields of physics and chemistry and biology, some of which will be considered in a later chapter. Though not all of these may be convincing, he does

73. Del Re, *Cosmic Dance*, 41.
74. Romero-Baró, "God's Mark."

however speak eloquently and helpfully to the matter of God's agency in the creative process through the Holy Spirit, the Lord and Giver of Life. He cites Denis Edwards in this regard:

> God is interiorly and intimately present in all that God creates. ... The Creator Spirit is present in every flower, bird and human being, in every quasar and in every atomic particle, closer to them than they are to themselves, enabling them to be and to become.[75]

This acknowledgment of the immanence of God, which is held together in Romero-Baró's tradition with the transcendence of God, by means of the Trinitarian mechanism of the Spirit's engagement, confirms the deep interpenetration of Trinitarian theology and science in his thought.

A theologian, Curtis L. Thompson, and a scientist, Joyce M. Cuff, (both in the Lutheran tradition) have also together explicitly employed the concept of coinherence grounded in Trinitarian theology[76] to speak analogously of the social nature of all reality as well as in human persons, as expressed in social theory and complex adaptive systems. Drawing especially on depictions of the Trinity in John of Damascus of the eighth century, who depicted the three persons in a perichoretic dance of mutuality and oneness, yet maintaining their distinctive personhood, they speak also of how human beings are by grace drawn by union with Christ, or *theosis*, into the Divine dance. As such they benefit fully from the rich interrelationship of the Divine persons in the inner life and love of the Trinity. In turn, the natural world also participates in the Divine life. In a manner reminiscent of Moltmann they assert that God is thus open for human relations and creation, and in love God draws that world into himself. The section on the human self in light of "religious coinherence," in which Kierkegaard is invoked, will be revisited in a later chapter. But these authors extend the concept of coinherence to all creation. They state that "the term coinherence, extended to a universal category, lifts up the way that each organism participates in the dance round of life, receiving sustenance from the whole

---

75. Edwards, *God of Evolution*, 91–92, 94.

76. David Bentley Hart's definition of perichoresis is cited: "The Christian understanding of God as a perichoresis of love, a dynamic coinherence of the three persons, whose life is eternally one of shared regard, delight, fellowship, feasting, and joy" (*Beauty of the Infinite*, 155). In their own definition of how John of Damascus describes perichoresis in the Trinity, there is just an ever so slight tinge of the anthropocentric: "three persons joining together in the dance, and in the process becoming united in that single activity while maintaining their own distinctive personas" (Thompson and Cuff, *God and Nature*, 135). The eternality of *both* the persons *and* the communion is shaded in the enthusiasm for this concept of perichoresis.

and donating its gifts to the whole. Nature is alive as it is included in the divine dance of love."[77] They speak of both *coinherence*, as life in one another by mutual donation, and of *consilience*, the coming-togetherness of reality in response to Divine love, so moving coinherence beyond the "context of the divine" to "all creatures great and small."[78]

It is hard to overestimate the contribution of John Polkinghorne to the holding together of theology and science. Especially since the writing of *Science and the Trinity* (2004) his approach has been one in which, exemplifying our own approach, he allowed theology to shape the agenda, rather than science. Rejecting deism (for its theological thinness), mere theism (which stops short of acceptance of the doctrines of conciliar theology), revisionism (which radically revises orthodox claims in a demythologizing manner), he affirmed a developmental theology in which he affirmed "a continually unfolding exploration" between and within the disciplines, recognizing the provisional nature of the language and concepts in both, with an emphasis on the continuity with theological orthodoxy, rather than discontinuity. This continuity would be assured by a bottom-up or empirical approach in theology, just as in science. This empiricism of the theology side was informed by three sets of historical data: (i) Scripture as properly interpreted, acknowledging genre, reevaluation of unedifying material in light of the progressive nature of revelation and the creedal or conciliar theological commitments which have arisen from its study over the centuries, and as evaluated by a polysemous view of Scripture (Scripture has more than one sense); (ii) the experiences and testimonies of the earliest Christians preserved in the apostolic tradition and New Testament writings, which Polkinghorne called "Trinitarian thinking";[79] and (iii), the ongoing experiences of all Christians and their witness as expressed in the liturgy of the church, which expands the empirical database toward a "liturgy-assisted logic," focused especially in the Eucharist. Thus he states, "Faith seeking understanding receives its impetus from religious experience." This is a sacramental vision of science and theology, a sacramental theology which "is as complex and sophisticated and ultimately as powerfully insightful, as the considerations that support a fundamental theory of science."[80] In response to the concern that theology and science, on this account, though both arrived at empirically, might because of the different object of their study lead to relativism or epistemic subjectivism, Polkinghorne's answer was that

---

77. Thompson and Cuff, *God and Nature*, 135.
78. Ibid., 133–38.
79. Polkinghorne, *Science and the Trinity*, 99–103.
80. Ibid.

there is only one world and that a unity of knowledge can be expected to be arrived at in this developmental model.

The belief that both science and theology are best done from the bottom up, from a faith seeking understanding perspective, is expressed by Polkinghorne in *Science and the Trinity*.[81] He develops the analogy between relationality in God the Trinity and in matter. Thus he states: "I shall make what some of my scientific colleagues might think was an over-audacious claim, that a deeply satisfying intellectual candidate for the title of a true 'Theory of Everything' is in fact provided by Trinitarian theology."[82] He clarifies that it is not that we can infer the Trinity from nature, but "that there are aspects of our scientific understanding of the universe that become more deeply intelligible to us if they are viewed in a Trinitarian perspective."[83] Later, he illustrates this in a number of ways, which we will explore in a later chapter. Suffice it to say that Polkinghorne is convinced that the Trinitarian perspective, such as is expressed in John Zizioulas' *Being in Communion*, which Polkinghorne suggests could equally well have the title, "Reality is relational,"[84] does indeed reveal deeply intelligible but otherwise hidden features of nature, such as non-locality. These themes in Polkinghorne will be developed in later chapters.

Drawing all these brief encounters of theologian scientists and scientist theologians together, we may conclude that there is a significant strand of thought in their scholarship related to coinherence. This begins within the doctrine of God, and within the doctrine of creation in Christian theology, and leads to postulations of the presence of coinherence by way of analogous imaging and traces in creation, as revealed by science. The idea then arises that theology itself and the discipline of science, that is, *knowledge* of the perichoretic God, and *knowledge* of the perichoretic creation, might themselves be found in each other, while maintaining their distinct identities.

The question now arises, what might such a perichoretic relationship look like, especially respecting the autonomy of these disciplines, and the Christian concern for the primacy of theology, given that God is the Creator and Reconciler and Redeemer of creation? The answer to this question will now be worked out as we consider the mutualities and particularities of theology and science that will be evident in the history of the development of science, and then with respect to knowledge (epistemology) and being (ontology) in each of the magisteria.

81. Ibid.
82. Ibid., 61.
83. Ibid.
84. Polkinghorne, *Trinity and the Entangled World*, 12–13.

Chapter 3

The Coinherent *History* of Ideas

"THE WAY WE WERE":
THE COINHERENT HISTORY OF IDEAS

THIS CHAPTER CONCERNS PRIMARILY the third aspect of this project: the *proposal* that Trinitarian theology and science, as areas of knowledge, may be considered to be coinherent. In particular it is with respect to history, and specifically the history of ideas, rather than epistemology or ontology, that we are concerned.

The unavoidable relationship between Christian theology and culture has always been a particularly challenging one throughout the church's history. For example, in the development of the doctrine of the Holy Trinity, controversy has surrounded the origin of the concepts employed by the Fathers, and even the terms employed. Though words like *ousia* and *hypostasis* seem to have been commandeered by the church and invested with its own meaning, it could not be denied that they came from Greco-Roman culture. The opinion on this expressed by T. F. Torrance leaves no ambiguity about which was, in the providence of God, the direction of this contextualization. He stated that "Nicaea represents the Christianizing of Greco-Roman culture rather than the Hellenization of Christian faith."[1] One might say that the church, upon the foundation of biblical revelation, inculturated or contextualized this doctrine, rather than being enculturated by Hellenistic ways. I wish to catch a little of Torrance's constructive spirit by proclaiming

---

1. Colyer, *How to Read T. F. Torrance*, 183n142.

the reality of the coinherence between theology and science in light of the gospel, and to seek to Christianize the culture of modernity in this regard. There is good reason to hope that this may be done, for, as Torrance and others have contended, science has in fact historically speaking, developed and prospered in the context of Christian civilization, and during and since the Reformation in particular, precisely because there is a consonance with respect to the history of ideas in each discipline.

The claim that with respect to the history of ideas, Christian theology and the natural sciences are deeply intertwined, will seem counterintuitive to contemporary scientists.

These surprising echoes of coinherence between their histories are the focus of our attention here. A significant voice drawing attention to this relationship was T. F. Torrance, whose account of the relation between Christian theology and natural science tended to "proceed from an assumption other than the fundamental separateness of the disciplines." His research reveals the "narrative of a complex, interdependent history in which ideas from the disciplines tend to cross-fertilize with one another," concluding that there is "substantial overlap between natural science and Christian theology . . . in their histories of development."[2] Building on Torrance's insights, this chapter traces the history of science with a particular eye toward the flourishing of science within a Christian context, in marked contrast to other cultural contexts—especially the ancient Greek context—as well as marking the shift away from Christianity in modernity with its particular view of reason. Noting the deconstruction of the modern hypothesis in the postmodern era will then present a view of reason and prejudice/faith that offers a kinder window for the coinherence of science and theology, that of critical realism. This way of doing knowledge receives some mention here and is expanded upon in the next chapter, along with the related notion that epistemology follows ontology.

The Birthing and Flourishing of Science within the Christian Context

Two ontological realities serve to demonstrate the overlap between theology or the Christian faith and science. The first is the clear distinction good theology provides between God and the creation, the metaphysical remove, as it were, between God and creation. Thus creation is *not* God. This distinction is implicit in a text such as John 1:3—"*Through him all things were made; without him nothing was made that has been made.*" Clearly the Word

2. Achtemeier, "Natural Science," 270.

who is God is distinct from "all things that are made," the creation. But even the fact that the triune God works through the agency of the Word-Son, here, (and the Spirit, elsewhere) is suggestive of some metaphysical distance between Father and Son, especially when it is most likely that in the eternal covenant of God, the Son, is *incarnandus*—that is, has an orientation toward the incarnation in eternity past, and therefore toward agency in the creation.

But this theological reality must not be emphasized to the expense of another one. What God through the Word creates is good. It may not be God, but it is good. It is not, as in the Greek world, inferior to spirit. This was emphasized in the Genesis account, and it is recapitulated here also in John 1:3, 14: "*Through him all things were made; without him nothing was made that has been made. . . . The Word became flesh and made his dwelling among us. We have seen his glory, the glory of the one and only Son, who came from the Father, full of grace and truth.*" The Son in creation, in a created body, is no less glorious than in preincarnate days, albeit that glory may be veiled. This goodness of the body of the incarnate Son vindicates the goodness of matter.

These two theological realities are actually the cornerstone for the widely held proposal that Christianity was the seedbed for the development of modern science in the first place. The Christian doctrine of creation always affirmed that creation was *good* and therefore worth engaging, and worth coming to know. The Christian doctrine of the incarnation reaffirmed the goodness of creation, and the resurrection forever sealed the goodness of the human body and, therefore, of creation and the new creation. That creation was *good* made it worth studying, and engaging with in an empirical manner. That it was *not God, not sacred in the sense of being Divine*, rendered it accessible. Some cultures of a pantheist variety could never develop science for they were simply too fearful of the matter they sacralized, too fearful of tampering with the gods. Other cultures, like the Greek one, did not develop science for they downplayed the importance of the material realm, and experimentation within it, as unnecessary. It is possible, then, to argue historically that the scientific culture and approach to life that arose in Europe from the sixteenth century onward is the offspring of a Western Christian culture and more particularly of Protestant thought.[3]

In a nutshell, the proposal that science is coinherent within Christian theology *arises* in part from a compatibility *stemming* from a high, but not too high, view of created matter. Matter matters and is worthy of study. It has its own identity, its own particularity. It is not inferior to things mental

---

3. See, e.g., Dillenberger, *Protestant Thought*. See also Cochrane, *Reformed Confessions*. See in particular Provan, *The Reformation and the Right Reading of Scripture*, chs. 13 and 14.

or spiritual, as in Platonism. Yet it is not sacralized, that is, imbued with the substance of divinity, as in paganism or animism. It may reflect the glory of God (Ps 19; Rom 1:20) in the sacred space that is creation, but it does not usurp the Creator. That is, it is not to be considered equal with God. It is God's creation, and he is distinct from it. It is not too sacred to study.

If it is true to say, then, that modern science was birthed within a Christian culture and that there are good theological reasons for this, the empirical manner in which Christianity as a *historic* faith was affirmed added to this compatibility. The faith was grounded in those who witnessed the advent of Jesus Christ—his life, death and resurrection from the dead—and passed this on from generation to generation in the history of the church. Though there is a strand of atomism and naturalism in the Epicureans which influenced the inception of scientism in modernity, for the most part, the Greek philosophical culture did not consider creation to be good, but something rather to escape in order to engage in the higher human pursuits of the intellectual realm, separated from the empirical.[4] The Greeks could offer human civilization mathematics, but not science.[5] The Greeks viewed

---

4. On this see Foster, "Man's Idea of Nature," 361–66, and "Christian Doctrine," 446–68; McGrath, *Science of God*, 51; Hooykaas, *Religion*, 5–6; and Judge, "Commentary."

5. This is not to minimize the reality that early Western scientists were influenced by Greek thought of both the Aristotelian and Neoplatonic variety. However, it is precisely in moving beyond Aristotle and Plato that science can proliferate. Kepler, for example, initially held on to the Aristotelian idea of formal causes, but moved from seeing mathematics as secondary to making it primary, "privileging instead the nature of the qualities that form gave to matter and all the teleological orientations this implied." Ultimately the Aristotelian notion of quality and teleology was collapsed by Kepler "into the act of mathematical quantification. This subtle shift in emphasis was actually of 'momentous importance'" for "it is a short step from equating the truly real with the mathematical to the idea that all certain and reliable knowledge is mathematical and not mystical/theological." Chapp, *God of Covenant and Creation*, 78. This paved the way for a deistic rather than Trinitarian view of the relation between science and theology. Chapp has asserted that both Copernicus and Kepler were more influenced by "spiritual Neoplatonism" of the Pythagorean kind, than by "secular Aristotelianism," and that it as the former influence that paved the way for the new scientific revolution. The relates to the mathematically harmonies nature. "Indeed," says Chapp, "Copernicus, who lacked real evidential corroboration that his heliocentric hypothesis was true, nevertheless held to its veracity due in large measure to its mathematical elegance compared to the ugly and clunky epicycles required by the Ptolemaic system." He adds that "the real crisis created by people like Johannes Kepler, and later Galileo, was not the oft-cited pseudo-crisis of geocentrism versus heliocentrism, but rather all the attendant entailments of the shift to a mathematical/mechanical view of the cosmos versus a theophanic one." This was the de-sacralizing of the "old cosmos of the form-giving intermediates in favor of a new model that, despite its cloak of Pythagorean mysticism, seemed for all the world to be devoid of direct divine presence" (78–79). In other words, this spawned the theological crisis of deism. In a similar vein, Isaac Newton seems to have followed Aristotle's traditional form theory which asserted that there

matter as unimportant and could never advance science beyond abstract reasoning.

These assertions are supported by an important thinker in this arena, Karl Popper (1904–94), the Austrian-British philosopher of science. Speaking against the school of Vienna,[6] he stated that at the heart of scientific endeavor is not accumulated evidence that proves the truth, but rather it involves attacking the hypothesis, and then successive disproofs, giving rise to the next hypothesis. Science does not work by what's in the mind already, though there may be a tentative hypothesis in mind. It works by the experimental method, not its concepts. Popper attacked Plato and the Platonic mirage of Idealism, with its idea that truth lies in the perfect form. Particular things were deemed to be faulty and truth lay beyond sensory data for Plato. In the Greek philosophical world, the world was utterly predictable on the basis of logic and it was not subject to change. From the pre-Socratic philosophers and then Plato and Aristotle, a manner of understanding the world was being developed using mind alone, thinking rationally to explain everything—and behind this was the assumption, the "great" hypothesis that the universe is logical and unsurprising. This Classical Greek philosophical contribution was, simply, all wrong. Not that there isn't a certain order and logic behind it that actually permits scientific discovery—an orderly Periodic Table, for example. But this axiom is simply wrong. The

---

are cosmic agents which are responsible for the mediation of the forms of substances from God, or at least to say that they were occult or inscrutable. Robert Boyle, however, employed the internal form principle, which suggests that the form of a substance has its formal cause in the shape and relations between the particles that constitute the substance which were regular and not random. The efficient cause for Boyle of an object's qualities was the mechanistic laws governing the relations of particles worked out by Newton. The result in both cases was again an incipient deism. It will take a more Trinitarian approach which is renewed in Calvin, and then Jonathan Edwards, and then Barth, to bring some resolution of the issue of causation and the engagement of God in creation. Regarding the latter, Bruce Hindmarsh has commented that Edwards knew Newton's work in the General Scholium, and that over against the assertions that we cannot know the inside of things but only external forms and final causes, Edwards not only boldly proposes "atoms" on five occasions and particulate matter built from the inside out, in the "Personal Narrative," speaks of how he would "behold the sweet glory of God *in* these things" and to see the "appearance of divine glory, *in* almost everything." Jonathan Edwards, *Works*, 16:793–94.

In a forthcoming book on early evangelicalism, D. Bruce Hindmarsh will suggest that in that era, spiritually speaking, it was all about the inside of things. Edwards' occasionalism may not be the ultimate foil for deism, but it pointed in a consciously Trinitarian way for a better, more coinherent resolution.

6. This school, also known as the Vienna Circle of Logical Empiricism or Logical Positivism, was a group of philosophers and scientists from the natural and social sciences, logic and mathematics who met regularly from 1924 to 1936 at the University of Vienna.

idea was that logic ruled all, that the mind can deduce necessary truth, as in mathematics, or music, the music of the spheres. Thus Aristotelian logic was absolute. Logic comes from Logos and comes from calculation. Mathematics was considered to be a form of knowledge. The universe was all musical spheres with balancing parts expressed mathematically. Therefore, following pre-Socratic Greek philosopher Parmenides (b. ca. 515 BC), who offered the statement "change is impossible," Empedocles (495-430 BC), best known for originating the cosmogenic theory of the four classical elements, accepted this, and suggested that what may look like change was actually delusion. He explained the appearance of change not just as a delusion. He suggested that the senses were recording a process of circular rotation. The cosmos was thus envisioned as a beautiful prison, one which cannot be changed, as it would then not be complete.[7]

The Christian doctrine of creation and the incarnation and the resurrection stands in contrast to this. And it is much more consonant with what we as humans know of the universe from modern science. And both this gospel and this science come to be known in the same way. They are post-intellectual, that is, they are discovered empirically.

Other cultures were unlikely to develop science for the opposite reason. They held creation in too high an esteem, as a result of their pantheistic notions that creation *is* God, and therefore did not engage with it for fear of incurring the wrath of the God or the gods. Christians viewed creation as good, but not God, a good space in which they had been authorized to steward and care for it on behalf of God. This would require getting to know it—a task immeasurably aided through the tools, methods, and aims of science. Indeed, acknowledging the confluence of aims is a matter at the very heart of this work.

The doctrine of creation is integral to the intelligibility of the world, as Michael Hanby has *reminded* us in his important book *No God, No Science*.[8] He asserts that the Greek problem with respect to science was not just its disparaging of matter, but its inability to differentiate God and creation. It was the Christian doctrine of creation and the incarnation which brought about "fulfillment" or that which was lacking, in Greek philosophy. He then argues that this cosmological achievement was all but eliminated during the scientific revolution, beginning in the seventeenth century. But before moving to that topic, we must first consider how the Christian culture of the

---

7. These reflections on the thought of the Greek philosophers are a summary of those of historian Edwin Judge in his commentary on Popper. See Judge, "Commentary." For a detailed description of Popper's thought on the history of science and falsification, see Popper, *Logic of Scientific Discovery*.

8. Hanby, *No God*, 2, 55–58, 72, 100–108, 129–32, 175, 305–9.

medieval period, influenced by the doctrine of creation and the incarnation in the apostles, the (apostolic/patristic) fathers, and the Renaissance, gave birth to science.

Compatibility with Medieval-Renaissance Christian Context

Empirical science through sensuous experience took root in distinctly theological soil. In particular, the Christian doctrine of creation and the incarnation validated matter was crucial to this. This is aptly expressed in Loren Wilkinson's statement that this empirical knowledge came to be valued "through the Christian experience of the Creator-God of love who invented physical reality, and who in Jesus, became a part of it."[9] The contingency of the Creator in his creating and the consequent contingency of creation, was a further theological understanding which was amenable to the development of science, in that it highlighted the need for empirical evidence. The creation, "like who God is, is inexhaustible, surprising and gracious. Knowledge comes through engaged experience, not detached contemplation."[10] The origins of science in the Christian tradition have been well documented in the work of the Oxford philosopher Michael Beresford Foster (1903–59) in the 1930s. These findings are all the more remarkable for the charged context in which they were made, a context where "any influence of Christianity on the development of science it had been negative."[11] The mood was captured by the words of Bertrand Russell at the beginning of his *History of Western Philosophy*, in which science, which gave genuine knowledge, was contrasted with theology, which "induces a dogmatic belief that we have knowledge where in fact we have ignorance, and by doing so generates a kind of impertinent insolence towards the universe."[12] The stage had been set for this conflict by Wilson Draper's warfare model expounded in his controversially titled *History of the Conflict between Science and Religion*. He opined that by its devaluing of science, Christianity had become "a stumbling block in the intellectual advancement of Europe for more than a thousand years."[13]

9. Wilkinson, "Cheeses, Chartreuse," 9.

10. Ibid., 9–10.

11. Ibid., 9. See also Teel, "Christian Theology." Teel contributes in part 1 a thorough and detailed synthesis of Foster's three *Mind* articles on "the Christian Doctrine of Creation and the Rise of Modern Science," and in part 2, "a critical literature review of published references to the Foster Thesis."

12. Russell, *History of Western Philosophy*, xiv.

13. Draper, *History of the Conflict*, 33.

It is worthy of note that these hard attitudes were not without reason. The church has not always had a great record with regard to listening to science. The oft-invoked refusal of the Catholic Church[14] to accept the discovery of Copernicus that the earth was not the center of the solar system and the excommunication of Galileo for believing this, is usually held up as irrefutable evidence of just this kind of incommensurability.[15] In light of this, Foster's work is all the more poignant. His "meticulously reasoned articles—written not as Christian theology or apologetics, but simply as a careful exercise in the history of thought—were the beginning of a slow but thorough change in this image of 'warfare' . . . and 'it is now widely acknowledged that some aspects of medieval Christianity were not only a fertile seedbed for modern science, but quite possibly a necessary condition for its eventual development.'"[16]

The primary thesis in Foster's argument was that "Greek science had never moved beyond its embryonic stage because it assumed that genuine knowledge was (as in a mathematical proof) always a matter of abstract reasoning from certain first principles." Crucial to his thesis was the reality that what modern empirical science and a Christian worldview share, in both cases over against Greek philosophy, is the "part which *sensuous experience* plays in it."[17] Not that sensuous experience was unknown to the Greeks. It was just that it was not valued highly in the realm of natural philosophy.[18] By contrast, knowledge of the God who created physical reality and by the incarnation became part of it, enhanced the value of things earthy and material. Emphatically, "we cannot know the world God has made simply

14. It should also be noted that some seventeenth-century Protestants were also deeply distrusting of the Galileo science. "The first anti-Copernican monograph to appear in the Lutheran sphere," Klaus Scholder reminds us (*Birth of Modern Critical Theology*, 53–58), "was that of Danish mathematician and theologian Peter Bartolinus . . . published in 1632."

15. Peter Harrison has in fact shown that this was not so much a conflict between the church and science, but between these astronomers and the scientists of the day who advised the church, and who considered the new evidence insufficient to overturn the prevailing view. See Harrison, *Territories of Science and Religion*, 172–73.

16. Wilkinson, "Cheeses, Chartreuse," 9.

17. Foster, cited in Wilkinson, "Cheeses, Chartreuse," 10, emphasis added.

18. Interestingly, empirical method was in fact essential to the work of the historian whose job was to arbitrate disputes by gaining knowledge of narrow particularities (*historia*) through receiving testimony and testing its claims. Ancient Greek historians such as Thucydides (as well as Roman successors such as Tacitus) proceeded in a similar manner, "convinced that true history could be written only while events were still within living memory, and they valued as their sources the oral reports of direct experience of the events by involved participants in them." Bauckham, *Jesus and the Eyewitnesses*, 8–9.

by thinking about it," says Loren Wilkinson, citing Psalm 34:8, "Taste and see that the Lord is good." The recognition that "sensuous experience is the source of knowledge," he concludes, "is basic to Hebrew understanding. And it is here, rather than in Greek ideas of the superiority of the knowledge abstracted from the senses, that the tradition of empirical science took root."[19]

Other authors have affirmed this Foster hypothesis also. Durham theologian of science, David Wilkinson states that

> the warfare language hides the fact that the modern tradition of empirical science has deep roots in the Jewish and Christian tradition. The point was first made clearly in Michael Foster's meticulously reasoned series of articles, "The Christian Doctrine of Creation and the Origins of Modern Science," published in the resolutely positivist philosophical journal *Mind* in 1934. It was only as late medieval Christian thinkers distanced themselves from the Platonic idea that creation was an imperfect manifestation of eternal and perfect ideas in the mind of a transcendent God that they began to be able to appreciate the contingency of creation, and thus the necessity of investigating it empirically, not in terms of what a rational Creator must do, but in terms of what a personal and loving God wills to do. It is no accident that, for better and for worse, science is a plant which grew primarily in Christian soil.[20]

Conflict Does Arise in the Late Middle Ages, and On into the Reformation Period

While this thesis—that the values of the doctrine of creation within the Christian faith did indeed have great consonance with what science is, and how it developed—can stand scrutiny, it must in fairness also be acknowledged that the Christian church did not always apply the empirics on which their historical faith was grounded to science as it developed. It did not always read and interpret Scripture well, compounded by the fact that the institution of the church and its politicking did not always draw on the best ideas of the Christian theologians in their traditions. As McGrath notes, to "critique the leading ideas of Christian theology on the basis of the actions of certain late medieval ecclesiastical figures is to assume a simple,

---

19. Wilkinson, "Cheeses, Chartreuse," 10.
20. Wilkinson, "One World."

The Coinherent History of Ideas   69

direct, and linear connection between these entities which rarely existed in practice."[21]

With respect to the above-mentioned Copernicus, he was ultimately vindicated in his observational approach to the heliocentric issue, accompanied by mathematical calculation, by the empirical approach of Galileo when the latter was able to use a telescope (1609–13). It was not just thinking, but empirical observation and mathematical calculation that resolved this issue. The primary issues of the conflict with the church arose from (i) a treasured Middle Ages worldview of geocentrism, with echoes of the Platonism of the Greeks which was sometimes influential in the medieval church; and (ii) the interpretation of Scripture, which was read through geocentric spectacles, and with a flat or wooden literalism. Interestingly, the view of the universe as geocentric went all the way back to Ptolemy, the Egyptian astronomer of the first half of the second century. The way in which this view changed to heliocentric is actually a remarkable reality, indeed "one of the most significant changes in the human perception of reality to have taken place in the last millennium"[22] in that it was such a radical change from the extant model. Of course, Copernicus' model of planets in circular orbits, because it could not account for the data on the motions of the planets, would give way via the work of Tycho Brahe and Johann Kepler to a more sophisticated elliptical model, and the mathematical relationship between the square of the periodic time of the planet (to complete one orbit round the sun) and the cube of its mean distance from the sun (they are proportional).

Jumping ahead for just a moment, there is a great deal of similarity between the issue of Copernicus and that of evolutionary theory in the twentieth century. Though there has been a strand of thoughtful theologians and scientists who have embraced the theory of evolution—what is after all, not "just a theory" (a theory holds high credibility in the scientific world, being accompanied by strong evidence of many kinds)—and found it to be compatible with the book of Genesis properly read, the majority of evangelical Christians reject it and are in grave danger of repeating the Galileo-Copernicus fiasco. The church in Copernicus' day was challenged to look again at its interpretation of biblical passages, and its indiscriminate enculturation into both Aristotelian philosophy and Pythagorean Neoplatonism.[23] In other words, the data, now clear in its insinuations, had to be taken into account in biblical interpretation. A coinherent view between

21. McGrath, *Science and Religion*, 13.
22. Ibid., 18.
23. Chapp, *God of Covenant and Creation*, 78.

theology and science assumes that there will be no contradictions between science and the Bible, but with the important proviso, as *properly interpreted*.

The methods and assumptions of biblical interpretation has its own history. Limning the progression, McGrath has outlined three primary ways in which Scripture was interpreted in the tradition over the centuries. I add a fourth, which arose from the "back to the sources" approach of the Reformation.

1. There was the woodenly literal approach. For example, Genesis 1 was assumed to refer to seven literal twenty-four-hour days. This approach, still alive and well in our times, is really not the literal, but the literalistic approach. That is, it neglects the literary genre of texts, and rhetorical, historical approaches which are in fact part of the literal or normal interpretation approach.

2. Second there has been the allegorical approach, especially evident in the church fathers so that three nonliteral senses of Scripture become admissible in the Middle Ages. Genesis is thus viewed as poetic or allegorical, giving rise to a theology of creation, not science. Interestingly, the Western church father of the fourth century, Augustine, knows that the six day account of Genesis 1 cannot be literal. Since he believed in a fiat creation, why would God need twenty-four hours to create what he did each day? Twenty-four hours was too long! So he allegorized it as a metaphor for the Christian life.[24]

3. The accommodation approach. This approach to Scripture has been very important for permitting dialogue between the physical sciences and theology. It acknowledges the reality that revelation is given in culturally and anthropologically conditioned ways that need to be researched and understood before the interpretive gap can be bridged. With respect to the early chapters of Genesis, the language and images that are used are acknowledged to be appropriate to the culture of the original audience, and are therefore not to be understood in a wooden literal way. Rather the key ideas are to be extracted recognizing that these have "been expressed in forms and terms which are specifically adapted or 'accommodated' to the original audience."[25] This approach is not new, but exists in Judaism and in the patristic Christian era. However, its full development comes in the Protestant Reformation, with significant input from John Calvin, which we will consider shortly.

---

24. St. Augustine, *Literal Meaning of Genesis*. See also Rüst, "Early Humans," 182–93.
25. McGrath, *Science and Religion*, 20.

4. I have added the *properly literal or normal hermeneutic* (rhetorical, historical), which treats biblical literature as literature (albeit God-breathed, it is mediated through human literature), and researches things like the literary genre of passages, and cultural and historical background (e.g., the ancient Near Eastern background of Genesis 1 and 2). This will certainly include the accommodation approach, but it is more broadly the historical critical approach which is practiced by biblical scholars like Waltke, Walton, Provan, Long, Wright, Watts, McKnight, etc. The crucial issues in this method is are related to these questions: What kind of text is this? What questions is it really answering for the original audience? What is the authorial intent? This reading of Scripture has been refined in the Modern period, but its roots go back to the Reformation. It is itself a science.

The mature development in biblical scholarship and interpretation reflected in especially the latter two approaches, which enabled the church to gain a better sense of the place of science, occurs *in the sixteenth century* with its impetus coming from the Renaissance "back to the sources" movement and the Reformation. The accommodation method spoken of above was important in the astronomy debates of the sixteenth and seventeenth centuries, and in particular the controversy regarding whether the sun revolves around the earth or vice versa. Psychologically speaking, Freud has opined that it was a wound for humanity and its sense of self-importance, to discover that humanity did not stand at the center of the universe,[26] one of three "narcissistic wounds" of the modern age. Interestingly, the second wound Freud highlighted was Darwinism, which seemed to suggest that humanity did not have a unique place on earth (the third, was that, in accordance with his own theory, humanity was not even the master of its own limited realm). When wounds occur, rationality sometimes goes by the board. The church digs its heels in by stubbornly sticking to its theological guns without real biblical warrant.

A hermeneutic or interpretive methodology that avoided this unnecessary conflict between theology and science may in fact be discerned in John Calvin (1509–64). In so doing, Calvin made three important contributions to the development of the natural sciences: (a) he encouraged them by positively affirming the scientific study of nature, grounded in his

26. It should be pointed out, as Dennis Danielson has shown, that the removal of geocentrism was *not* in fact considered to be the wound that Freud maintained it was. He states that it is an "old cliché" that the "geocentric cosmology is said to locate the earth in the place of greatest importance in the universe." In fact, this view "dissolves before the sophisticated clarity of Aristotle's account." Danielson, *Book of the Cosmos*, 39, 41.

positive theology of creation, and its orderliness, and the ways in which it reflected the wisdom and power of God; and (b) he upheld the principle of the perspicuity of Scripture. Calvin, like other Reformers, did engage with long-standing issues in the tradition, but he also clarified other issues that have been considered to be novel. The mark of the Reformation is the belief that Scripture was the sole, final authority of the church, and that it was capable of being so because it was perspicuous.[27] It did not require the guidance of the church hierarchy (the magisterium), which is not to say it could be interpreted individualistically, that is without the church present and past. However, as Iain Provan affirms, "Possessing both the Bible in its original languages (or, at least, in an accurate, vernacular translation), and some rudimentary rules of reading, the Reformers believed that no-one should have undue difficulty in understanding what Scripture had to say."[28] The whole matter of going back to the sources in biblical interpretation and exegesis no doubt provided a powerful impetus in the pursuit of knowledge in other areas, including science. It also gave permission for interpretations outside of those of the magisterium that were related to matters of science, thus permitting integrative work. This is illustrated even within the Catholic tradition, for example, where the accommodationist approach of Carmelite friar Francisco Foscarini was hugely important to the debate in the church regarding Galileo (1564–1642) in Italy (as evident in Foscarini's *Letter on the Opinion of the Pythagoreans and Copernicus*);[29] (c) Calvin removed obstacles to theology/science integration in particular by eliminating a literalistic approach to the Bible, and by offering instead the "accommodationist" viewpoint of biblical interpretation. Calvin's view was that the intent of the Scripture is not to be a scientific textbook, but rather it is for the knowledge of God in Jesus Christ. McGrath expresses Calvin's view when he avers that the Bible "is not an astronomical, geographical, or biological textbook. And when the Bible is interpreted, it must be borne in mind that God 'adjusts' to the capacities of the human mind and heart. God has to come down to our level if revelation is to take place. Revelation thus presents a scaled-down or 'accommodated version' of God to us, in order to meet our limited abilities. Just as a human mother stoops down to reach her child, so God stoops down to come to our level. Revelation is an act of divine condescension."[30]

---

27. That is, "plain to the understanding especially because of clarity and precision of presentation" (*Merriam-Webster*).

28. Provan, *Reformation and the Right Reading of Scripture*, pp. 283–84.

29. See Blackwell, *Galileo, Bellarmine, and the Bible*.

30. McGrath, *Science and Religion*, 21.

The Coinherent History of Ideas 73

It is important to hear directly from John Calvin in a way that illustrates this accommodationist principle, in the context of a science issue, that of astronomy. In his commentary on Genesis Calvin wrote that Genesis 1 and 2 were written from the perspective of a Hebrew observer and were not to be considered as a modern scientific account (79, 86). It is important to note in Calvin's discourse the validation of the expertise of the astronomer, and we may extrapolate to the scientist, and the encouragement of all who have time and ability to acquaint themselves with the science also:

> Verse 16. *The greater light.* I have said, that Moses does not here subtilely descant, as a philosopher, on the secrets of nature, as may be seen in these words. First, he assigns a place in the expanse of heaven to the planets and stars; but astronomers make a distinction of spheres, and, at the same time, teach that the fixed stars have their proper place in the firmament. Moses makes two great luminaries; but astronomers prove, by conclusive reasons that the star of Saturn, which on account of its great distance, appears the least of all, is greater than the moon. Here lies the difference; Moses wrote in a popular style things which without instruction, all ordinary persons, endued with common sense, are able to understand; but astronomers investigate with great labor whatever the sagacity of the human mind can comprehend. Nevertheless, this study is not to be reprobated, nor this science to be condemned, because some frantic persons are wont boldly to reject whatever is unknown to them. For astronomy is not only pleasant, but also very useful to be known: it cannot be denied that this art unfolds the admirable wisdom of God. Wherefore, as ingenious men are to be honored who have expended useful labor on this subject, so they who have leisure and capacity ought not to neglect this kind of exercise. Nor did Moses truly wish to withdraw us from this pursuit in omitting such things as are peculiar to the art.

However, when Calvin comes to explain why Moses excluded science from his account of the creation, the burden of that explanation has to do with the authorial intent of Moses. He wrote for people who were not scientists, so as not to exclude uneducated people, in order that all may acknowledge the creatorial power and majesty of God at whatever level they can perceive it:

> But because he was ordained a teacher as well of the unlearned and rude as of the learned, he could not otherwise fulfill his office than by descending to this grosser method of instruction. Had he spoken of things generally unknown, the uneducated

might have pleaded in excuse that such subjects were beyond their capacity. Lastly since the Spirit of God here opens a common school for all, it is not surprising that he should chiefly choose those subjects which would be intelligible to all. If the astronomer inquires respecting the actual dimensions of the stars, he will find the moon to be less than Saturn; but this is something abstruse, for to the sight it appears differently. Moses, therefore, rather adapts his discourse to common usage. For since the Lord stretches forth, as it were, his hand to us in causing us to enjoy the brightness of the sun and moon, how great would be our ingratitude were we to close our eyes against our own experience? There is therefore no reason why janglers should deride the unskilfulness of Moses in making the moon the second luminary; for he does not call us up into heaven, he only proposes things which lie open before our eyes. Let the astronomers possess their more exalted knowledge; but, in the meantime, they who perceive by the moon the splendor of night, are convicted by its use of perverse ingratitude unless they acknowledge the beneficence of God.[31]

It is important to re-emphasize that Calvin's viewpoint that Genesis 1 was written for the uneducated, relating to what they can see, did not mean that he did not encourage those who were pursuing knowledge of the science of astronomy, as is evident from this quote. Thus, while on the one hand avoiding wooden literalism, Calvin in his *Institutes* espoused a robust theology of creation grounded in Christology, which pervades the whole narrative of Scripture, and focused texts such as John 1 and Colossians 1. Calvin's robust theology of creation became foundational to the world-affirming worldview and scholarship which developed in the Reformed tradition after him.[32] The Calvinist tradition that promoted healthy theology-science dialogue continued into the era of Modernity, reaching its epitome in T. F. Torrance, and we will consider his work now in some detail. He has written at length about the gains, or the "promise and excitement," that have arisen since the time of the Reformation, that is, "since the ground

---

31. Calvin, *Commentary on Genesis*.

32. The work of Edward Wright is one example. In a preface to William Gilbert's treatise on magnetism, he echoes Calvin when he expresses the opinion that Scripture is not concerned with physics, and that Scripture was "accommodated to the understanding and way of speech of the common people, like nurses to children." See Hooykaas, *Religion and the Rise*, 122–23. Randall Zachmann has also developed the theme of the compatibility of theology and science and of the freedom of scientific inquiry in Calvin, as revealed by his particular interest in astronomy and his sense of wonder concerning the grandeur of God and the smallness of humans. Zachmann, *Reconsidering John Calvin*, 1–21. See Zachmann, "Free Scientific Inquiry." See also Stump, "Randall Zachman."

has been cleared in the most remarkable way of the old dualist and atomistic modes of thought that have plagued theology for centuries." The dualisms Torrance countered will be described in more detail in chapter 8. A new and exciting era had for Torrance been ushered in not only by the developments in empirical science, but also by the recovery of the importance of the doctrine of the Trinity, through Karl Barth, with the incarnation as its historically empirical revelation. The fact that creation is made real by the incarnation, even for the triune God himself, removes all dualism and justifies the study of creation, and invites us to look for echoes of the onto-relational in creation, in science.

Thus the onto-relational grammar of Christian theology, centered in the Trinity seen as perichoretic persons-in-relation, can inform science, justifies and invites the exploration that inspires science, and keeps science in a priestly and doxological mode. But science with its stringent methodology and its insight into all reality, in turn influences theology to be equally rigorous and empirical in its approach (a theological science). Theology and science done in cognizance of each other, together in this coinherent way, is what excited Torrance. However, Torrance was not naïve about this new era. The "onto-relational way of thinking" he knew to be difficult for us in the West due to the "impact of atomism, ancient and modern, in our culture." He speaks of "long-ingrained habits of mind and of speech with which we are beset in the Latin-Greek tradition of Western culture, and the static connecting with which we have been accustomed to operate in our linear logic."[33]

I suspect Torrance would have been disappointed with how things have unfolded in Christian theology since his time. Much theology has moved in precisely the opposite direction altogether, becoming all too enamoured with renewing old Greek dualisms, clouding the distinctness of God and creation with notions of material participation and sacramentalism of a concomitant type.[34]

---

33. T. F. Torrance, *Ground and Grammar*, 174.

34. I refer here to the Radical Orthodoxy. While I admire RO's critique of modernity and secularity, and its theologically inspired, postmodern informed re-narrations of many disciplines, such as economics (Daniel Bell and Stephen Long), culture (Graham Ward), politics (William Cavanaugh), and theology/philosophy (Milbank and Catherine Pickstock), as well as its Augustinian vision (avoiding the Nietzschean vision of postmodernity), its allergy to the particular lead it to express a deep ambivalence about the concrete particularity of Christ and the atonement and the authority they exert over the Christian life. Its Neoplatonic framework and its emphasis on material participation (methexis) to accomplish its aims seems to cloud Divine and created identity. For more on this, see Reno, "Radical Orthodoxy Project."

Torrance's aspirations were profoundly missional. He had hoped for the "kind of theology that can support the message of the gospel to mankind, as, in touch with the advances of natural science, theology comes closer and closer to a real understanding of the creation as it comes from the hands of God."[35] The mission is before us still. A physicist associate of T. F. Torrance, Jim Neidhardt, asks the question, "Why would a theologian be willing to commit valuable time and effort to acquire substantial understanding of another discipline: i.e., natural science?" His response was that all of Torrance's integrating efforts "are grounded in and guided by the recognition that the early Christian church not only communicated the gospel to the Greco-Roman world but also transformed the prevailing cultural framework, thereby allowing the gospel to take deep root and grown from within. As then, so for every age, the gospel's creating, reconciling, and redeeming power can have a renewing-transforming impact upon the whole frame of human culture, science, and philosophy."[36] In particular, it is Torrance's integrative framework of the "*perichoretic* interpretation of theology and natural science" that might serve "as a base for both scientists and theologians as they build bridges between the disciplines."[37]

For T. F. Torrance the onto-relational way of thinking is a crucial historical link between theology and science. With respect to the first, the basic grammar of *theology* is onto-relational.[38] As described already, historically the theological usage of the concept and term coinherence or perichoresis went from its first use in describing the union of the two natures of the Son incarnate, through the relations of the persons of the economic Trinity into the ontological or immanent Trinity, by way of the concept of the *homoousion*, the shared deity of each of the persons. Thus the term perichoresis in its refined state ends up being used to describe the holding of each of the persons in the other, or their mutual interpenetration, in one God. This refined concept could then no longer be applied back to Christology, as noted above. It would result in a diminishing of the full humanity of Christ, for one thing. Within the context of the Trinity, however, this refined conception of perichoresis, as Torrance notes, "in its application to intratrinitarian relations in God" led to the development of the "onto-relational concept of the Divine Persons—or, rather, an understanding of the three Persons in the one God as onto-relational realities in God."[39] Thus arose "a new *concept of*

---

35. T. F. Torrance, *Ground and Grammar*, 178.
36. Neidhardt, introduction to *Christian Frame of Mind*, xxxviii.
37. Ibid., xl.
38. T. F. Torrance, *Ground and Grammar*, 174.
39. Ibid., 173.

person, unknown in human thought until then, and to the onto-relational person at that, which is applicable to our interhuman relations in a created way, correlated to the uncreated way in which it applies to God."[40] This was in stark contrast to the derivation of persons in Western theological thought, whether Catholic or Protestant, which involved the "individualization of rational nature (see in the famous definition of Boethius)." Rather, this understanding of personhood is "ontologically derived from the Communion of Being in Love in God himself."[41]

This understanding of personhood and a relational ontology which was present in the Cappadocian Fathers, has been perpetuated in the Eastern tradition. It appears less often in the West, though present in Richard of St. Victor in the twelfth century, then making its way through Duns Scotus to Calvin. It then "petered out in Western thought in the face of the atomistic, individualistic thinking of Locke."[42] The resurgence of this thought, and the relational nature of personhood, leads Torrance to expect it to have wide and profound impact on "world thought and culture."[43]

With respect to *science*, Torrance comments that it was the individualism which is the context for Western science which made it difficult for the transition from a particulate view of matter, which involved particles with external relations (Newton, Bohr), to particles as being dynamic and continuous fields (Einstein, Maxwell, Heisenberg) as in modern particle physics and quantum theory. These fields of science, notes Torrance, have been "forced to develop something like onto-relational notions—for example, where we find that the interrelations between particles as space-time entities, or dynamic energy-knots, are as significant, if not more significant, than the so-called particles. Thus, within the indivisible connection of particle and field, we operate not with discrete particles, but with onto-relational realities which we find it rather difficult to bring to precise expression in our traditional subject-object predicate language and its grammar, not to speak of its logic."[44] Torrance speaks of communication he had with a physicist at London University, Fritjof Capra. The latter, having read some of Torrance's work, expressed to him that in his work on particle theory he had found it "so difficult to express the way in which he found particles containing one another, as it were, within then strictures of language of the Western type, that he had been forced to take over relational ways of thought from Hindu

40. Ibid.
41. Ibid., 173–74.
42. Ibid., 174.
43. Ibid.
44. Ibid., 175.

and Buddhist thought and also from Taoist thought, in order to develop appropriate modes of thought and speech for scientific understanding."[45] In his reply, Torrance duly informed Capra that the relational thought of Hindu and Buddhist origin "is not correlated with the empirical realities of nature," and was therefore inappropriate for physics.[46] "Then I drew his attention to the *concept* of *perichoresis* in the Christian tradition," says Torrance, ". . . which Christian theology refined and developed to express the mutual coinherence of the Persons of the Holy Trinity,"[47] which though it is a lofty concept, was, as Torrance asserts, "reached through a movement of thought that took its rise from the empirico-theoretical ground of the incarnational activity of God within the spatio-temporal structures of our world, and it remains, indirectly, through the level of the economic Trinitarian relations, empirically correlated with that ground." Thus, Torrance concludes, "it would not be surprising if a perichoretic relation, with appropriate and adequate change in relation to the nature of the subject-matter of the field, could be applied to the problem of quantum theory or of particle theory."[48] He then cites Christopher P. Kaiser,[49] physicist, for his efforts in precisely this direction.

The very essence of the empirical or scientific approach to theology is expressed in pithy fashion in this interchange, as well as its historical rootedness. Torrance speaks first of the way in which the onto-relational reality of the Divine and human nature of Christ as incarnate was witnessed empirically by the apostolic community, and in history which in turn is the empirical justification via the concept of *homoousios*, for how we think of the onto-relational nature of the Trinity as persons-in-relation. It is the grounded-ness of the first, the incarnational reality, that provided the connection with things created, thereby justifying the use of the onto-relational or perichoretic concept in science.

The late Trinitarian theologian Colin Gunton expresses a very similar sentiment to that of Torrance, when in *The Promise of Trinitarian Theology* he writes, "The development of modern field theory in Faraday and Clerk Maxwell—two of the predecessors to who Einstein repeatedly refers, has

---

45. Ibid.
46. Ibid.
47. Ibid., 176.
48. Ibid.
49. Kaiser, *Toward a Theology; Doctrine of God; Creational Theology; Creation and the History of Science.*

led inexorably to the conceptual echo of Trinitarian theology in relativity theory and its developments."[50]

This is borne out from the science side, in a number of instances. One significant landmark example was in the work of physicist Clerk Maxwell. In looking "for a deeper way of interpreting nature that was not linked to the classical, Newtonian notions of mechanical necessity as manifested in isolated particles interacting causally with one another," Maxwell developed "his theory of the electromagnetic field which brought about a seminal paradigm shift in scientific understanding." At the heart of this theory was the idea of the "field concept" which was "first formally articulated as a relational way of describing particles as never separable from their interactions." Maxwell noted that the "relationships between particles as represented by the continuous, space-filling electromagnetic field were an intrinsic *part of what the particles really are*. Thus, this relational notion of fields of radiation and their structure became an independent reality in their own right."[51] This led theologian T. F. Torrance to affirm the onto-relational nature of being, in that sense analogous to the being-in-relation of God. Thus he affirmed that "the relations he (Clerk Maxwell) referred to were not just imaginary or putative but real relations, relations that belong to reality as much as things (particles) do, for the interrelations of things are, in part at least, constitutive of what they are. Being-constitutive relations of this kind we may well speak of as 'onto-relations.'"[52]

This onto-relational nature of particles has also been seen to be analogous to the nature of the human "person" derived from patristic understanding of the Divine persons in the Trinity. Thus Neidhardt states,

> This field notion concerning physical reality introduced by Clerk Maxwell is heuristically analogous to the biblical concept of the person which was developed by the early Church Fathers in order to understand the biblical evidence pointing to the triune nature of God.

He goes on to claim that "central to the biblical understanding of the person is the *reality of human relationships as an integral part of what persons really are*. You as a person are not an isolated individual, like the Newtonian particle separated from other autonomous particles. Rather, you as a person are interrelated with others, your parents, your friends, even

---

50. Gunton, *Promise*, 151.
51. Neidhardt, "Biblical Humanism," 137–42.
52. T. F. Torrance, "Christian Faith and Physical Science," 215–42.

people with whom you disagree. These *interrelationships constitute the very stuff of personal* being."[53]

The direction of Maxwell's postulations about the onto-relational nature of particles in fact seems to have been from the Trinity, through human personhood, and onto nonhuman particles. Torrance's seems to imply precisely this when he states that it was a "Christian theological understanding" that was "a possible motivating factor in creating Clerk Maxwell's deep appreciation for Michael Faraday's interpretive vision of charged particles or magnets being interrelated to one another by invisible lines of force which fill all of space,"[54] and that "this deep appreciation led to Clerk Maxwell's development of the electromagnetic field in order to describe particles as never separable from their interactions."[55]

This phenomenon is echoed in the work of others. For example, from the perspective of the theoretical physicist, the electron also is "relational," being in relation with photons (units of light energy) and positrons (electrons moving backwards in time) all the time, as depicted in Feynman diagrams. These are pictorial representations of mathematical expressions which describe the behavior of subatomic particles, introduced in 1948, and named after their inventor Richard Feynman, an American physicist. From the perspective of the chemist, the electron is the foundational entity in the discipline, and it is an important case in point for the identity-in-relationality of all matter. It is always "in relation" with other electrons, as well as the particles of the nucleus of an atom. And electrons themselves defy momentum/position precision also. I can remember well in early university years coming through the revolution in understanding of the nature and positioning of electrons in an atom. The old perfect circles that represented orbits in which it was imagined that particulate electrons circulated, a model originating in the work of Danish physicist Niels Bohr, were summarily replaced with quantum mechanically derived orbitals, s, p and d, and f, that represented probabilities for the presence of an electron, which as waves, obeyed mathematical wave functions. There were now such things as hybridized orbitals, such as sp3 orbitals in methane, for example. Were they waves or were they particles? How well could we predict their distance from the nucleus? Or is our desire to ascribe position and momentum to a particle just reductionism on our part, as physicist M. D. Stafleu suggests.[56] The work of Nobel Prize–winning physicist Werner Heisenberg, known best for

53. Neidhardt, "Biblical Humanism," 137–42.
54. Neidhardt is referring to T. F. Torrance, *Faith and Physics*.
55. Neidhardt, "Biblical Humanism," 137–42.
56. See Stafleu, *Time and Again*.

his uncertainty principle, was important in this transformation. Heisenberg did more than introduce new models for atoms but indeed "elaborated a very important model of levels of reality." Though he first outlined his models in his *Manuscript of 1942*, they would be published only in 1984.[57] In his own words, Heisenberg's philosophical thinking was shaped by "two directory principles: the first one is that of the division in levels of Reality, corresponding to different objectivity modes depending on the incidence of the knowledge process; the second one is that of the progressive erasure of the roles played by the ordinary concepts of space and time."[58] For Heisenberg, reality is "the continuous fluctuation of the experience as gathered by the conscience. In this respect, it is never wholly identifiable to an isolated system."[59] Nicolescu concludes therefore that, in Heisenberg's view, "reality could not be reduced to substance." She adds that "for today's physicists, this fact is obvious: matter is the complexus substance-energy-space-time-information."[60] In a way that resonates strongly with the Trinitarian sentiments of theologian T. F. Torrance, Werner Heisenberg "states incessantly, in agreement with Husserl, Heidegger, Gadamer, and Cassirer (whom he knew personally), that one has to suppress any rigid distinction between Subject and Object."[61]

Calvin's influence was also present in another historical lineage. Abraham Kuyper's worldview may be thought of as Calvin's creation theology come to roost, his love of creation being expressed in the words, "There is not a square inch in the whole domain of our human existence over which Christ, who is Sovereign over all, does not cry, Mine!" The Christian metanarrative of "creation, fall, redemption and consummation" actually stems from the work of Abraham Kuyper as particularly expressed in his Lectures on Calvinism in 1898.[62] In fact, we owe in large part to Kuyper (and the "Kuyperian" school of thought) the now popular notion of "worldview," which refers to the fundamental and global perspective with which one or one's community sees the world, or the beliefs and "stories" about the world and reality that are so basic as to be not so much rationally proven as they are presupposed. In particular, Kuyper presented the idea that Calvinism was more than just a set of doctrinal propositions, but an all-encompassing Christian worldview grounded in the sovereignty of God, and expressed

57. Nicolescu, "Idea of Levels," 11–25.
58. Heisenberg, *Philosophie*, 240.
59. Ibid., 166.
60. Nicolescu, "Idea of Levels," 11–25.
61. Ibid.
62. Kuyper, *Lectures on Calvinism*.

in the trajectory, "creation, fall, redemption." As such, Kuyper's view of the mission of the church and the Christian was holistic and it was one that encouraged the engagement of Christians in the human endeavor, not withdrawal. The sovereignty of God over all realms of creation, the prominence of the cultural mandate given to humanity in Genesis and fulfilled in Christ, and the salvation-historical markers of creation-fall-redemption all contributed to Kuyper's world-affirming theology. Equipped with this worldview, the people of God could profitably engage in all areas of culture including politics, science and the arts, toward the redemption of humanity and creation in this era of history.

A Kuyperian genealogy may also be traced through to the worldview and theology of philosopher theologian Nicholas Wolterstorff,[63] whose pilgrimage took him away from intellectual foundationalism[64] into a more holistic way of knowing and educating that includes more than just the mind, but involvement of the whole person in the pursuit of justice and *shalom*. James Smith similarly builds on Kuyper but advances the category of "worldview" (ensconced as it is within a Cartesian anthropology) beyond the merely cognitive, in light of the fact that humans are "desiring beings" or "persons-as-lovers," not cognitive "thinking things."[65] The influence of Kuyper is also evident in the important work *The Transforming Vision: Shaping a Christian World View*,[66] by Brian J. Walsh and J. Richard Middleton who, in turn, had a profound influence on the work of N. T. Wright as indicated by the dedication of his seminal *The New Testament and the People of God*[67] to Walsh. Wright's work and his influence of Christian mission, though impossible to summarize in a few words, has drawn attention rightly to the "story" dimension of the Christian worldview by seeking to point out the continuity between the story of God's redemptive dealings with Israel and the Christ story. Christ in fact recapitulates the story of Israel. He fulfills the mission of God in all the ways that Israel failed. But in turn, just as Christ is for Israel, so also the people of Christ, linked in union with him as the church, recapitulate the cultural mandate, which must include the pursuit of science, and become *for* the world. In all these ways, the Reformation tradition has developed a generally healthy view of science and freedom of

---

63. Wolterstorff, *Educating for Shalom*.

64. For a discussion of foundationalism, see Placher, *Unapologetic Theology*, and Thiel, *Non-foundationalism*.

65. Smith, *Introducing Radical Orthodoxy*.

66. Walsh and Middleton, *Transforming Vision*.

67. Wright, *New Testament and the People of God*.

inquiry which prepares the way for our proposal of its coinherence within the framework of a world-affirming theology.

The "Scientific Revolution" of the Seventeenth Century Saw Great Consonance between Christianity and Science, and the Beginnings of Great Conflict

Possibly as a consequence of the Copernican revolution, partly in the medieval universities in which Christian theology was deemed to be consonant with science, partly as a result of the Renaissance in Europe, and significantly as a result of the Baconian account of knowledge that begins with experience of the world, a very Christian notion, the scientific revolution occurred. It is crucial to note that science began with observation and then principles drawn up to account for the observations and data. This rediscovery of empiricism was key.

Despite the complexity of the origins of scientific revolution, there is wide agreement that Sir Isaac Newton (1642–1727) was its most important influence. Building on Kepler's law (the square of a planet's periodic time is proportional to the cube of its mean distance from the sun), the question of its significance was asked—what is its significance and could the motion of the earth, moon and planets all be accounted for on the basis of a single principle? Newton believed so and called it "celestial mechanics." His demonstration of the mechanics of the solar system led poet Alexander Pope to write:

> Nature and Nature's Law lay hid in Night
> God said, *Let Newton be!* and all was Light.

As McGrath states, "Newton is often presented as a noble monument to rationality and cosmic order, a beacon of scientific orthodoxy in the midst of a still superstitious society."[68] However, Newton was not quite the scientist (being fascinated by alchemy) and not quite the theologian (a Deist) he is touted as being, though he did make a massive contribution to the development of science.

Newton's scientific genius was in extrapolating principles that govern the behavior of objects on earth (an apple falling to the ground) to celestial bodies, giving rise to Newton's law of universal gravitation. This equation describes the force between any two objects in the universe:

---

68. McGrath, *Science and Religion*, 27.

$$F = \frac{GMm}{r^2}$$

[where F is the force of gravity (measured in Newtons, N), G is the gravitational constant of the universe and is always the same number, M is the mass of one object (measured in kilograms, kg), m is the mass of the other object (measured in kilograms, kg) and

r is the distance those objects are apart (measured in meters, m)].

This is the inverse square law, and applies anywhere in the universe.

Gravity is now most accurately described by the general theory of relativity (proposed by Albert Einstein in 1915) which describes gravity, not as a force, but as a consequence of the curvature of spacetime caused by the uneven distribution of mass/energy; and resulting in time dilation, where time lapses more slowly in strong gravitation. However, for most applications, gravity is well approximated by Newton's law of universal gravitation, which postulates that gravity is a force where two bodies of mass are directly drawn (or "attracted") to each other according to a mathematical relationship, where the attractive force is proportional to the product of their masses and inversely proportional to the square of the distance between them. This is considered to occur over an infinite range, such that all bodies (with mass) in the universe are drawn to each other no matter how far they are apart. True for an apple falling to the ground, as well as two planets.

Newton's three laws of motion and his theories involving concepts of mass, space and time meant that all of these could be handled mathematically. The religious implications of this were that the world was a machine and was clearly the product of design. It was William Paley who likened the world of Newton's science to a watch. Just like a watch, the mechanistic worldview of Newton implied design and purpose, and so pointed to a creator. It was proof of the existence of God. Yet, as a result, God was no longer Shepherd and King of the cosmos but the Divine clockmaker, who had wound up the clock and was not required to intervene. This account opened the door to a naturalist understanding in the universe in which God was not needed. Its religious analogue arose as deism, even if unwittingly on Newton's part. Deism maintains that God is Creator, but it also insists that God is not continuously involved with creation, and has no guiding presence within its sustaining and development. This as opposed to *theism* which professes God's continuing involvement with creation, and *Trinitarian theism* which specifies the agency of the Son and the Spirit with and in creation. Evolutionary creationists of the teleological kind, for example, are not deists, but Trinitarian, invoking the agency of the Son and Spirit, yet in ways that permit the freedom of creation to be creation, including being able to participate in its own future.

Deism characterizes those influential British writers who defined the "Age of Reason": Lord Herbert of Cherbury, Thomas Hobbes, David Hume. Not all would have accepted the title, and some were skeptical of the need for Divine revelation, but "the Newtonian worldview," as McGrath indicates, "offered Deists a highly sophisticated way of defending and developing their views, by allowing them to focus on the wisdom of God in creating the world."[69] This challenges us to arrive at a theology of the engagement of God in creation, a biblically important theme. God not only created but is constantly and intimately engaged all the time, not just when his so-called intervention is needed. This will be revisited under the theme of agency in chapter 5.

In sum, one can see that there was a very close link between Christianity and the development of science in this period. No doubt some of the tenets of the Christian faith which we have highlighted as conducive to science applied in Newton's case and motivated his scientific pursuits: the clear distinction between God and creation, the order in creation derived from a wise God, and so on. However, the *kind* of theology present in Newton, and a significant number of the other scientists of his time, actually served ultimately to create a distance between the disciplines as science developed. Deism, with its loss of the belief in the immanence of God, not only led to a detrinitization of theology but to a decontextualizing of science as well, thus obviating the concept of its agency in participational agency of the triune God, and robbing it of meaning.

Yet a fully Trinitarian theology actually returns us to a fuller engagement with the world, rather than a separation from it (and from science as a means for knowing it). As Hanby reminds us, "Trinitarian love is the coincidence of infinite unity and infinite difference,"[70] and in relation to the creation, this means he is both transcendent *and* immanent, that there is "*both* the transcendent fullness of the cause (God) with its superiority to the effect (the cosmos) *and* the genuine novelty of the effect." And once "one acknowledges the coincidence of infinite difference and infinite unity in the Trinity, and once the apparent contradiction of affirming the transcendent superiority of the cause and the irreducible 'more' of the effect is removed, the effect becomes an image of the cause—and ultimately, an image of love—precisely in its novel otherness to it." "The world," Hanby concludes, "is a vestige or an image of God, in other words, not simply in

---

69. McGrath, *Science and Religion*, 29.
70. Hanby, *No God*, 344.

virtue of its similarity to him but in its difference from him, in the very fact that it is *not* God."[71] The difference is what seemed to impress Newton, and less so the immanent presence of God to creation. This easily made possible the prevalent concept of the world as a machine, and provided the seeds for the separation of theology and science in Modernity.

Deism served to give rise to a secular theology. As such it radically undermined a rich Christian doctrine of creation—one that warrants the claim that "theology and science, that is, conceptions of God and conceptions of nature are necessarily and *intrinsically* related."[72] It is consonant with some aspects of the revealed God of the Bible, even inspiring a sense of awe in response to the grandeur and the wisdom of God. Hanby poses the question, "What difference does it make if Newton used God to help formulate his laws of motion, after all, if these laws *work* without reference to God?" He answers the question by asserting that the "God of modern nature is dispensable as a consequence of the *content* of this new secular theology almost as a matter of planned obsolescence."[73] One can easily foresee a major facet of modernity being birthed here, that of the absence of God in the public square, not just in science.

The untraditional theology of Newton and Descartes brought about a new view of nature. Both "radicalized the voluntarism of the fourteenth century, employing 'the principle of annihilation' to destroy the intrinsic intelligibility of the world" and this "decoupling of divine volition from the transcendental attributes of being amounts to an *a priori* 'detrinitization' of God arguably more radical than Ockham's, and indeed, Newton secretly rejected the doctrine of the Trinity."[74] This in turn affects God's relation to the world, and it especially radically alters the meaning of Divine and human freedom. Viewed in a Trinitarian way, Divine freedom is a function of the relation between the Father and the Son, which is to say that "it is fundamentally an expression of *love* and inseparable from all the other predicates with which it is convertible." By contrast in the Unitarian doctrine of the deist, this new secular theology, "divine freedom becomes a matter of power, unqualified by goodness, beauty, or truth, closely akin if not indeed identical to the new concept of force."[75] This exalting of power isolated from love, coupled with the loss of autonomy and actuality which the immanent God has conferred upon the world through his gift of *esse* (being as op-

71. Ibid.
72. Ibid., 120.
73. Ibid., 121.
74. Ibid.
75. Ibid.

posed to mere existence, or being-in-relation), ironically led these natural philosophers to invoke Divine agency in the operation of the world in a way that moves well beyond the tradition.

Interest in and the relevance of theology proper, that is, questions about who God really is, are seriously marginalized by means of deism and its concomitant view of nature. As Hanby puts it, "God ceases to be immanent in creatures, more interior to them than they are to themselves as Augustine puts it, for the simple reason that creatures emptied of *essence* and *esse* no longer have any real interior to be related to." This is what makes this theology inherently obsolescent, for once "God's relation to the world becomes extrinsic and accidental, he is rendered superfluous for the intelligibility of the world." And if God is no longer fully immanent, he cannot be fully transcendent either. He can no longer be the "subsistent act of being itself, in whom all things participate by virtue of the act of being." Rather, in the Newtonian and Cartesian realm, God is merely a "singular within the 'positivity' of being—a substance, in Descartes' words—extrinsically confronting the world through relationships of power and force." Hanby concludes that this is premised not only on the detrinitization of God, but his finitization, being "premised upon the eclipse of that very difference between God and the world which the Incarnation revealed and which the doctrine of creation secured and protected."[76]

The God of deism finds a keen expression in English philosopher John Locke as a theology of Idealism (which was, in turn, a great influence on Jonathan Edwards's theology). Locke's *Essay concerning Human Understanding* (1690) encourages projecting onto God attributes deemed philosophically appropriate for God, by extrapolating them to infinity. God is made up of human rational and moral qualities projected to infinity. Later deism deemed this to be honoring to the deistic God. Others, however, saw through the reductionism of deism by which God became a clockmaker, and the world became a machine not requiring God. Newton did not actually believe God could not intervene, but saw no evidence that he did. It was all nice and tidy for some who could pursue science without interference from God, and it paved the way for a universal religion based on bottom up observation of humanity, resulting in a common but vacuous belief in a wise but distant Creator. In Europe, Voltaire (*Philosophical Letters*) was influenced also by this mechanistic view of the universe, in ways that led to the development of Enlightenment rationalism. On the other hand, there

---

76. Ibid., 122.

were some appeals to God as active in creation, even if only in the biological realm, and not in the world of planets and objects and mechanics.[77]

The most significant appeal to God as designer and creator of the natural world, and especially in life forms, came from William Paley, Archdeacon of Carlisle. His *Natural Theology; or, Evidences of the Existence and Attributes of the Deity, Collected from the Appearances of Nature* (1802) "had a profound influence on popular English religious thought in the first half of the nineteenth century, and is known to have been read by Darwin."[78] However, like that of Matthew Tindall, Paley's view of the world was static and could not cope with the dynamic worldview underlying Darwinism, the next major influence on science.

What Caused the Turn from This Fruitful Dialogue into the Warfare Model, the Making of Science into a Rebellious Teenager?

The thesis that the history of the ideas of science is intertwined with the history of Christian theology is validated by the adjoining of some form of Christian faith with science in the Newtonian era. That there were aberrations in the theology of some principal thought leaders does not negate this. In fact, as we have shown, their deficits only serve to punctuate the reality of coinherence of science with good theology. However, the science which has been birthed in a Christian cradle, rebelled altogether against God, protecting its autonomous identity. It even negated the valid identity of the Christian faith when it seemed like the source of that faith, the Bible, could not stand the test of scientific scrutiny. Theology was in fact consigned to irrelevance by means of the false dualism of "faith and science," with the assumption that the latter was done with empiricism and pure objective reason, and no faith. Thus science came to occupy a public space of recognized legitimacy, while theology was relegated to the realm of private value judgments.

Before turning to examine the causes of this teenage rebellion of science and naturalism or scientism, one caveat is necessary. To avoid the tendency toward Modernity bashing—as if Modernity is all bad, as if we aren't glad of modern medicine and electric light and computers (sometimes!)—we must proceed with caution. As with all eras and cultural identities, Modernity too is a mix of accomplishments reflecting both the image of God in his glorious human creatures as well as the fallenness that leads to idolatry. The particularly modern form of idolatry is that of technology and science,

---

77. See, e.g., John Ray (1627–1705).
78. McGrath, *Science and Religion: A New Introduction*, 31.

which have in fact contributed significantly to the global warming and imminent ruination of the planet. We have argued, on the other hand, that the freedom to study creation in its own right, which the Enlightenment prospered, in fact had its proper *roots* in a Christian doctrine of creation with *roots* as far back as the patristic and medieval churches. It could be argued that the cultural mandate given to humanity by God in Genesis 1 has been better fulfilled than in any other era. That deep and clear thinking has triumphed over superstition. That the arts have prospered. However, it is the elimination of the explicitly triune God as the true source of all being, and the neglect of the incarnate life, death, and resurrection of Christ as the mediating influence for the study of creation and science that has, on the part of both the church and the world of science, led to the breakdown of the coinherence of the two disciplines—unleashing a monster that cannot be contained.

The primary factors in the separation of theology and science seem to have been the following: (i) Enlightenment naivete about reason, which is considered in the following chapter; (ii) the proposal of the biological origin of humanity by Charles Darwin and then, building on the elucidation of genetics, in neo-Darwinism (a second "Copernican" revolution); (iii) the enculturation of evangelical Christians into the rationalism of Modernity that was manifest in rationalistic apologetics which were *of* Modernity, and belied the "faith seeking understanding" or critical realism approach of the tradition which is compatible with science; and lastly, included in this, (iv) the literalism of the Bible reading of some evangelicals, a literalism not justified in the Reformation heritage of the movement.

Regrettably, the modern enculturation and the biblical literalism has persisted within the contemporary church. Despite postmodern influences, the "political (and academic) rhetoric indicates that modernity is a thriving project."[79] This has been most notable in theologies of both a liberal and conservative kind which are apologetic projects of correlation with secular thought, employing supposedly autonomous reason.[80] Fundamentalism in particular is "but a mirror of modernism"[81] in its engagement also on the assumption of neutral, objective reason. The literalism associated with

---

79. Smith, *Introducing Radical Orthodoxy*, 32.

80. Smith cites Dooyeweerd in relation to this point: "Theology is itself in need of a transcendental critique of theoretical thought" (*ITWT*, 6). He cites the influence of Tübingen on much twentieth-century theology including fundamentalist and early evangelical theology which presumes upon a "neutral, 'objective' reason to warrant their theological project" and by so doing ends up being "correlationist and accommodationist." Smith, *Introducing Radical Orthodoxy*, 37.

81. Smith, *Introducing Radical Orthodoxy*, 37.

interpretation of Genesis 1 is an example. It is a very modern approach, ironically for people wanting to be against modernism!

What happened outside of the church to make science divorce its partner, and become supreme in modern society in ways that were not healthy for science, as well as society at large? The real culprit in the advent of modernity, according to two independent sources, has been the resurgence of the influence of the Greek philosopher Epicurus and his student Lucretius. A philosophy of the reductionism of the cosmos to atoms, Epicureanism is an elite philosophy of the ancient world which taught that even if God or gods exist, they are distant and do not concern themselves with the world, so that our world makes itself as it goes along, evolving without any influence of God. The influence of the two thousand-year-old poem of Lucretius *On the Nature of Things*, on the development of the modern world, after its rediscovery after a millennium of obscurity has been noticed by Stephen Greenblatt and chronicled in his book *The Swerve: How the World Became Modern*. Though Lucretius believed that the sun circled around the earth and also in the spontaneous generation of worms in wet soil, at the core of his poem "lay key principles of a modern understanding of the world." "The stuff of the universe," according to Lucretius' proposal, "is an infinite number of atoms moving randomly through space, like dust motes in a sunbeam, colliding, hooking together, forming complex structures, breaking apart again, in a ceaseless process of creation and destruction."[82]

This poem thus actually represents "the scientific vision of the world— a vision of atoms randomly moving in an infinite universe." Surprisingly, the poem is "imbued with a poet's sense of wonder." But this wonder "did not depend on gods and demons and the dream of an afterlife; in Lucretius it welled up out of a recognition that we are made of the same matter as the stars and the oceans and all things else."[83] Greenblatt offers the opinion that the culture which "best epitomized the Lucretian embrace of beauty and pleasure and propelled it forward as a legitimate and worthy human pursuit was that of the Renaissance." Greenblatt declares that "something happened in the Renaissance, something that surged up against the constraints that centuries had constructed around curiosity, desire, individuality, sustained attention to the material world, the claims of the body. The cultural shift is notoriously difficult to define, and its significance has been hotly contested."[84] While this is most obviously evident in works of art and aesthetics, Greenblatt states that "it helps to account for the intellectual

---

82. Greenblatt, *Swerve*, 5.
83. Ibid., 8.
84. Ibid., 9–10.

daring of Copernicus and Vesalius, Giordano Bruno and William Harvey, Hobbes and Spinoza." The shift to modernity was in fact still, in its first instincts, a return to many aspects of a Christian doctrine of creation which had been neglected by the church, and it in fact confirms the thesis that an incarnational, creational faith was coinherent with the develop of science. Listening to some aspects of the description of its development reads precisely like a vindication of a coinherence thesis: modernity was "not sudden or once-for-all, but it became increasingly possible to turn away from a preoccupation with angels and demons and immaterial causes and to focus instead on things in this world; to understand that humans are made of the same stuff as everything else and are part of the natural order; to conduct experiments without fearing that one is infringing on God's jealously guarded secrets; to question authorities and challenge received doctrines . . . to imagine that there are other worlds beside the one that we inhabit; to entertain the thought that the sun is only one star in an infinite universe. . . . In short, it became possible—never easy, but possible—in the poet Auden's phrase to find the mortal world enough."[85] The Christian viewpoint is not that the mortal world is enough, but it is that the mortal world matters. And it encourages the exploration of the created world in precisely the ways here described. Realistically, modernity did cast off belief in the incarnate Son and the triune God who gives meaning and ethical groundedness to the scientific endeavor.

This distancing of theology from science in the advent of Modernity is accredited to these "ancient atomists" by Catherine Wilson, with special attention on Lucretius and Epicurus.[86] Lucretius' poem *On the Nature of Things* is once again at the heart of this study of the influence of these ancient philosophers in the articulation of the major philosophical systems of the seventeenth century, and, more broadly, their influence on the evolution of natural science and moral and political philosophy. Following eras of critique by Cicero, on the hand, and the church fathers, on the other, "the Epicurean philosophy surfaced again in the period of the Scientific Revolution, when it displaced scholastic Aristotelianism. Both modern social contract theory and utilitarianism in ethics were grounded in its tenets." The Epicurean imprint became "an acknowledged, and often unacknowledged presence in the writings of Descartes, Gassendi, Hobbes, Boyle, Locke, Leibniz, Berkeley."[87] The overall effect, despite the Christian faith of some of these

---

85. Ibid., 10–11.
86. Wilson, *Epicureanism*, 5.
87. Ibid., frontmatter.

key influencers of modernity was the separation of science and theology, in particular because the Christian synthesis was one of deism.

This Epicurean influence in Modernity has been noted also by biblical scholars and theologians. For example, the role of deism, at the theology end of things, in the development of this split has been acknowledged by New Testament scholar N. T. Wright. The dualism of this way of being motivates him to say, "We have lived for too long in the split-level world of Enlightenment fantasy."[88]

The reason for the fissure between theology and science from the *science* end is that science carries a naiveté about its own endemic metaphysical assumptions and theology. In this vein, Michael Hanby states that there are "metaphysical and theological judgments latent in modern science since its inception and passed down to posterity primarily through Descartes and Newton," which "persist as part of the ontological structure of modern science even though subsequent science has superseded the philosophies that gave them birth."[89] At the heart of this ontology is a reduction of being from "act," the idea of givenness *plus* contingency, the idea of the real being or "thisness" of a thing, to mere "facticity," that is, the mere givenness of created things. This ontology of modern science also involves "a theological extrinsicism which reduces God to a finite object, nature to artifice, and creation to manufacture, and it lays the ontological groundwork for modern naturalism's juxtaposition of natural and supernatural agencies and forms of explanation."[90] All this is "exacerbated by a new 'active' conception of science itself, which replaces an ontological conception of truth with a functionalist conception, thus dampening the desire for truth and making the very notion of truth, in its original ontological meaning, all but unintelligible."[91] A particular case which demonstrates the implicit theological and ontological commitments in science is the development of Darwin's theory of evolution. Hanby, though not averse to the theory *per se*, shows that the manner in which the theory was conceived was according to the "functionalist" tradition of British biology and in Darwin specifically as a result of the natural theology of William Paley. Paley, considered by many Darwinians to represent "the apex of Christian thought on creation," transmitted to the functionalist tradition of Darwinian biology the ontological assumptions of Newtonian physics. He thereby gave to this biology its "defining problem," which is "its view of the living organism and the 'God' that Darwinians

---

88. Wright, "Wouldn't You Love to Know," 5.
89. Hanby, *No God*, 3.
90. Ibid.
91. Ibid., 3–4.

do not believe in." With respect to the latter, Hanby states that Darwin's own Darwinism is a "sometimes uneasy amalgam of Malthusian theodicy, Smithean political economy, and continental morphology, with more than a dash of Humboldtian Romanticism thrown in."

The primary influence, however, is Paley, whose theological and ontological assumptions become "endemic to the subsequent Darwinian tradition,"[92] and are as such theologically incoherent and "metaphysically disastrous," precisely because they "compromise the Darwinian conception of nature *as natural*."[93] This then influences how the organism is conceived by Darwin. Nature "displaces the living organism as both the subject of its own being and the subject matter of evolutionary biology, thus bringing the mechanistic ontology of modern naturalism to its logical and nihilistic conclusion." This in turn anticipates "the disappearance of the organism as the defining drama of evolutionary biology after Darwin" including the "modern synthesis" of Darwinian evolution and Mendelian genetics. Most importantly, what Hanby shows is that metaphysics always accompanies scientific theories in a way that is often "unrealized by its protagonists," and thus reveals thus the "'Catholicity' of reality" which "propels science beyond the debilitating confines of its own ontology."[94] Scientific theories and God are distinguishable, but they are just not separable. They are coinherent, in other words.

The Reclaiming of the Rebellious Teenager: Deconstructing Modernity and the Positivist Claims of Scientism, Offering a Thoughtful Trinitarian Theology of Science

The great opportunity of our times for thoughtful, missional Christians is to offer fresh articulations of the Christian doctrine of creation, grounded in the Trinity and the incarnation, which allow theology to be theology, and science to be science, yet which also affirm the profound mutuality and inter-enhancement of each. That is, accounts of theology and science which manifest the coinherence of the epistemology and the ontology of these disciplines. In an era when scientism is less and less credible, in which modern certainty has been deconstructed by postmodernity, in which global warming threatens our existence, there is, I believe, a hearing for a world-affirming, science-embracing gospel. A gospel that offers a humble

---

92. Ibid., 4.
93. Ibid.
94. Ibid.

apologetic, a holistic and communal worldview, (or better, world-love), a gospel that is grounded in the triune Creator God, supremely transcendent and yet infinitely immanent; a gospel that leads to human flourishing and creational *shalom*. These themes of coinherence will now begin to unfold in the following chapters.

Chapter 4

The Coinherent *Epistemologies* of Theology and Science

Resonances between Theology and Science related to Knowing (Epistemological Commonalities, Models, and Analogies)

In him was life, and that life was the light of all mankind.
(JOHN 1:4)

That which was from the beginning, which we have heard, which we have seen with our eyes, which we have looked at and our hands have touched—this we proclaim concerning the Word of life ... so that you also may have fellowship with us. And our fellowship is with the Father and with his Son, Jesus Christ.
(1 JOHN 1:1)

GROUNDED IN THE COINHERENCE of the triune God and his revelation in the incarnate Christ, and echoed coinherence in creation and ideas, we continue to explore our proposal that theology and science may be coinherent. One of the most significant misconceptions blocking productive conversation is the belief that science and Christian theology operate according to different ways of knowing. Accordingly, any way forward—be it my proposal or any other—must examine the epistemologies at the heart of each, or else risk missing the point. To suggest, as we will in this chapter, that knowing, or the process by which we come to know what we know, is very similar in each of these disciplines, would be expected to turn some heads. If, in the words of the physicist we encountered in the introduction, a "deeper, clarified understanding of the *perichoresis* between theology and natural science could have a substantial healing impact upon our scientific-technological society,"[1] then that perichoresis must apply to how we know, or to epistemology, in each discipline, which is precisely what we hope to show in this chapter. By exploring the particular epistemology practiced in each discipline—which I characterize as *critical realism*—we can begin to formulate a response to this important challenge. Exploring the coinherence of theology and science with respect to knowing will then enable us to go on to address the issue of the intelligibility and the beauty in God as expressed in Divine revelation, and the question of the human capacity to perceive the orderly intelligence and beauty of the Creator who manifests each of these in his creation by image and trace.

"The Way We Know"... in Theology and in Science: General Resonances

The core issue with respect to how we know is the relationship between the knower and the object they wish to know. Modernity proclaimed the possibility of an unembroiled distance between the knower (who possesses the possibility of objectivity) and that which she seeks to know. The advent of postmodernity in its more moderate forms has given the lie to this possibility and has instead served to narrow the gap between science and theology, particularly on the grounds of epistemology. Postmodernity has done this by demonstrating that reason is never unprejudiced. Christian theologians of the Radical Orthodox (RO) school have also shown convincingly that there is specifically no neutral secular sphere, including that of science, thus unveiling the religious status of the whole modern vision.[2] In light of this, author Jamie Smith exhorts Christians to engage in the public

---

1. Neidhardt, introduction to *Christian Frame of Mind*, xl.

2. Theologian Jamie Smith comments that these RO conclusions in fact mirror the postmodern critique of metanarratives made by Lyotard, for example. See Smith, *Introducing Radical Orthodoxy*, 127.

square of ideas on the basis that all engagement by everyone is faith-based, given the fideistic nature of reason itself and the myth of neutral secularity.[3] The eclipse of pure reason has not yet pervaded modernity. Secularism and scientism seems still very much publicly viable, its core being the conclusions of the Enlightenment. The Enlightenment has as its heart the notion of "prejudice against prejudice"[4]—where the most dangerous prejudice is the religious. As Smith concludes therefore, "political (and academic) rhetoric indicates that modernity is a thriving project."[5] Thus, postmodernity still has its work to do in secularistic science.

It is science in particular that has been seen as the realm of *certainty* in the quest for indubitable *certainty* in modernity, led by Immanuel Kant and René Descartes. It was the method of Descartes that specifically led us down the blind alley of seeking absolute certainty in science, and the Kantian disjunction of knower and the known. Two important voices which have exposed the fallacies of this rationalistic worldview, scientism and the reliability of pure reason, and the myth of total objectivity, even for scientists, are Michael Polanyi (*Personal Knowledge*) and Alasdair MacIntyre (*After Virtue*). The idea which dominated many Western countries of the infallibility and supremacy of reason of the autonomous human mind, and of a pristine secular space untarnished by religious faith has been exposed as a hopeful but deleterious myth by means of postmodernity's critique. Postmodernity's contribution to the contemporary postfoundationalist milieu has affected both science and theology. With respect to the latter, it has created some windows for the gospel and a "faith seeking understanding" confessional theory and practice of the Christian church. The realist revelation-ism expressed in Karl Barth's commitment to the epistemological convictions of Anselm that theology is "faith seeking understanding," provides a window arising from a consonance between postmodernity and Christian theology done in this way. Reflecting this, theologian Martin Davis has stated, "Against the Kantian disjunction between the knower and the known, God's own 'eloquent self-evidence' has sounded through to us both in the mediation of revelation in ancient Israel . . . and particularly and most

---

3. See Hastings, *Missional God*, 52. Hearing the naturalistic rhetoric of someone like Richard Dawkins with its lack of awareness of the prejudiced nature of reason, makes one wonder if somebody should write a book called *The Scandal of the Secular Mind* as a counterpoint, of course, to theologian Mark Noll's book *The Scandal of the Evangelical Mind*.

4. A phrase coined by Hans-George Gadamer, *Truth and Method*, 276.

5. Smith, *Introducing Radical Orthodoxy*, 32.

clearly in the incarnation of the Word (Logos) of God in Jesus Christ, who is 'of one being with the Father' (*homoousios to Patri*)."[6]

In science, on the other hand, the advent of quantum physics has had an effect on rationalist certainties. The work of scientist-turned-philosopher, Michael Polanyi, has of course, placed a significant dent in the knower-known dichotomy. It was he who coined the term "personal knowledge." He specifically exposed the objective-subjective dualism as fallacious and that in fact "all knowing of reality involves the personal commitment of the knower as a whole person,"[7] which must include the role of the imagination. The radical force of Polanyi's critique is that it has leveled all knowing—even scientific knowing. The crucial issue is the "starting point" of knowledge, as Lesslie Newbigin has pointed out. Descartes' was anthropological: "his own existence as a thinking mind" ("I think, therefore I am"). This was for Descartes a self-evident and irrefutable truth. The thinking self, as opposed to the feeling self or the acting self, once made the starting point, opened up *three dualisms* which became part of modernity:

1. The dualism between the thinking mind and the world of things outside of the mind, extended in space (*res cogitans* and *res extensa*). As Newbigin states, for Descartes, the "thinking mind was not extended in space" but was, "so to speak, a single point, an eye looking from outside into the cosmos extended in space. The mental world and the world of material things belong, as it were, to two quite different and separate realms of being." But, as Newbigin concludes,

    > This has led to the popular idea that God, who belongs to the mental or spiritual world, cannot influence or interfere with the material world. The world of pure thought, as for example in mathematics, hovers above the "real"—that is, the material—world but is not part of it. This dualism is very similar to that which dominated classical thought, namely, the sharp distinction between a world of pure forms or ideas and the sensible world with which we are in contact through our five senses.[8]

    Of course, the modern mind-set does involve the empirical approach that tests the theory of the mind with experiment. Mathematics goes with science as the means of the expression of empirical findings. Yet, still within modernity, this dualism persists. In fact, the moment a mathematical formula is expressed, though it may describe a created

---

6. Davis, "T. F. Torrance: Scientific Theology."
7. Newbigin, *Proper Confidence*, 39.
8. Ibid., 36–37.

reality, it can become distant from that reality. Into this dualism comes the pronouncement of the heart of the Christian gospel that has implications for all reality: "*And the Word became flesh and dwelt among us*" (John 1:14).

Newbigin explains how the early church had to overcome this dualism in order to affirm as "public truth the gospel's central statement that the *logos* was identical with the Man, Jesus of Nazareth." It could do so, he confirms, "because the starting point of its thinking was in the Bible, where this dualism is absent."[9] Saint Paul affirmed that the one God in Christ was the Creator of things visible and invisible (Col 1:15–16: "*The Son is the image of the invisible God, the firstborn over all creation. For in him all things were created: things in heaven and on earth, visible and invisible. . .*"). Newbigin also states that as long as this dualism persists, the gospel can never be accepted as "public truth," but only as "private opinion." He believes that developments in physics and mathematics in the past hundred years has sought to overcome this dualism, and especially quantum physics, in which "the observer and the object of observation do not belong in separate worlds" but "interact."[10]

2. The second dualism is closely related to the first. It is that expressed in the words "objective" and "subjective." This dichotomized language is so much a part of our vocabulary today that it is hard to think in a way that escapes them. Of course, there is always a subject and the object of the subject's inquiry, but it is the wide separation between the two that Descartes' method encouraged, resulting in two types of truth claims: those which communicate objective knowledge, and those which express subjective experience. In the nineteenth century, science came to be known as the source of objective knowledge and the locus of public truth,[11] consigning religion to the realm of subjective experience. Only science could offer objective facts that were universally true irrespective of culture and other contingent elements of a human person.

What is truly radical about the Christian gospel is its proclamation that there is only *personal* encounter, and that objectivity is imperfect and uncertain, always mixed with some subjectivity and always accompanied by use of the imagination. If true, this proclamation validates historical encounter as a valid arena for truth seeking, and as an arena in which there can be real objectivity, though not of

9. Ibid., 37.
10. Ibid.
11. Ibid., 38.

a disembodied and disconnected kind. Christian theology, therefore, enters into the space between objective and subjective, even as it redefines both in its pursuit of personal, embodied, historically embedded knowledge. This is reflected in the gospel's central and epistemologically audacious proclamation: *And the Word became flesh and dwelt among us. And we beheld His glory* (John 1:14) . . . *That which was from the beginning, which we have heard, which we have seen with our eyes, which we have looked at and our hands have touched—this we proclaim concerning the Word of Life.* (1 John 1:1)

3. The third dualism was that between *theoria* (theory) and *praxis* (practice). Newbigin comments on the fact that these two words are absent from the Bible, "because they express a way of understanding which is foreign to the Bible" but which are deeply entrenched in our culture. We picture a thing in our minds as it ought to be and then, as a second step we check out what is "real." In Hebrew, there are only concrete and not abstract realities. For example, the word for "anger," an abstract concept in English, is concrete in Hebrew. It is the word for "nose." When one is angry, one's nose flares and draws in and expels air. Being angry is thus concrete. In the world of the Bible, the ultimate reality is personal and, as Newbigin states, we are "brought into conformity with this reality not by the two-step process of theory and practice, vision and action, but by a single action compromised of hearing, believing and obeying."[12] "The operative contrast," continues Newbigin, "is not between theory and practice; it is between believing and obeying on the one hand and the refusal of belief and obedience on the other." These two actions of believing and obeying are one in Hebrew thought where to know is not a reality until we do. Take for example the words "knee" and "gift," which in Hebrew come from the same root word, because they are related, not by their appearance, but by action. The Hebrew word for knee literally means "the part of the body that bends." The Hebrew word for a gift means "what is brought with a bent knee." One has not brought a gift, in other words, until one has bent the knee. Both Hebrew verbs and nouns have action associated with them where the Greek and English nouns do not.[13] Similarly, in the New Testament, when Jesus calls Simon Peter, it is not to a world of disembodied belief which he calls him. His calling is instead expressed as "Follow me." It requires a holistic response. As Newbigin affirms,

---

12. Ibid., 38–39.

13. This example is taken from the *Ancient Hebrew Research Center*, http://www.shamar.org/articles/hebrew-thought.php#.WCMQ6eGLSdE.

the theory-practice dualism is a denial of good anthropology: "the human person is not a mind attached to a body but a single psychosomatic being. This again poses a challenge for Christianity in the public square" for it cannot be "propagated as a theory or a worldview and certainly not as a religion."[14]

The overcoming of these dualisms ultimately lies in Jesus, the Son of God made human—truly God, truly human, truly a part of the creation he created, yet distinct as God. The belief that there is a real God who corresponds to the revelation of God in the tangible, visible, audible person of his Son, is at the heart of how humans come to know God. It suggests there is something real that we can know, with the use of our critical faculties. But it does require faith. Knowledge by critical realism cannot function without faith.

That this is true in the realm of Christian theology is well known and acknowledged since Augustine, through Anselm and on to Karl Barth. Knowledge in theology is always faith seeking understanding. It is always first *a posteriori* and not *a priori*.[15] What many may not accept quite so easily is the proposal that science, indeed all knowledge, is arrived at in a similar way.

Contrary to the scientism of logical positivism, which is the belief in the privileging of scientific knowledge or the primacy of science over religion, there is no science until we have criticized the critical, and deconstructed the notion of pure reason. In science, despite the aversion of scientism to metaphysics, "explanations are always attached to some metaphysical commitments."[16] I do not practice science until I have first understood faith, or prejudices, or tacit (that is, knowing has unspoken, implicit or intuitive aspects) understanding, or knowledge as personal knowledge. In that sense, to be an honest scientist is to be post-scientist.

The compatibility and coinherence of Christian theology with science lies in how we know what we know. It is a compatibility by way of *empiricism*. In the previous chapter, it was noted how, in some surprising and very significant ways, the gospel was and is compatible with, indeed instrumental in the development of science in the Western world of cultural Christianity. This in contrast to the world of the ancient Greek philosophers, who

---

14. Newbigin, *Proper Confidence*, 39.

15. A more direct way of speaking of the relationship between faith and reason is to say, as Jim Houston, a modern intellectual giant and founding principal of Regent College, has been wont to say, that reason, the life of the mind, and its pursuits, come *after* faith. This is not anti-intellectual, he insists, but it is post-intellectual, that is, reason is always post-faith. James Houston, personal correspondence.

16. Padgett, *Science and the Study*, 13.

did not and could not develop empirical science. This had everything to do with epistemology. We may conclude that there is a profound consonance between scholarship in theology (Torrance's *Theological Science*) and scholarship in science. Sometimes the word integration is used in this regard. Yet integration assumes that theology and science are not already one. The move from integration to coinherence[17] is warranted on the grounds that God is the author of both, and though these disciplines have their own particularities and methodologies, they are one in their epistemologies, and, to persons of open mind, they can be one in their conclusions regarding the universe and God. They do not *need to be* integrated except in our own dualistic Western minds.

In sum, then, we may now debunk the myth that science is discovered through reason and objective, empirically accumulated knowledge that is public, while theology is subjectively perceived and privately appropriated. Knowledge in science, just like in theology, is *tacit* and *personal* and *motivated*, terms we will explain through the contributions of various scientists and theologians. The common epistemology in all human knowing is the "faith seeking understanding" approach which Augustine elucidated back in the fourth century. Faith, or prejudice, or motivation, and reason are always intertwined. The person (subject) and that which is known (the object) cannot be separated. The common epistemology of theology and science always involves what is empirical. That is, it is based in experimental evidence, be it physical or historical. It also involves a process of the proposing of hypotheses or theories, involving use of the imagination, which are then verified or falsified by further experiment which either establish the theory or not. In both cases, and this is the essence of *critical realism*—an underlying "faith" assumption that theories or doctrines and their language actually express what is actually going on in reality.

"The Way We Know"... in Theology and in Science: Specifically, Critical Realism

Science manifests critical realism in its own particular way. Chemists assume that when they draw out orbitals which reflect the probability of the positions and numbers of "electrons," there is such a thing as an electron particle or wave that corresponds to these calculations. Or, if a chemist

---

17. As expressed elsewhere, the actual term integration is problematic in that the oneness of theology and science are construed as merged without distinction. Coinherence allows for mutuality and correspondence but preserves the irreducible identity of the disciplines.

submits a crystal to the x-ray crystallographer—which actually provides a picture of the atoms in the molecule and their spatial relationships to each other—that this is a picture of something that really exists. X-ray crystallography is a phenomenal tool that does indeed provide pictures of molecules.

Similarly, theologians who, after carefully sifting through the witness of the apostles and the early church, and after serious study of the available texts of Scripture (this reflects the *critical* in realism, the critical process of sifting and evaluating the evidence, or the data), used the language that God as one in *essence* (*ousia*) and three in person (*hypostaseis*) should be referred to as "Trinity," they assumed that this reality is in fact reality. They assumed that God is indeed who he has revealed himself to be, in Christ and by the Spirit (this is the *realism*). That he really is three persons-in-relation, and that the language used, provisional though theological language always is (this too is the *critical* part of critical realism), was adequate for the task of representing for the church who God really is. Correspondingly in science, the crystallographer assumes that the placing and identity of the atoms of a molecule depicted in his final crystallograph realistically conveys where atoms really are and their relative positioning and bond distances between them. This is realism. However, the same crystallographer's realism is not a naïve, but a critical one, meaning that she knows that the best the active human mind can do with the tools at hand is to come up with models and mathematics that approximate to reality. The critical piece refers to both the fact that the knower is active in the process, and that she knows the limitations of her findings.

In fact, the step of faith required in making the assumption that reality (ontology, being) is really there (realism) beneath our epistemological probings and theorizing, and indeed, the whole process of reasoning which scientists and theologians undertake, points for the Christian to mediation in Christ, God's agent in creation, God's revealer of himself, and God's reconciler of all things. In fact, at the most fundamental level, Christology is precisely what inspired theologian of science T. F. Torrance to speak confidently of correspondences in knowing and being in the theology/science interface. We will consider Torrance's illuminating work in this area now at some length, simply because his is the most theologically articulate expression of the epistemological coinherence of theology and science.

It was precisely the commonality of the ways of knowing in science and theology that prompted T. F. Torrance to suggest that *critical realism* is common to both.[18] What was desired was a specifically *Christian* epis-

18. Similarly, John Polkinghorne expresses the opinion that in the comparison of science and theology, "both are best understood as leading to a critical realist account of what is the case." *Quantum Physics*, xi.

temology and that meant "one that took seriously the starting point for all knowledge of God in Christology, mediated by the Word written through the Holy Spirit."[19] This search took Torrance in the direction of interaction with the natural sciences, but it had everything to do with the incarnate Christ. The starting point which Torrance discovered to be in common for the study of creation and the study of God was what drew Christ and the sciences together for him. This was "a commitment to a realistic view of the world and then the adoption of a methodology in conformity with the nature of the object under study," which Torrance called a *kata physin* form of scientific inquiry. Underlying this is the idea that all true knowledge involves the nature of the object impressing its inherent rationality on our minds, which requires therefore that thinking be in accordance with the nature of the given object.[20] What Torrance saw in the work of James Clerk Maxwell (who discovered the properties of an electromagnetic field of force, a "paradigm shift" which led to the birth of modern physics) and Einstein (who built on Maxwell's work and expressed the general and special theory of relativity, doing so in a manner that supremely illustrated the scientific method of *kata physin*) became the conceptual basis for Torrance's theological methodology.

Torrance viewed Maxwell and Einstein to be the apex or culmination of scientific development since the second century, and as the third of three paradigm shifts in the history of scientific thought. The first of these was that associated with the Ptolemaic cosmology in the second to fourth centuries, which had a significant influence on the church's thought with respect to cosmology, and found its chief expression in Augustine and his Aristotelian theological/philosophical thought which Torrance opines canonized this approach in Christian theology for many centuries. The second shift involved a move to a Copernican and Newtonian cosmology, with a mechanistic worldview and a deist understanding of God which negated his involvement in the world, which Torrance spoke of as a modified form of dualism, one that reflected a move from Augustinian-Aristotelian dualism to a Augustinian-Newtonian dualism. The third shift was the Maxwellian-Einsteinian revolution which spelled the end of dualism, it being a unitary approach based on the concept of continuous fields.[21] Torrance saw in Einstein's scientific realism an important resource and resonance for doing theology.

---

19. Habets, *Theology in Transposition*, 21.
20. Ibid.
21. For more on this, see ibid., 52–54.

The Coinherent Epistemologies of Theology and Science 105

This epistemological correspondence between theology and science relates to the fact that all reality is just that—reality, whether Divine or human—and reality that is discoverable. This was a correspondence that Torrance found in the incarnation. He was comfortable in making this move on the grounds that Christ is Lord over all realms, but also because he observed that this was the method by which the church had discovered the identity of the person of Christ (1 John 1:1, *"That which was from the beginning, which we have heard, which we have seen with our eyes, which we have looked at and our hands have touched—this we proclaim concerning the Word of life"*) and for the crafting of the doctrine of the Trinity based on the revelation of the incarnate Son by the Spirit.

One of the greatest challenges for the ordinary Christian wrestling with the relationship between theology and science is christological: how to put together the Jesus of Nazareth—the Jesus of history, the Jesus of reconciliation and redemption—with the cosmic Christ who was the agent within the Trinity for creation *ex nihilo*, has been the Divine agent, along with the Spirit, in the providential (not deterministic) evolution of the universe and of life on earth, and is perpetually the sustainer of all things.[22] Yet the mood or tone of the rich christological passages of the New Testament specifically on creation, which usually also pull together creation and redemption (John 1:1-18; Heb 1:2-3; Col 1:13-20), richly convey the grandeur and scope of the work of the Christ in the cosmos.

Though Torrance first uncovers his epistemology in science, and recognized it to be in common with that of theology, and then moved beyond Barth in that he *engaged* the natural sciences,[23] he did not, as McGrath emphasizes, leave behind Barth's central affirmation that "the distinctive nature of theology is determined by its object, which is defined as God revealed in

---

22. Torrance's theology is aptly summed up by Dawson and other scholars in conference on the theology of T. F., James, and David Torrance, as *Discovering the Incarnate Saviour*. See Dawson, *Introduction to Torrance*. Similarly, Habets in his recent work on T. F. Torrance, *Theology in Transposition*, expresses the christocentricity of Torrance's theology throughout, and in particular with reference to chap. 7, he states the following: "As Christology forms the center of his entire theology on the foundation of the doctrine of the Trinity, this chapter will highlight the coherent, consistent, and comprehensive nature of Torrance's dogmatics and how the reality of Jesus Christ the incarnate Word comes to inform and structure the entire content of a truly Christian dogmatics" (2).

23. Barth treated theology and science as non-interactive disciplines in a manner that has resonance with Stephen Jay Gould's non-overlapping magisteria viewpoint, although differently motivated and conceived. Torrance found in the theology of Barth the construction of a unitary approach to reality, an approach he found also in Einstein. Barth was not aware of this but apparently seemed pleased about it when Torrance informed him of this (see T. F. Torrance, *Transformation and Convergence*, ix).

Jesus Christ."[24] In fact, "Torrance invokes the theological principle of the *homoousion* in making the point that this epistemological insight is ontologically determined. God already is in himself what he is in his historical self-revelation in Christ. Epistemology is thus correlated with ontology."[25] Torrance already stressed this point from 1938 onward. Even in his Auburn Lectures, he states that "the *ordo cognoscendi* is only possible on account of the *ordo essendi*."[26]

A mutually beneficial conversation between theology and science which is possible concerning *formal methodological* matters is what emerges in Torrance's work. This refers to a correspondence related to the reality that the "scientific" method is employed in both disciplines. Another way to say this is that *critical realism* applies in both disciplines as the humble yet constructive way of gaining knowledge.[27] There is an undergirding assumption in both disciplines that there has to be some kind of *correspondence* between what is in the researcher's mind and what is being studied, between the models and patterns of the scientist's or theologian's mind and the actual reality under investigation (again, the *realism* of critical realism). Another way to say this, as indeed T. F. Torrance did in fact say it, is that knowing follows being, epistemology follows ontology.[28] As a consequence, "true rationality never seeks to impose a preconceived pattern on to the material it wishes to know. Instead it humbly enquires of a given field of reality; it puts questions to it, and then—as Torrance so often says—it lets its questions be questioned."[29] The process of research will thus involve "purifying the active concepts that form the matrix of their encounter" as well as eliminating "distorting impositions of alien thought patterns that derive from outside sources."[30] In science, it will be fairly clear that this involves the empirical process that moves from hypothesis, to carefully designed experiment, to evaluation, toward a thesis. Less obviously for some, in theology, this involves hearing the apostolic and ecclesial testimony concerning God's self-revelation in Christ. It also includes exegesis of the text of Scripture in light of its cultural historical background, its literary genre, its grammatical meaning and its rhetorical forms, and so on.

24. McGrath, *T. F. Torrance*, 208.
25. Ibid.
26. Ibid., with reference to Torrance, "Christian Doctrine of God," 93.
27. For a fuller discussion of epistemological realism in Torrance's work, see Achtemeier, "Natural Science," and Kelly, "Realist Epistemology," 75–102.
28. See Kelly, "Realist Epistemology," 76. He notes that this is discussed in Barth in *Church Dogmatics* I/2, 5ff.
29. Kelly, "Realist Epistemology," 76.
30. Achtemeier, "Natural Science," 272.

Caution is required at this point, of course. For *scientists* who might baulk at the idea of coming under the control of theology or even associating with its epistemological method, it is clear that Torrance did not intend that there should be a hegemony of theology over the sciences. He acknowledged that each science had its own freedom for the development of its idiosyncratic procedures, analytical tools, thought structures, criteria and language in the pursuit of its own subject within the natural order, without interference from theological science. Yet, Torrance, from a faith perspective, and grounded in a high Christology, will have no doubt that whatever science discovers, it can never contradict first-order, creedal theology. He will also invite scientists as priests of God's good creation to reflect on what their discoveries reveal of the glory of Christ, inviting them evangelically into the response of worship and into the building of a theology which must include all reality, a theology that is encyclopedic. He would, if you like, invite the scientist to find the meaning of her work in the light of Christ the Creator and Sustainer and Priest-King of the cosmos.

Theologians, for other reasons, might balk at the idea of crassly and uncritically employing scientific method for discerning theological truth from Divine revelation, be it general, special or personal revelation. Torrance did believe that scientific method should be applied in theology, if critical realism was indeed applicable in both. Thus he freely spoke of theology as "scientific theology" or "theological science." "Scientific theology," according to Torrance, "is active engagement in that cognitive relation to God in obedience to the demands of His reality and self-giving."[31] The emphasis in a scientific theology then is on God's objective revelation of himself "so that the truth of God may shine through unhindered and unobscured by the 'opacity' of the human mind."[32] On other words, "we seek to allow God's own eloquent self-evidence to sound through to us in His Logos so that we may know and understand Him out of His own rationality and under the determination of His divine being."[33] Torrance's scientific theology is thus, in this sense, a *via positiva* (though it does not rule out the *via negativa*) approach to knowledge of God developed in accordance with God's historical self-revelation in the history of Israel and the incarnation of Jesus Christ.

However, it is important to clarify that Torrance did not think method from the natural sciences could be uncritically employed for the pursuit of the knowledge of the transcendent God. Furthermore, when he spoke of theology as a "science," Torrance was using the term in a much broader

---

31. T. F. Torrance, *Theological Science*, ix.
32. Davis, "T. F. Torrance."
33. T. F. Torrance, *Theological Science*, ix.

sense than its sense in the scientific world might convey. "Science," for Torrance, and in this he was not original,[34] was conceived of as "an investigative discipline whose goal is to faithfully expound the intelligible structure of its own particular object."[35] It could be thought of more generically as knowledge, as in *scientia*. This for the natural sciences is knowledge focused on the properties and behavior of the particular aspect of the natural order under consideration in that particular science, whereas for theology the focus "is upon God's self-disclosure in the history of Israel that culminates in the incarnation, life, death, and resurrection of Jesus of Nazareth."[36] What Torrance wished to emphasize in speaking of theology as a science, on the one hand, is that theology, like natural science, involves both a vigorous commitment to disciplined investigation, one "as methodologically rigorous as the hard sciences."[37] It also entailed a warranted belief, on the other hand, that thought structures in the engraced human mind do mediate a true encounter with the reality of what is being encountered. The subject of inquiry in theology is principally the person and work of Christ as this reveals the nature of God. The apostolic accounts of the incarnation, life, death and resurrection of Jesus are grounded in the real history of their historically empirical encounter with him. They heard and saw and touched the living Word (1 John 1:1). Then the church throughout the centuries has had ongoing encounter with that living Christ.

A key theological tenet in Torrance that undergirded this was the eternal, Divine nature of the living Word within an immanent eternal Trinity. Torrance's practice, following Barth, and over against Moltmann, was to deny any idea that God's eternal being is constituted by his relations with creation or humanity in history. The revelation of the Son as Jesus of Nazareth was the revelation of the eternal Trinity in which the Son lived in coinherent relations with the Father and the Spirit. The noetic road to the immanent Trinity might be through the economic Trinity, or the revelation of the incarnate Word and the Spirit, but the reality of the eternal being of God was necessary to the reliability of this economic revelation. There could be no God "back of"[38] the immanent Trinity and there could be no *meaning*

---

34. Thomas Aquinas speaks of theology as a science. In fact, he does so in the very first article of the first question of the *Summa Theologiæ* I, Qu.1, Art. 1.

35. Achtemeier, "Natural Science," 271.

36. Ibid.

37. Colyer, *How to Read T. F. Torrance*, 40.

38. The phrase "back of" reflects a phrase in Karl Barth's discourse on the God revealed in Jesus Christ by the Spirit (*CD* I/1, 350–53). He wished to emphasize that behind the revealed God is the real God, and that there could be no God "back of" or "behind the Trinity," like a Quaternity for example. He preserved the transcendence of

to the incarnational revelation of God in Jesus Christ in the economic Trinity without its correspondence to the immanent Trinity.

Torrance, like Newbigin, also skewered dualisms of multiple kinds, but none more so than cosmological dualism, which proposes a "separation between the reality or essence of something and the empirical sources of our knowledge about it—between substance and appearance."[39] This relates to what is "really real," and in this regard, Torrance was critical of the ancient Greek thought of both Aristotelian and Platonic or Neoplatonic sources, and precisely so in consequence of the theology of the unconfused union of the Divine and human natures of the incarnate Christ. Any philosophy that proposes that the really real is in the heavenly, or eternal realm of pure thought forms, and that concrete creation is itself not real, he saw as a denial of the goodness of God's creation, and a confusion of God and creation. He was well aware that this philosophical orientation regarding creation explained the absence of science in the Greeks precisely because they treated experimentation and the observation of concrete particulars as unimportant, preferring to speculate in a top-down manner in an *a priori* rather than *a posteriori* way. Torrance knew that the ultimate theological reality of the Trinity was arrived at in an *a posteriori* way, as a response of the early church to the empirical reality that God had walked in their midst in the fully human person of Jesus Christ, who shared the Divine essence and communion with the Father and the Spirit. As Achtemeier states, reflecting Torrance accurately: "The Nicene *homoousion*, which stands at the center of orthodox Christology, is the Church's emphatic declaration that the fullness of the divine being has become present and knowable within the realm of space and time in the historical, flesh-and-blood reality of Jesus Christ."[40]

In theology, this incarnational reality reflected in the term *homoousion* is vital for the *realism* piece in critical realism. That God is really revealed in the incarnation may be affirmed at the level of objective Divine revelation; however, the human reception of that revelation is also necessary. The correspondence between objective reality and human knowing of it in both

---

God in that he did not insist that the immanent Trinity was identical to the revealed or economic Trinity, but did insist on their correspondence, if revelation was to be trustworthy.

39. Achtemeier, "Natural Science," 271.

40. Ibid. See also John of Damascus in *The Three Treatises on the Divine Images*. In his defense against iconoclasm, John offers the argument that the Son of God become matter and therefore can be depicted in icons, and that to deny this is to reject that Christ was fully man, a heresy already corrected at earlier ecumenical councils. Crystal clear on his sole worship of God, John reflects a general appreciation of created matter as a means for seeing through to God, in a manner that supports the view that God is revealed by way of trace in creation.

theology and science that defines the *realism* in critical realism is assumed on the basis of another theologically foundational concept for Torrance. This is the principle of the *intelligibility* of revelation, be it general or special, or, to use a related term describing the capacity of the human recipient to perceive what is intelligible, *perspicuity*. The intelligibility of the creation to humanity finds its source ultimately in the *Logos*, the living Word who created all things in a manner that reflects wisdom, with an order that is discernible. This is an assumption that already shaped the Wisdom tradition of the Hebrew Scriptures.

Not that this makes everything simple. God who is the God of revelation is also the God of *hiddenness*. We are too feeble to endure the full light of the blazing glory of God. Just as the Son was here on earth as, to use Luther's term, the Divine *incognito*, so, by analogy, theological and scientific findings are not always, or even mostly, found in facile ways. Jesus exhorts his followers to ask, seek, and knock, to persevere in prayer. The early church takes almost four centuries to articulate its most crucial doctrines relating to the deity and humanity of Christ and the Trinity. Similarly, scientific knowledge is gained mostly slowly with painstaking work in the laboratory by often lonely researchers who can become dispirited. What's more, the discoveries of science often have an element of the serendipitous in them that confound any postulation of a directly proportionate relationship between hard work and "success." This is what gives meaning to the descriptor "*critical*" in critical realism as Torrance understood it. The correspondence between the human mind of the researcher and the reality she probes is not always direct and immediate. Some element of mystery remains, though "mystery" must not be conceived of as preventing further probing.

Torrance was significantly influenced by Michael Polanyi in his understanding of epistemology, both with respect to the tacit and personal nature of knowledge, but also with respect to the fact that reality-mediating theories or doctrines both in science (Einstein's general relativity, for example) and in theology (the Niceno-Constantinopolitan Trinity) were not facile, either in their discovery, or in the straightforwardness of their correlation between empirical apprehension and theoretical construct. Torrance noticed that "creative leaps of cognition" were often involved in the crafting of theory, and that there were tacit aspects to the comprehension of the deep structures of reality that were grasped intuitively, not just by formalized processes of rational inference. This did not imply an epistemological dualism for Torrance. The mind of the knower and the object of knowledge were not separated by an unbridgeable gulf. The assumption that there is a bridge was based for Torrance in the presupposition of the goodness of God and in the reality of the incarnate Logos who made and sustained the objective reality of creation, and who mediates its accessibility because he is intelligible and has made humans in his image to be capable of perceiving the intelligible in a perspicacious way.

Moving beyond a merely non-dualist view of knowledge and the cosmos, Torrance on the basis of a christological doctrine of creation, also argued for a non-monist view of God and creation, and therefore of theology and science. In this respect of his thought, Torrance owed a debt to renowned physicist and theologian John Philoponos (490–570). He eschewed Neoplatonic notions of material participation (*methexis*) of the creation in God, believing them to be harmful to both theology and science. Theologically they were harmful in that they led to the limited description of God as an "Unmoved Mover" rather than the living God capable of acting within creation without being conditioned by creation or limited by it. Instead he proffered the view that creation was distinct from the Creator, and real and valuable in its own right as created, and at the same time, profoundly dependent upon the Creator Son and under the life-giving influence of the Creator Holy Spirit. As such the relational triune God, through the Son and the Spirit, is in *koinōnia* with the creation—a relationship of participation which in turn permits the creation certain degrees of freedom to be and to become, participating in its own development. In sum, Torrance was above all convinced that both disciplines, theology and science "result from *a posteriori* reflection on an independent reality which they attempt to describe in their respective manners."[41] An epistemology of a faith seeking understanding, then, pertains to both. Which is to say that *critical realism* applies to both also.

This epistemology is expressed also in the work of John Polkinghorne.[42] Polkinghorne suggests five points of comparison between the ways in which science and theology pursue truth: moments of enforced radical revision, a period of unresolved confusion, new synthesis and understanding, continued wrestling with unresolved problems, deeper implications.[43] This process, familiar to most scientists, is also familiar to any exegete of Scripture moving toward discovery of the exegetical idea of a passage—a process just as rigorous as any in science.

Polkinghorne particularly uses the term *motivated* belief. By "motivated," Polkinghorne meant belief that is warranted by reason and empirics. Polkinghorne, who was both a priest and a quantum physicist believed that

---

41. McGrath, *Science and Religion*, 226.

42. Michael Polanyi was once again the philosopher of science most influential in determining Polkinghorne's adherence to critical realism.

43. Polkinghorne, *Quantum Physics & Theology*, 15–22.

When he "turned his collar around" he did not stop seeking truth.[44] In fact, following T. F. Torrance in this regard, the trend in Polkinghorne's very helpful work in the theology science discussion was increasingly toward becoming more and more theological, and specifically Trinitarian.[45] Like Torrance, he made each of these disciplines the context for the other. Theology that is not contextualized by science is defective, and science not contextualized by theology may lack imagination and meaning.[46] Of the contribution he made in this regard, Edward Davis affirms that "Polkinghorne offers an open-minded, critical attitude toward both science and theology that constitutes a powerful, deeply insightful case for the truth of Christian theism. I know of no more attractive alternative to the narrow bibliolatry of the fundamentalists or the reckless modernity of many liberals."[47] It may simply be added that Polkinghorne advocates in particular for a Trinitarian theism, one in which the coinherence of theology and science are grounded in the coinherence of methodologies with respect to knowing.

In this vein, Alister McGrath can also rightly claim that his work on the methodological and conceptual convergence between the natural sciences and Christian theology operates on the same basis. In fact, McGrath suggests that he "represents the first theological application of the form of 'critical realism' developed by Roy Bhaskar (born 1944), which allows the recognition of a degree of social construction in the human representation of reality, while at the same time insisting that ontology determines epistemology."[48]

A significant influence on Michael Polanyi, who speaks of all knowledge as "personal," was the work of Scottish philosopher John MacMurray, whose personalism led him to argue that the nature of human beings is personal, rather than mechanical or organic. Epistemologically, how we "know" what we know is the same in all spheres of knowledge. It is personal knowledge. It is tacit. It is empirically arrived at. When God revealed himself to Moses in the burning bush as "I am who I am," he was really saying don't try and guess who I am intellectually in some kind of disembodied way. There's mystery but it is revealed ultimately in the embodied person of the Son, who could be seen and heard and touched, as John tells us (1 John 1:1–4). In the same way in science, we don't discover things by guessing but by experimentation, through trial and error, and what we discover is

---

44. See, e.g., Polkinghorne. *Exploring Reality*, ix.
45. See Polkinghorne, *Science and the Trinity*.
46. See Polkinghorne, *Theology in the Context of Science*.
47. Davis, "Motivated Belief."
48. McGrath, *Science and Religion*, 226.

often surprising. In addition to some aspects of quantum physics, the contribution of Michael Polanyi thus deployed the suggestive term "personal knowledge" we encountered above, confirming that "all knowing of reality involves the personal commitment of the knower as a whole person."[49] It would therefore seem impossible to find any coinherence between theology and science unless we share a common epistemological commitment to the fearless pursuit of truth no matter its source—the dictum that all truth is God's truth. But we must also all acknowledge that faith commitments affect how we see truth in theology, and plead with others to see that this is always true in *all* pursuit of truth, including scientific. As Polanyi and others have shown, all knowledge is humble knowledge.

In evaluating the way of knowing in theology and in science, one has to admit that while prejudices or faith or tacit influences do influence science, the levels of certainty achieved by science seems higher. This is especially the impression one gets in the harder sciences in which conclusions are tested by instrumentation and reproducibility. The accuracy of a technique like x-ray crystallography which chemists use is utterly remarkable, as we have observed. This "high" certainty may seem to contradict our hypothesis of the similarities in ways of knowing of hard science and theology, or "theological science," using Torrance's term. Two comments may be made here: first, it is at the higher level of the *philosophy* of science, that is the meaning of science, that theology and science especially share the common limits of reason; and second, even ways of arriving at so-called hard science are actually by the way of falsification, rather than verification, and therefore involve a faith approach and personal knowledge validated or invalidated by empirical data.

By way of further explanation, in the twentieth century, the manner in which beliefs could be confirmed in science was considered to run in two possible directions. Verificationism, which, as McGrath explains, "held that the natural sciences were capable of stating their ideas in forms capable of being confirmed from experience," and falsification which "held that they were able to state their ideas in such a way that defective approaches could easily be shown to be false, even if it was rather more difficult to confirm valid theories than verifications had once thought."[50] These ways of knowing within science arose from within a very important philosophical movement called the "Vienna Circle," which involved philosophers, physicists, mathematicians, sociologists, and economists, led by the philosopher Moritz Schlick (1882–1936). Interestingly, the core belief of this group was that

49. Newbigin, *Proper Confidence*, 39.
50. McGrath, *Science and Religion*, 67.

"*beliefs must be justified on the basis of experience.*"[51] This empiricism was reflective also of the work of Scottish philosopher David Hume. This school thus held empiricism in high esteem and disavowed metaphysics (something impossible to do, as we have noted). All statements had to be related to what is experienced. It also employed with rigour in the symbolic logic of Bertrand Russell (1872–1970). The person who developed verificationism was Rudolph Carnap (1891–1970), most notably through his work *The Logical Structure of the World*. The only two sources of knowledge he validated were sense perception and the analytic principles of logic. This gave the natural sciences high priority in the Circle, in the pursuit of knowledge.

For Carnap, "only statements which are capable of being verified are meaningful." Philosophy was "seen as a tool for clarifying what had been established by empirical analysis."[52] Only some mathematical truths required no empirical verification ($2 + 2 = 4$, for example). In all other cases, empiricism was required for meaningfulness. Logical positivism emerged from this verificational approach. Some theologians like John Hick sought to maintain Christian theology under this philosophical approach by opting for "eschatological verification," the idea that there will be an "endpoint" which will verify all.[53] However, the verification principle actually self-destructed, insomuch that logical positivism does not work for anything in the past. As McGrath illustrates, the statement "There were six geese sitting on the front lawn of Buckingham Palace at 5:15 p.m. on June 18, 1865" is definitely meaningful and it could have been verified, but we are not in a position to verify it.[54] Second, logical positivism was plagued by a problem of scale: it could not, for instance, deal with subatomic particles, which cannot be "observed." This led to modification of the principle based on what may reasonably be *inferred* from experimental observation. Interestingly it was developments within science itself which led to the dilution of the verification principle. This led to the development of a rival approach, that of falsification, championed by Karl Popper (1902–94), a very important contributor to the development of the philosophy of science in the twentieth century. Popper thought of the development in scientific knowledge as an evolutionary process. Preliminary theories are offered and then subjected to rigorous strategies for falsification, in a way that was thought to parallel natural selection in evolutionary biology. Popper thought of the verification principle as too rigid, and liable to excluding valid scientific conclu-

---

51. Ibid., italics original.
52. McGrath, *Science and Religion*, 68–69.
53. Ibid., 70.
54. Ibid.

sions. Crucially, verificationism excluded the most important scientific statements, that is, the "scientific theories, the universal laws of nature."[55] It also, on the other hand, allowed pseudosciences such as Marxism and Freudianism to be legitimized, based on the verification by these authors of virtually anything they viewed as meaningful and corroborative of their ideologies. Popper's description of the contrastingly humble attitude he saw in Einstein contributed to his conclusion that falsification was a better way to do science. Around 1920, Popper read that Einstein, in relation to his general theory of relativity, had averred that "if the red shift of the spectral lines due to the gravitational potential should not exist, then the general theory of relativity will be untenable."[56] This demonstrated that Einstein was actually holding his theory in humility, and looking for something that might falsify it. Although Einstein's statement proved to be an overstatement based on the fact that the redshift might have been too small to be observed by the technology available in the 1920s, nevertheless the principle remained.

Popper was convinced that theories needed to be tested against experience, which would then lead to their being either verified or falsified.[57] Popper in fact accepted some of the fundamental themes of logical positivism, especially the notion of the foundational role of experience of the real world. However, the acid test was that whereas logical positivism "stressed the need for stating the conditions under which a theoretical statement could be verified, Popper held that the emphasis must fall upon being able to state the conditions under which the system could be falsified."[58]

Philosopher Anthony Flew actually takes up the falsification way of knowing in order to demonstrate that religious claims cannot be meaningful given that "nothing drawn from experience can be regarded as falsifying them." It turns out, however, that the demand for falsification is much more complex than this.[59] Flew's absolute demands could not even be met by the natural sciences, because they too, as in Flew's critique of religious claims, introduce the modifications or qualifications of which Flew is so critical in religion. As McGrath confirms, "In reality, anomalous data is generally accommodated within theories by a subtle and complex process of adjustment, modification, and qualification."[60] Popper himself had really hoped to eliminate metaphysics from science. However, his way of attempting to do

---

55. Popper, *Conjectures*, 281.
56. McGrath, *Science and Religion*, 72.
57. Ibid.
58. Ibid., 73.
59. Ibid.
60. Ibid.

so—by demanding that they be falsifiable—was much more difficult than he had imagined.[61] The conclusion of this discussion of verifiable and falsifiable methodologies is that the confirmation of scientific theories is more challenging than expected, that anomalies may either disprove a theory or be accommodated within it, and that even the "philosophy of science cannot itself determine which of these possibilities is right . . . only a simplistic positivist philosophy of science holds that an anomaly forces the abandonment of a promising theory."[62]

In the end, the falsifiability of religious claims is not really different to those of the natural sciences. As McGrath again confirms, "The dialogue between science and religion often proceeds on the assumption that there is a shared commitment to an external world, which the human mind is able to discern and represent, to some limited yet significant effect." This, he ascribes to a group of philosophies under the term, "realism," which we now consider specifically as applied to science and then theology.

"The Way We Know" . . . in Theology and in Science: Critical Realism in the Sciences

The explanatory and predictive successes of the natural sciences have led to the widely held conclusion that the reality suggested by the theories involved in these sciences point to the existence of the independent reality they describe, not in the foundationalist way of Descartes, for whom certain realities were *a priori*, but in a realist way. For example, particles or waves called electrons by chemists, actually exist as electrons whose electron density can be predicted on the basis of the Heisenberg uncertainty principle and the Schrödinger wave equation, leading to accurate orbital maps, and predictability about reactivity patterns of molecules on this basis. Daniel Bernoulli's account of the relation between pressure and kinetic energy accords enough with reality that planes can actually fly when built around this relation. Natural sciences can actually explain the world, in other words, because their theories describe what really is in the world. This is realism. As John Polkinghorne has stated,

> The naturally convincing explanation of the success of science is that it is gaining a tightening grasp of an actual reality. The true goal of scientific endeavour is understanding the structure of the physical world, an understanding which is never complete

---

61. Ibid., 74.
62. Ibid., 74–75.

but ever capable of further improvement. The terms of that understanding are dictated by the way things are.[63]

If the successes of the scientific theories in the natural sciences were not reflective of reality, this would be a massive coincidence, which seems unlikely.

It is important to stress that scientific realism is grounded in *empiricism*. As McGrath states,

> Its plausibility and confirmation arise from direct engagement with the real world, through repeated observation and experiment. It should not be thought of primarily as a metaphysical claim about how the world is, or ought to be. Rather, it is a focused and limited claim which attempts to explain why it is that certain scientific methods have worked out so well in practice.[64]

Realism explains scientific theories in such a way that doesn't "make the success of science a miracle."[65] Scientific realism, expressed as theory replicating reality, is thus justified by its successes. These statements reflect two realities worth commenting on, however: (i) they do reflect the reality of the world and not just what it signifies, a reality consonant with the doctrine of creation that affirms both the real reality and goodness of the created order; and (ii) they reflect the fact that within empiricism, the setting up of experiments has its own limitations, which accounts for the reality that in hard sciences, the level of certainty may be high, give that the experiment has eliminated variables. Thus, experiments and results in hard science may look much more concrete and convincing than in the soft sciences or theology. However, the nature of the experimentation must be borne in mind.

With respect to both science and the theology/science dialogue, *critical realism* has been advocated in this chapter as that form of realism most appropriate to these disciplines. Critical realism simply conveys a distinction with naïve realism which maintains that reality impacts directly on the human mind without any critical reflection on behalf of the observer by means of mathematical formulae and mental models. Nonrealism or antirealism stands in contrast to naïve and critical realism, maintaining the viewpoint that the human mind constructs its ideas without any reference to a world outside of itself. What is essential to *critical* realism is the acknowledgment that the human mind is active in the process of perception and correlation of the phenomena observed. It constructs *mental maps* based on what it discovers from empirical processes. This also stands in contrast with two

---

63. See Polkinghorne, *One World*, 22.
64. McGrath, *Science and Religion*, 78.
65. Putnam, *Mathematics*, 73.

alternatives to knowing, idealism and instrumentalism.⁶⁶ A mediated position is that held by Bas von Fraassen, "who drew a distinction between a realist, who holds that science aims to give a literally true description of what the world is like, and what he calls a 'constructive empiricist,' who argues that acceptance of a theory does not involve commitment to the truth of that theory, but to the belief that it adequately preserves the phenomena to which it relates." Thus, for the constructive empiricist, to invoke the word "electron" as if it represents a real reality is to introduce "unwarranted and unnecessary metaphysical element into scientific discourse."⁶⁷ One can see that scientism seeks freedom from metaphysics.

"The Way We Know" . . . in Theology and in Science: Critical Realism in Theology

To say that these options, critical realism, idealism and instrumentalism in the philosophy of science, have parallels in contemporary theology is to understate the case. Don Cupitt represents the nonrealism position ("abandon ideas of objectivity and eternal truth, and instead see all truth as a human improvisation").⁶⁸ A major issue in our time relates also to whether Christian theology is determined by real and personal revelation of the real God in real time by his incarnate Son, someone who the historical church community heard and saw and touched. Or whether theology is done in a manner that corresponds with Idealism. This is prefigured well in the manner in which two great Reformed theologians arrived at the doctrine of the Trinity. Jonathan Edwards, in the interests of contextualizing theology in early Mo-

---

66. *Idealism* is the philosophy holding that physical objects do exist in the world, but it avers that "we can have knowledge only of *how things appear to us*, or are experienced by us, not things as they are in themselves." Alister McGrath, *Science and Religion*, 80. Kant, who is best known in modernity for this viewpoint distinguished between phenomena from the world of observation, and things as they are in themselves, called noumena, which can never be known directly, and which only metaphysics can inform us about. This view is thus called phenomenalism in the philosophy of science. It is uncommon in the sciences (Ernst Mach is one proponent). *Instrumentalism* is the viewpoint that scientific concepts and theories are useful in a pragmatic kind of a way. That is, they are useful instruments for explaining and predicting phenomena, and only as useful as they do explain them, but are still not true descriptions of unobservable reality. They are merely a further organization, a step on the way. Osiander in the Reformation was an exponent of this viewpoint, thus enabling him to discount the Copernicus hypothesis. Ernest Nagel's commentary on the kinetic model of gases, in which gas molecules are likened to billiard balls, is merely a useful instrument for understanding the observations that are made in experiments on these gases, but nothing more.

67. See McGrath, *Science and Religion*, 80–81.

68. See ibid.

The Coinherent Epistemologies of Theology and Science 119

dernity, relies on Lockean Idealism to construct a Trinity on psychological grounds, and he does so, as William Danaher has said, by way of a psychological account of the Trinity, not even analogy.[69] Karl Barth, by contrast, is a critically realist theologian, whose road to the Trinity is historical and personal revelation as received by the church, in such a manner that the economic Trinity is the road into the immanent Trinity. Furthermore, the sacramental move of the Radical Orthodox theologians reflects a return to the Neoplatonism that undergirds the Idealism above.

As McGrath states, most theologians "who have engaged with the natural sciences tend to be persuaded of the merits of realist approaches to theology." This has been true to my own experience. I can imagine that it is difficult for scientists with no theological background whatsoever to relate to the statement that doing theology and doing science involve the same epistemological process. But that is precisely the case. The ethos of being in a chemistry research lab grappling with the evidence that various spectra have revealed about a compound, and the ethos of being in a Greek text grappling with the evidence that the authorial intent (and ultimately that of the Divine authorial intent) was always the same for me. As was the wonder when each puzzle was unveiled! Other examples cited by McGrath of theologians who have engaged with science in the critically realistic way, are Ian Barbour, Arthur Peacocke, and John Polkinghorne, all of whom draw on the emphasis in William James on "the active role of the knower in the process of knowing."[70] T. F. Torrance is another case in point, as noted above. Though he was not a scientist *per se*, he made it a consuming passion for twenty years to engage with science, a factor influencing his realist approach in both disciplines. I am convinced that the study of creation keeps theology and theologians appropriately grounded. Theologian and scientist Alister McGrath similarly adheres to realism in both disciplines, but he cordons off his own version of critical realism in that he draws on the insights of Roy Bhaskar and his stratification of reality. That is, the sciences and all fields of knowledge reflect an account of reality according to its (their) distinct nature (*kata phusin*).[71] The idea of critical realism is that when what has been proposed by way of a thesis or hypothesis is self-consistent and when the evidence points in a direction, epistemology is following ontology, and the theory is probably right. Absolute certainty is rarely achievable. The emphasis on the reality that critical realism must be applied according to the distinct nature of the object concerned, reflected in Torrance and Mc-

---

69. Danaher, *Trinitarian Ethics*, 63–65.
70. McGrath, *Science and Religion*, 83.
71. Ibid.

Grath, is an appropriate one especially given the nature of theology which has a transcendent (and immanent) object of study. This leaves room for the reason expressed in an earlier chapter for the *asymmetric* nature of the coinherence between theology and science. Why does conciliar theology have primacy? Can this position really allow science to be science? I do acknowledge that this is a stance of faith, but one that in fact is critically realistic. It is a belief grounded first in the doctrine of creation, leading to the conclusion that study of the Creator must surpass, but never exclude, study of the creation. It is grounded also in the conviction that God has revealed himself in his Son and by his Spirit, in an authoritative and perspicuous way for humanity, through the church, and that therefore, although God's two books of creation and Scripture cannot contradict, for he is the one God, and this is one world, not two, nevertheless the *personal* revelation of God in Christ through the Scriptures, must take precedence over general revelation. The truth is that theology, because it must account for *all* reality, not just that revealed by science, is a bigger discipline.

One of the basic convictions of critical realism in theology, in sum, then, is that certainty is not possible to reason alone, and theological language, although it does represent revealed reality, as in science, is always provisional. Another conviction is that truth is arrived at empirically in a historical sense, and in the sense that it responds to the data of biblical studies; "both result from *a posteriori* reflection on an independent reality which they attempt to describe in their respective manners."[72] A third conviction is that there is an active role of the knower in what is known; that is, complete "objectivity" is not possible. There is a Trinitarian and incarnational circle of hermeneutics involving our knowing, in participation with the Revealer, and the church.

There is an epistemological coinherence between theology and science in this regard. As Torrance stated, in his rigorous form of theological realism, "Theology and every scientific inquiry operate with the correlation of the intelligible and the intelligent."[73]

Critical realism is thus a philosophical system grounded in faith that the Revealer of truth in every realm is neither capricious nor obscurantist, and yet also not controlling, in that he does not make things plain easily, for he has created persons in his own image who he expects to be inquisitive, and to explore, and to think, and to worship.

The place of metaphysics in both science and theology are contested, but in both cases are frankly, unavoidable. This has been addressed with

---

72. McGrath, *Science and Religion*, 226.
73. T. F. Torrance, *Reality and Scientific Theology*, xii.

respect to science. In theology and biblical studies, the view that any ontotheological statements made from study of the text are suspect is corrected by the critically realistic approach which keeps the text always in conversation with the theology and vice versa, in faith that the real is being revealed by the text. Gathering all of this together we may conclude on the basis of critical realism, that *ontology determines epistemology*!

It is most appropriate to bring this chapter to a close with a summary definition of critical realism which can in fact be applied to theology as well as science, that of N. T. Wright, a practitioner of the science and art of New Testament scholarship, who speaks of it as

> a way of describing the process of "knowing" that acknowledges the *reality of the thing known, as something other than the knower* (hence "realism"), while also fully acknowledging that the only access we have to this reality lies along the spiralling path of *appropriate dialogue or conversation between the knower and the thing known* (hence "critical").[74]

We have now therefore set the stage for developing the theme of the remaining chapters of the book which have to do with *being*, rather than knowing, which will confirm that, in fact, being or ontology is the foundation of knowing, or epistemology. That is, in the spirit of critical realism, we will confirm that our knowing of the triune God, and our knowing of his creation, reflects the reality of who *he* really is, and what *it* really is.

---

74. Wright, *The New Testament and the People of God*, 35.

Chapter 5

The Coinherent *Ontologies* of Theology and Science

The Being of God and the Being of Creation, Part One

Worship and praise belong to you, Father,
in every place and at all times.
All power is yours,
You created the heavens and established the earth;
You sustain in being all that is.
EUCHARISTIC PRAYER 1, SCOTTISH LITURGY, 1982.

BEING: COMMON MATERIAL INTERESTS

IN THIS CHAPTER, WE move from consideration of the common epistemologies of the disciplines of theology and science to discussion of the ontology that makes this possible. If the epistemologies of theology and science are in common, in the spirit of critical realism, we may expect that this must be because there is also a correspondence with respect to ontology, or being. That is, the being of God discerned in response to Divine revelation given

The Coinherent Ontologies of Theology and Science

in Christ and through the Scriptures, is the source of all that is, and he puts his stamp upon all that is. We have expounded the reality accepted in the tradition that coinherence is definitive of the being of the triune God who brought the creation studied by scientists into being. We have noted also that coinherence defines the essence of the incarnation, by which God and humanity/creation are related. Based on these assertions, the doctrine of creation leads us to assume that there is evidence of this coinherent God in humanity (as image), in creation, and therefore in science (as trace). This chapter thus addresses mainly the second of our objectives, which is to support the idea that there are echoes of coinherence in the being of creation as unveiled by science, that account for the commonalities in epistemology, which in turn have led us to propose the coinherence of the disciplines of theology and science.

We will in this chapter focus on reflections of the coinherent nature of the triune God in the nonhuman world, which we observe as *traces* of the Trinity. In the next chapter we will continue this discussion extending it to further traces of the Trinity in nonhuman creation. In chapter 7, we will then consider the reflection of the coinherence of the triune God in humanity, which is spoken of in Scripture as the *image* of God.

The assumption carried forward concerning the nature of critical realism is that reality or ontology, be it Divine, in the case of theological science, or nature, in the case of the natural sciences, is truly reflected in the knower's knowing, or in epistemology. It needs to be stressed that realism is *critical*—that is, there is not a facile or always obvious correspondence between the empirical process of the investigation and its reality. Nevertheless, the assumption is that epistemology follows the ontology that undergirds it, a notion which has been expressed succinctly with respect to the work of T. F. Torrance:

> The critical realism advocated by Torrance connects the knower and the known together in personal union, thus putting the knower (theologian) under a certain obligation to offer a rational account of that which exists independently of the knower (theology). By this means it is obvious that for Torrance and his scientific theology, as for Einstein and his natural science, epistemology follows ontology.[1]

The ontology to which Torrance was referring (and what is most relevant to the theology/science interface) was with respect to the nature of creation, in light of the nature of the triune God. The concern of the sciences is obviously the physical universe. Yet theology (theological science)

---

1. Habets, *Theology in Transposition*, 56.

expresses in various ways the nature of the physical universe in light of who the God of creation is, and provides explanation as to why it is contingent and intelligible and beautiful. We are going to see that the person of Christ as a Trinitarian person, and the nature of the Trinity as revealed in him, and by the Spirit, will be crucial to giving evidence for the notion that epistemology corresponds to ontology. That is, what we know of the being of God and what we know of the being of creation, and the reliability of what we know, is grounded in the incarnational and mediatorial and revelatory nature and history of Jesus Christ. This assertion is arrived at in a manner that is consistent with critical realism, one that reflects a way of knowing that is empirical and that follows a faith seeking understanding methodology. The person and work of Christ as the second person of the Trinity assigned in the eternal councils of God to be the agent of God in creation, and to be incarnate, and to reconcile a fallen creation, is crucial to the gracious correspondence that God has granted between our knowing and what really is. And herein lies the confidence for the proposal of the coinherence of theology and science. Foundational to the union of theology and science has been the reality that God has chosen to make the physical universe the medium for the expression of his self-revelation, and indeed has appropriated it "as the created medium of our knowledge of himself by entering our time and space as the man Jesus of Nazareth, who is fully (including spatio-temporally!) a human being without thereby ceasing to be God."[2] It is the mediation of the Son in creating and becoming incarnate and reconciling, and what this tells us about the Trinity, that leads us to look specifically for traces of the *being* of God as triune, in his creation.

However, as expressed before, it is *not* that we wish glibly to find in nature things that have some facile resemblance to threeness in oneness! This is critical realism, *not* naïve realism. Unwarranted analogies for the Trinity all fall short and can indeed be heretical. What is being looked for are aspects of the creation (as known through science) which by way of imaging and by way of trace reflect some of the essential *concepts* of the Trinity, and which we might indeed expect to find, given that the God of creation is, after all, the triune God.

In order to prepare the way for investigating the analogy between relationality in God and in creation, it is important to refresh ourselves on some aspects of the doctrine of the Trinity. The first aspect we wish to re-emphasize is that the triune God is a *"being in relation."* As already noted, some theologians express the revealed reality that the one God of the Old and New Testaments is one in essence and communion and three in person,

---

2. Achtemeier, "Natural Science," 274.

by the phrase three "persons-in-relation." This is the preferred description of theologians who stress both the personal and the social nature of the Trinity. This includes Orthodox theologians, such as John Zizioulas, as well as some theologians like Moltmann, the Torrances, or Volf in the West. These theologians have often been called "social Trinitarians" though they have just recently been labelled as "relational Trinitarians" to distinguish them from the anthropological and sociopolitical Trinitarians within the social Trinity label. Other theologians prefer to use the language of "three persons *as* relations." This includes theologians like Pope Benedict XVI, and others of a more Western and Scholastic orientation who call themselves *classical* Trinitarians.[3] Encouragingly, then, the tradition as a whole does not question the relationality of the being of God. This is unsurprising given that all must surely agree that God is love. However, it is for this reason that the use of the term "relational Trinitarian" above is a very unfortunate one, for surely all Trinitarians believe that God is relational within his own being and toward creation and humanity. It is almost as unfortunate as the term "classical Trinity" which aside from conveying a certain hubris, actually lays claim to what, in my opinion, is more truly the legacy of the social Trinitarians—the theology of the Cappadocian Fathers. The point I wish to make here is that no matter what viewpoint (classical, social/relational) one takes on the matter of personhood, all within the Great Tradition agree that God is a "being in *relation*." Other controversies around the doctrine of the Trinity—the relationship between the economic and the immanent

---

3. See Holmes et al., *Two Views*, for a description of the controversy between contemporary theologians with respect to the correct "model" for understanding the Trinity. In the midst of the revival of interest in the Trinity in the last thirty years, this books seeks to clarify for the contemporary church the model of the Holy Trinity that Christians should follow. On the side of the so-called "classical Trinity" which purports to reflect the most nuanced interpretation of the Cappadocian Fathers and Nicaea, are theologians like Sarah Coakley, Michel Barnes, Lewis Ayers, Brad Green, John Webster, George Hunsinger, Kevin Vanhoozer, Orthodox Khaled Anatolios, and Catholic Karen Kilby, represented, in the one corner, by Evangelical theologian Stephen Holmes (Classical Trinity, Evangelical Perspective) and Catholic theologian Paul Molnar (Classical Trinity, Catholic Perspective); and in the other corner, there are Tom McCall (Relational Trinity: Evangelical Perspective) and Paul Fiddes (Relational Trinity: Radical Perspective), who though they have their own particular nuanced understandings, nevertheless have built on and represent analytical philosophers and theologians like T. F. Torrance, James Torrance, Alan Torrance, John Zizioulas, Colin Gunton, Cornelius Plantinga, Catherine LaCugna, Richard Swinburne, Jürgen Moltmann, Miroslav Volf, Wolfhart Pannenberg, Stanley Grenz, Millard Erickson, and David Brown. Please note that the term "Social Trinity" is out altogether, according to this book, as it represents an extreme which even the "Relational Trinitarians" cannot espouse, having become associated with the anthropological and sociopolitical approach to the Trinity in Leonardo Boff and the panentheist approach of Moltmann.

Trinity,[4] whether the Holy Spirit is spirated by the Father alone or the Father and Son together (the *filioque* controversy), who the font of the Trinity is—do not negate the one thing all in the tradition agree upon, that God is a relational God. And, as we have already indicated, there is also wide agreement that the persons, or relations, if preferred, in the Trinity are coinherent, that is, that each is in the other, and each is mutually internal to the other. Given that Jesus said, "I am in my Father and my Father is in me" (John 14:10) makes this unsurprising. The three persons are considered to be in a perichoretic relationship, which means that each holds the other, each is interpenetrated by the other, that each *is* in the other (a perichoresis of essence that accounts for the oneness of the Godhead, Latin: *circuminsessio*) and that each *acts* only with and in the other (Latin: *circumincessio*) in inter-animating ways. Thus, despite some nuanced differences, the Christian tradition confessionally expresses the reality that God is one in essence (*ousia*) and three in person (*hypostases*), and as such is the God of love, the relational God. The God who is *both* one in essence and communion, and *also* the God in three persons of irreducible identity (the Father is not the Son, the Son is not the Spirit, the Spirit is not the Father). God is neither atomistic nor collectivistic, but three persons in communion.

A final point to be made in this brief introduction to the doctrine of the Trinity which is foundational to a great deal of what interaction between science and Trinitarian theology is about, is that when it comes to the ways in which the persons of the Trinity function in the economy of creation and redemption, there is a complete equality of essence and honor even though there may be functional asymmetries. Coinherence helps to overcome what look like subordinate relations or actions and attitudes. Even as the Son is sent by the Father, the Father is present in the Son. The Spirit is the Spirit of the Father and of the Son at all times. Each is in the other. And, as Jonathan Edwards was anxious to show, all three persons, including the Spirit, receive equal honor[5] in what they do and in the outcomes of the creation and reconciliation of the cosmos.

Before speaking of the ways in which ontology undergirds epistemology, or how the being of the Trinity as revealed by the Divine-human

---

4. There are at least 7 ways of conceiving of the relationship between the economic and immanent Trinities. These can be found in Baik, *Holy Trinity*. Barth represents the best of these, in my opinion. The economic Trinity is not all we can know of God (preserving transcendence, *"no one has ever seen God"* (John 1:18), *"now I know in part"* (1 Cor 13:12), but nor can the immanent Trinity be inconsistent with what has been revealed (*"but the one and only Son, who is himself God and is in closest relationship with the Father, has made him known"*). The relationship is consonant, if not complete.

5. I have maintained that the desire to honor the Spirit is a driving force in Edwards's theology. See Hastings, *Jonathan Edwards*, 36, 81, 97.

incarnate Son is reflected in what we know of creation through science, it must be emphasized that nothing in creation can actually *replicate* Trinitarian coinherence in light of the transcendence of God. It can *echo* it, however. It has an image in humanity and traces all over creation. In other words, the relationship between coinherence in the mystery of the Trinity, who is God over all blessed forever, and coinherence of things like the study of theology and science, is *not* a univocal one. It *is* one of analogy, however. This analogy works for two reasons—creation is *modeled* or mimics the Godhead in certain ways that are true to a Creator-created relationship, and it does so because creation does more than model. It actually *participates* in the life of the Godhead in Christ, in whom God and created humanity participates by the Spirit, in a manner that is personal and relational on God's part. That is, all things are held together in Christ, the Lord of creation, and all things are under the influence of the Holy Spirit who broods over creation. The validity of these "*bridging concepts*" of *model* and *participation* allow us to say something about human identity, and about creation, and about human ideas, on the basis of who God is. This has been proposed and expounded at length by Christoph Schwöbel and Colin Gunton.[6] It should not be surprising then, that in creation there are *echoes* or traces of coinherence. These Trinitarian foundations will thus form the basis of our discussion of appropriate vestiges of the Trinity in creation, including in subatomic matter (quantum physics and chemistry), in light, in chemistry, in ecology. The way in which the providence of the triune God functions through the agency of the Son and the Spirit, and how this can be integrated with the order of creation at the macro-level and "disorder" at the quantum level will also be discussed. The age and emergence of the universe, of the earth, of humanity and how these reflect the kind of God we say we believe in will be discussed also. These coinherences explain our contention that in the thought world or the realm of knowledge of created human persons in relation with God through the God-Man Jesus Christ, that the worlds of theology and science might also be coinherent partners, each having its own identity, yet each thoroughly entwined in the other, each having equal honor, even if revealed theology may have functional priority. The first area of ontological coinherence we consider is that of relationality.

6. Schwöbel, *Trinitarian Theology Today*. See also Schwöbel and Gunton, *Persons Divine and Human*. See also T. F. Torrance's tightly argued exposition of the "onto-relational" understanding of personhood in both God and humanity in Torrance, *Reality and Evangelical Theology*. John Witvliet, drawing on their work, has suggested that these bridging concepts are of two main kinds: those based on the idea of a model, that is, that human existence models Divine existence; and those based on the idea of the participation of human persons and communities in the Divine communion. Witvliet, *Doctrine of the Trinity*, 259–96.

Relationality

The realistic aim of these ontological discussions must be borne in mind. It is not to prove the Trinity from nature, but to notice that certain aspects of our scientific understanding of the universe "become more deeply intelligible to us if they are viewed in a Trinitarian perspective."[7] The relationality of the persons of the Godhead is where we begin, keeping this qualification in mind. God is both profoundly relational and profoundly personal. One cannot use the term "person" properly in Trinitarian context without the qualification that each of the persons is in relation to the other, in fact, each is mutually internal to the other. Each has space for the other, yet each has irreducible identity. It might be expected that the "stuff" of creation might also show signs of this being-in-relationality. Take for example, the nature of electrons, fundamental to all matter. When we first learn chemistry our teachers draw electrons as if they were particles that fill shells around the atom. As we advance we learn that electrons have both a particulate nature and a wave nature related to the particle (they obey the Schrödinger Wave Equation).[8] They show particulate nature and wave nature all at the same time, and their location is described more by a cloud of probability than by a dot. Something called the Heisenberg uncertainty principle reflects the non-locatedness of electrons, which are described as present in orbitals, not as particles in circular orbits. The common occupation of orbital space, the relationship of electrons to other electrons within their own energy levels and with electrons of other energy levels, as well as their relation to protons and other "particles" of the nucleus is indeed the "stuff" of matter. This ontology surely is an echo of a higher one.

There are many more obvious traces of a relational God in matter, as reflected in the science of chemistry. Take the Periodic Table which reflects the intelligibility of the creation, on the one hand. The fact that we can organize all known elements according to the number of protons in the nucleus and electrons in the orbitals, surely reflects a God who is intelligent and who makes himself intelligible to us, his image bearers. But the Periodic Table is also indicative of relationality in a number of different ways. For example, the atoms of each elements are made of common constituents, such as electrons, protons, gluons, and so on. Yet the numbers of electrons

---

7. Polkinghorne, *Science and the Trinity*, 61.

8. The Schrödinger wave equation is the fundamental equation of physics describing quantum mechanical behavior. It is a partial differential equation that describes how the wavefunction of a physical system evolves over time. It is a *wave* equation in that the wavefunction predicts analytically and precisely the probability of events or outcome.

in their orbitals constitutes their particular identity. The elements are related in a horizontal fashion into *periods*, on the basis of the number of protons (atomic number) they have in the nucleus, which usually corresponds to the number of electrons each element possesses. For example, in the second period, the symbols of each element are arranged sequentially (the number after each is the atomic number): Li (3), Be (4), B (5), C (6), N (7), O (8), F (9), Ne (10). The elements are related vertically also into *groups* in which each element has the same number of electrons in their outer orbitals, giving rise to similarities based on valencies and reactivity patterns. For example, the elements iron (Fe), ruthenium (Ru), osmium (Os), and hassium (Hs) form Group 8, because they all have the same electron configurations in their valence shell, and have similar catalytic properties. At the same time, there is a uniqueness to each element in this group (in all groups) based on the total number of electrons in each atom, and their distance from the nucleus. Thus elements in the same group reflect patterns based on the individual atomic radii, ionization energies and electronegativities. Moving from top to bottom in a group, the atomic radii of the elements increase, as they have more filled energy levels, and so their valence electrons (electrons in the outer orbitals available for bonding) are found farther from the nucleus. Thus, each successive element as we move from top to bottom has a lower ionization energy because it is easier to remove an electron since the atoms are less tightly bound. Likewise, electronegativity decreases from top to bottom, due to an increasing distance between the valence electrons and the nucleus. There are further aspects of relatedness in the Periodic Table. For example, in general, the elements on the left-hand side of the table are the metals and those on the right are non-metals. This is generally based on whether they donate electrons when they bond with the atoms of other elements, or receive electrons. The pattern of sameness of essence in each element, and yet distinctness of identity, and the relatedness patterns of the elements provide traces of the nature of the triune God.

It is the reality that the very essence of the science of chemistry has to do with the capacity of elements for reaction with each other, the reactivity patterns of elements and their chemical bonding to one another, which is most interesting. If elements did not bond in the rich variety of ways that are described by covalent and ionic bonding, the cosmos would not exist. Oxygen, which we breathe and upon which our survival depends, is made up of molecules containing two oxygen atoms bonded together by electron sharing. The "motivation" or driving force for atoms of the same element or from different elements to bond is a lower energy state than the state in which the atoms existed before the bond. The oxygen molecule (O_2) is more stable than two separate oxygen atoms. There is a drive toward a lower energy, more stable state, in chemical bonding. This phenomenon, so seminal and constitutive in matter, evokes the possibility that it is a trace of the relational nature of one God in three persons. This has led one theologian chemist, José Romero-Baró, to specifically draw an analogy between chemical bonding as the "Order of Love in Chemistry" and the theology of the intra-divine love of God, which is the bond of the Spirit, in an Augustinian Trinitarian way. Speaking specifically of the fact that the most important, almost defining property of all elements is their electron affinity, based on their electronegativities, Romero-Baró acknowledges that electrons are filled following "Pauli's principle of exclusion, according to which there cannot be any electron (any particle in general) with four quantum numbers that are the same." But Romero-Baró observes that beyond this mechanical orbital building up (Aufbau), the most profound reason for the chemical linking lies in this electronic "affinity" or *philía*, which would explain the fact that an element is more or less "thirsty for electrons." He goes so far as to say that we could in this way "recover the need for a metaphysical (non-material) principle to explain the movement of material elements" which he postulates is that of "love or friendship (*philía*) which Empedocles employs with the same intention."[9]

One does need to exercise caution in this regard. One might immediately object that the noble gases which are very non-reactive, don't seem to fit the picture. Romero-Baró is only suggesting that electron affinity or "thirst for electrons" is in general how we describe all elements and assess them for reactivity and bonding. The bonding of atoms of different elements, as predicted by electron affinities, is the very essence of chemistry. The way in which chemists can synthesize compounds by paying attention to these relationalities as well as the particular nature of the elements that form them, reflects something of the creativity and wisdom of God. But the very phenomenon of bonding does, it seems to me, merit some attention as a trace of the triune God.

Moving to the realm of physics, similar realities pertain. Above we commented on the profound relationality of the triune God. This is an emphasis that transcends the traditions, as we have noted. One cannot speak of persons, even in the more Cappadocian social Trinity, without speaking of relations, or persons-in-relation. The Western tradition, as noted above, has spoken more of relations *as* persons. This simply illustrates that exploring Trinitarian reality is always a dialectical exercise. Hans Urs von Balthasar asserts wisely that truth concerning the Trinity "can only be developed

---

9. Romero-Baró, "God's Mark on Nature."

The Coinherent Ontologies of Theology and Science 131

in two opposite lines of being and thought that point to each other."[10] In science, and especially in physics, while the eighteenth century had an atomistic flavour about it, the following two centuries saw a recovery of an emphasis on the importance of relationality in science. One noteworthy example, one of the great breakthroughs in nineteenth-century physics, was the theory of electromagnetism postulated by James Clerk Maxwell.[11] The relational significance of this theory was "the intimate linkage it revealed between electricity and magnetism, two sets of phenomena which superficially had seemed completely unrelated to each other."[12] Einstein's theory of general relativity went on to show "how space, time, and matter form an integrated system in which matter curves space-time and this curvature in turn influences the motion of particles of matter."[13] Thus, as Polkinghorne has stated, the "Newtonian picture of isolated atoms colliding in the container of absolute space, and in the course of the unfolding of absolute time, has to be replaced by an altogether more relational account, in which space, time, and matter are joined together in a kind of physical package deal."[14] This is a reference to the possibility of a grand unified theory, which though elusive, many physicists entertain, one that is "capable of combining a single account of all forces of nature, including gravity."[15]

Beyond forces that may be unified in a relational way, attention has been drawn by physicists to relational phenomena within chaos theory and quantum theory. In this regard, Polkinghorne speaks of "the most striking discovery of intrinsic relationality in physics," the phenomenon referred to above as "quantum entanglement."[16] Einstein and two of his students (Podolsky and Rosen) noticed that "quantum theory implied that two quantum entities which have once interacted with each other could, in consequence, be in a state in which they retained a power of instantaneous influence on each other, however far they may become separated."[17] This phenomenon is thus known as Einstein's EPR (Einstein-Podolsky-Rosen) effect, which showed that once two quantum entities have interacted with each other, they remain mutually entangled.[18] In fact, Einstein initially thought that

10. Balthasar, *Dramatis Personae*, 525.
11. Polkinghorne, "Trinity and Scientific Reality," in *Blackwell Companion*, 528.
12. Ibid.
13. Ibid.
14. Ibid.
15. Ibid.
16. Ibid.
17. Ibid., 528–29.
18. Ibid., 73–74.

this togetherness-in-separation was so "spooky" that it must imply that there was something wrong with modern quantum theory, which he had always disliked, or, at minimum, that the quantum account was incomplete. However, in the 1980s, well-designed experiments demonstrated that quantum entanglement is indeed a property of nature, leading to the conclusion that "the subatomic quantum world cannot be treated atomistically."[19] On this basis, the mutual connection was shown to be a "true ontological effect, producing real change in both entities."[20] Non-locality was confirmed also indeed to be "a property of nature." This was extrapolated by Polkinghorne to suggest that "twentieth-century science has revealed a deep-seated interconnectivity present in the fabric of the physical world."[21]

The phenomenon of relationality within quantum mechanics is particularly interesting. Drawing on this relationality, Polkinghorne makes the specific connection with patristic Trinitarian theology, to claim that all reality is relational, and that this perspective leads to the uncovering of otherwise hidden features of nature like non-locality. A number of other authors have developed this theme further, probing relationality in both matter, including the property of quantum entanglement, and in God.[22]

Creation is thus both *substantial and relational.* The classical Trinitarian theological assertion of God as both being and being-in-relation, or in fact, persons-in-relation, thus has some parallels in the scientific shift from classical physics to relativity and quantum theory. The concept of complementarity in micro-physics presents an analogous problem to the question about being and becoming; how can a physical phenomenon like light have qualities of both a wave and particle?

The paradigm shift in Barth's thought with respect to relations in the Godhead, is analogous to the shift in the new physics. Once the shift is made, the possibility that there could be a being which is apart from relations is nonsense, as is the notion that light must be either wave or particle, but cannot be both. Being and relations are simultaneous to one another. Being is inseparable from the relations which constitute any human person's existence: all of which relations are simultaneous, multileveled and complex.

19. Ibid., 529. Polkinghorne refers here to these as the "beautiful experiments of Alain Aspect and his collaborators."
20. Ibid.
21. Ibid., 73–74.
22. See Polkinghorne, *Trinity and an Entangled World.* Chapters 2 (Jeffrey Bub) and 3 (Anton Zeilinger) deal with this theme of quantum entanglement, a phenomenon hinted at above. This is a phenomenon in the subatomic world, where interaction "can bring about states that have to be considered as a single unified system, even though composed of constituents that may spatially be widely separated" (vii).

Moving beyond the realm of micro-physics and chemistry, the interdependence of all global reality as observed by the "butterfly effect" gestures toward a common Creator of all things, and specifically one who is himself profoundly relational. The butterfly effect is the concept that small causes can have large effects. The term arose from the metaphorical example of the flapping of the wings of a butterfly having a disproportionate effect on the details of the formation and course of a hurricane. Edward Lorenz, who coined the term, observed that the predictive runs of his weather model were widely different if the initial condition data was varied by only miniscule amounts.[23] The butterfly effect is known also in chaos theory where it describes the sensitive dependence on initial conditions in which a small change in one state of a deterministic nonlinear system can result in large differences in a later state.

The oneness and the interdependence of animal and plant life, and abiotic systems, in ecosystems and indeed of the single ecosystem that is the earth, points in the same direction. The term "ecology" was coined in 1866 by the German scientist Ernst Haeckel. Its etymology is the Greek word *oikos* for house, which is suggestive of the oneness and interrelatedness of the diversity of entities in the world. The concept of the one and the many is again a trace of the Trinity who is one and three. In this vein, Colin Gunton has offered a powerful theology of creation in which proper weight can be given to both the universal and the particular, in light of the triunity of God.[24] He was particularly concerned to express the fact that a dualistic or Platonizing doctrine of creation, such as is present in Augustine's account of it, "militates, despite its intention, against an affirmation of the true plurality and diversity of creation."[25]

The idea of a global and even cosmic ecology also resonates with the created oneness of the earth and its eschatological oneness in the second person of the Trinity, when his reconciling work will have taken effect. Paul speaks of this as "an administration [Gk. *oikonomia*] suitable to the fullness of the times, that is, the summing up of all things in Christ, things in the heavens and things on the earth" (Eph 1:10 NASB).

These examples of oneness and diversity prompt us to stress the care that must be taken with respect to the Trinitarian analogy. It is not that the doctrine of the Trinity is an exercise in mathematics. Christian apologists, for example, in response to the charge that $1 + 1 + 1 = 3$, not 1, have countered naively that $1 \times 1 \times 1 = 1$. But God is not and cannot be the result of

---

23. Lorenz, "Deterministic Nonperiodic Flow," 130–41.
24. Gunton, *The One*, 129–231.
25. Ibid., 2–3.

multiplication! Barth has correctly emphasized the reality that the oneness of God is not to be confused with the "singularity" that is connected with numerical unity. It is a revealed unity and unlike numerical oneness, the "revealed unity (of God) does not exclude but includes a distinction."[26] In other words, the doctrine of the Trinity, God as Father, Son and Holy Spirit, three persons of irreducible identity sharing the same Divine nature or essence in a oneness of communion, was formulated in response to revelation. That revelation was centered in the historical event of the incarnation, and the presence in history of a man who was God the Son. The immanent Trinity, who God is *in se*, is understood from who he is *pro nobis*, or for us, in the economy of redemption. Thus our understanding of oneness must be grounded in this revelation. To sum up this section on relationality in the nonhuman creation, this insight that reality is relational is a trace of the God who is "Being in Communion,"[27] to use the phrase used by John Zizioulas.

The relational nature of matter is just one insight into how ontology is reflected in epistemology. The personal and relational God who is invisible, is reflected in what is visible in the being-in-relation of creation. But God also gives *the capacity to discern* these relations to human persons, the pinnacle of his creation, who act on God's behalf in completing and stewarding the creation. These human persons are capable by grace of understanding relationality, that is, epistemology is possible, given they are made in the Divine image and that they too can perceive themselves to be persons in relation. It is for this reason that the Eastern Orthodox Church readily expressed the human person, and especially the human person-in-ecclesial-relation as the icon of the Trinity. The nature of the human self is social and the telos of its existence, or deification, is to be like the Trinity in this relational sense. "Selfhood is social, or it is nothing," affirms Polkinghorne, insisting that we are "only truly human, truly personal," as we "relate to others after the likeness of the Holy Trinity," expressing ourselves "as God does, in a relationship of 'I-and-Thou.'"[28] In the next chapter, this relational nature of being will be expanded upon with respect to humans and the church as the image of God (as we work out a coinherent theology and anthropology). But for our immediate purpose here, the crucial point is that the relational

---

26. Barth, *CD I/1*, 354–55.

27. This is reflected in the title and in the contents of Zizioulas, *Being In Communion*.

28. Polkinghorne, *Trinity and an Entangled World*, 126. Polkinghorne is here summarizing the Orthodox Trinitarian anthropology of Kallistos Ware. Barth makes the same claim; it is the central theme of his vol. 3 of the *Church Dogmatics*. The relational implications of his anthropology are highlighted by his adoption of the Latin phrase: *si quis dixerit hominem esse solitarium anathema sit* ("If anyone will have said that man is solitary, let him be anathema").

ontology of the cosmos is epistemically accessible because humans are made in the image of God.

In addition to, or related to the ontology of God as personal and relational, there are other vital aspects of his being that correspond to the nature of the being of creation. One of these aspects is the *freedom* of God, and the corresponding contingent nature of creation.

Freedom

Before developing a dialogue between theology and science around the theme of freedom, based in the Trinity, it will be important to revisit the Apostle John's great summation of the gospel in his prologue, John 1:1–14, and look at how this, among other passages, informs Trinitarian theology, and particularly the freedom of God:

> *In the beginning was the Word, and the Word was with God, and the Word was God. He was with God in the beginning. Through him all things were made; without him nothing was made that has been made. In him was life, and that life was the light of all mankind. The light shines in the darkness, and the darkness has not overcome it.*
>
> *... The true light that gives light to everyone was coming into the world. He was in the world, and though the world was made through him, the world did not recognize him. He came to that which was his own, but his own did not receive him. Yet to all who did receive him, to those who believed in his name, he gave the right to become children of God—children born not of natural descent, nor of human decision or a husband's will, but born of God. The Word became flesh and made his dwelling among us. We have seen his glory, the glory of the one and only Son, who came from the Father, full of grace and truth.*

In the beginning . . . . This phrase is an echo of Genesis 1:1, and the creation statement in John 1:3, which provides the first major verb of the Logos' action ("*through him all things were made*") confirms this. John 1 is the fullness of revelation about creation, indicating the specific role of the Son in creation. We learn here of a being (the Son) who existed *as* God with respect to identity and essence, and *with* God with respect to personhood and communion, before creation took place. So our passage starts before the beginning, before the big bang 13.7 billion years ago, outside of time and space, in eternity. To truly understand who Jesus is, John says, we must begin with the relationship he shared with the Father "*before the world began*"

(John 17:5, 24). This relationship is the central revelation of the gospel and the key to understanding all that Jesus says and does. But it also provides insight into the councils of the triune God prior to creation, which in turn provide insight into the nature of creation and the nature of the creatures chosen by God to lovingly care for and manage it. This takes us into the interface between theology and science, into the area of *coinherence* we are investigating here—that of *ontology*. That is, reflection on issues of *being*, that is, who God is, who we are, what matter is. These reflections will lead us into the theme of the freedom of God and the corresponding freedom imparted to humans and to matter, to be what they are created to be.

Above we spoke of the triune God as "being in relation." In preparation for exploring the concept of freedom in God and in creation, we must now also speak of the triune God as "being in *act*." Here I am going to reference specifically Karl Barth, who made much of God's premundane, precosmic act of election, that is, his election to create the cosmos, through the agency of the Son, his election to have the Son enter creation and become human. This electing act of God is, for Barth, the very best news of the gospel. God has in his freedom, in the very eternal act of the eternal generation of the Son that defines the immanent Trinity (some Barth scholars would say), and at least in the eternal covenant of God (for other scholars of Barth), chosen the Son to become human,[29] to become Jesus, the one Man who defines humanity in its freedom, the one Man in whom God has chosen to be for humanity. This primal decision in God from all eternity thus made Jesus of Nazareth the prototypical human, after whose image we have been created.

---

29. What exactly this means for the essence of the triune God is a hotly debated topic among Barth scholars, and principally, Bruce McCormack and George Hunsinger. For an able summation of the controversy, see Cary, "Barth Wars" (all quotes in this footnote come from this article). The issue is not just that Barth is saying that this one human being is present at the beginning and foundation of all things, but that, on McCormack's "hyper-Protestant" account, the Divine act of electing this incarnate human being in which the Son participates as electing God, actualizes the immanent Trinity. This radical understanding is termed "Barth-revisionism" by Hunsinger. As Cary says, "Even after he worked out his mature doctrine of election, Barth kept talking as if the Trinity could be conceived independently of Jesus Christ." Instead, Hunsinger "asks us to read Barth 'with charity,' seeking to discern the fundamental coherence of his thinking," and his conscious debt to the tradition, not modernity. Hunsinger appeals to "the 'doctrine of antecedence,' according to which all that God does in the world finds its ground in what God is antecedently in himself, prior to the work of creation and redemption. God's grace toward the world in Christ corresponds to, but is not identical with, what he is in himself as the triune God. In this context, there is a place for the notion of a logos *asarkos* or unincarnate Word, not as a principle of rationality to which we have access apart from Christ, but as a necessary concept in the doctrine of the immanent Trinity."

By his participation in humanity as an ontological entity, in the Son, God imparts that intended identity-in-freedom to humanity, at least by design.

In the freedom of God's act of election, the Son is both the *electing God*, a free agent in his nature as a person within the Trinity, and also the *elect man*, receiving freedom vicariously for humanity. As Robert Osborn has stated, this ensures both that Jesus, as the electing God is the "beginning of all God's ways," and that as the elected man he is "the goal and fulfillment of God's eternal will . . . the event in which God's eternal will is actualized. *The creation comes from Christ, and it is fulfilled in him.*"[30] Osborn clarifies by saying that as "Jesus is at the beginning and in the middle, he is also at the end. . . . Whatever comes to man in the freedom of God and in the fulfillment of his eternal will comes first of all to Jesus as *the* elected man."[31] This is the very heart of the gospel for Barth. He is, in his christological expression of election, defending it against "all non-Christological interpretations of divine and human freedom in orthodox Calvinism and Lutheranism, and in philosophical versions of the same in modern Protestantism . . . he is endeavouring to correct deterministic construction of God's freedom on the one hand and existentialistic, indeterminate constructions of human freedom on the other hand."[32]

But what does the freedom of God communicate about the act of God in creation? It communicates that it was created in freedom, and not out of necessity, and that its nature as created thus, is one also of contingency and of freedom. And what does this communicate about our human identity? What we are elected for in Christ, is *freedom*. I venture to say that this is the most crucial descriptor of identity in Barth's anthropology. It is *derivative*, a freedom *received*, received from the freedom of God to be God, his freedom to love, his freedom to create through Christ, and his freedom to elect Jesus and all humanity in him. Yet it is *real*, for the end goal of that election is the creature living in freedom. This is not freedom of a modern kind that says, "I can do or be whatever I want." The free creatures live into their identity-in-freedom, paradoxically, by being bound to the freedom of God in Christ, and are never more themselves by being ever in union with him. I want to argue that matter itself, that is all created being, has its identity-in-freedom in a similar, qualified way.

The freedom of God in creating is essential to understanding the freedom for what has been created, to be what it has been created to be, which is in some sense analogous to the freedom of God to be who he is. It is a

30. Osborn, "Karl Barth," 118, emphasis mine.
31. Ibid.
32. Ibid.

real freedom even though it is bestowed by God, and it is a "being in activity in line with God's own goodness,"[33] reflecting his own triune being in activity. This articulation of the relationship between God and creation is crucial to the avoidance of pantheism on the one hand, or even participation of a *methexis* variety in which Creator and created are conflated. On the other hand, it also averts notions of the freedom of created matter or beings in a way that implies their independence or "self-initiated self-making."[34] It adeptly describes how matter as created can be real and active, with a measure of freedom, and still be under the providence of God. This not only provides an analogy for the relationship between theology and science, but is vital to understanding something crucial for the big bang theory and for the theory of evolution, that is, the fact that God gives some degrees of freedom for creation to create itself, yet still guides these processes in providence. This aspect of Trinitarian theology, which relates to how the uncreated triune God relates to his creation, will be important also for the elements of a theodicy.

Pertinent to this theme of the freedom of God, T. F. Torrance speaks of three ideas which were present in the church fathers around the notion of creation *ex nihilo*, all of which relate to the influence of theology on the sciences, and all of which concern the underlying ontological realities of God discovered in the discipline of theology. These are expressed in *The Ground and Grammar of Theology*.[35] The first, which we will develop in the following chapter, concerns the rational nature of the universe reflecting the good and rational being of God. The second idea is closely related. It is that the universe is intelligible or has a contingent rationality. Its rationality is grounded in the nature of Creator, the Son. This involves the rejection of another dualism, the old Greek idea that the human mind was eternal and that it was a participant (*methexis*) in the Divine nature, ultimately leading to the apotheosis of the creature. Christian theology eschewed this dualism, and maintained the distinction between created and uncreated light. The human mind was a created, temporal entity and therefore not Divine. This means that God gave human intelligence its own contingent rationality. That is, a rationality that is real and yet derived from and dependent on the Creator, in a communion of persons, not a participation of substance. The fact that this given rationality is real makes both theology and science possible, and in a mutuality in this respect. It also influences the pursuit of knowledge in humility rather than in arrogance.

---

33. Couenhoven, "Karl Barth's Conception(s)," 248.

34. Ibid.

35. T. F. Torrance, *Ground and Grammar*, 48–50.

The Coinherent Ontologies of Theology and Science   139

The third patristic idea Torrance refers to and writes much about is the *contingent* freedom of the universe, which is a corollary of the first two. This freedom is found first in the being of God. Torrance reflects the view of Athanasius that creation was a free act of the *will* of God. It is to be distinguished from the generation of the Son by the Father or the procession of the Spirit which come from within the *being* of the Father. The triune God did not need to create, as if to overcome some deficit, or under any necessity, but created in an overflow of Divine love expressed in Divine volition. Thus what he created, was distinct from himself, having its own particularity and degrees of freedom. The contingency of God in creating (below the surface of the iceberg) is reflected in the contingent nature of creation (above the surface of the iceberg). The cosmos "depends from moment to moment upon the free grace of God in order to sustain it and its orderly operations" which "suggests an openness and capacity for novelty in the cosmic process which is reflective of the transcendent freedom of God."[36] Thus is expressed succinctly in *Ground and Grammar*:

> [God's] creation of the universe out of nothing, . . . far from meaning that the universe is characterized by sheer necessity either in its relation to God or within itself, implies that it is given a contingent freedom of its own, grounded in the transcendent freedom of God and maintained through his free interaction with the universe.[37]

In a manner that speaks to the issue as to whether participation of the creation in God is substantial or relational, Torrance significantly adds,

> It was this doctrine of the freedom of the creation contingent upon the freedom of God which liberated Christian thought from the tyranny of the fate, necessity and determinism which for the pagan mind was clamped down upon creaturely existence by the inexorably cyclic processes of a self-sufficient universe. Just as there is an *order* in the universe transcendentally grounded in God, so there is a *freedom* in the universe transcendentally grounded in the freedom of God.[38]

Having introduced the foundation of our considerations by way of this summary of the key concepts of Trinitarian theology, and particularly the freedom of God, we now continue our discussion of how the being of the triune God, by means of the incarnate Christ, is echoed in the mutuality

36. Achtemeier, "Natural Science," 277.
37. T. F. Torrance, *Ground and Grammar*, 4.
38. Ibid.

between God and the being of creation and of humans. The focus through each concept, related to coinherence and to ontology as the ground of epistemology, will be on the nature of God, flowing from the concepts of relationality and freedom. We will be cognizant as to how ontology might anticipate epistemology. The grounding of the each of the various aspects of the being of the triune God (relationality, freedom, goodness, immensity-with-immanence, agency, fecundity, particularity, mutuality, intelligibility, beauty—treatment of the latter two awaits the treatment of humanity in chap. 7), is what we have empirically discovered of these aspects of the triune being of God through the incarnation, as the church, through the perspicacious Scriptures. And evidence of the reflection in image and trace of these ontological realities in humanity and creation, will arise from how we have empirically discovered humanity and creation to be.

The third aspect of the *being* of God, or the ontological aspects of the relationship between the Trinity and creation, which we wish to highlight, is the concept of goodness.

Goodness

The fundamental goodness of the created order is a trace of the triune Creator God who as three persons in perfect love created out of that love, in accordance with will and not his essence. His goodness, which makes creation knowable through science, relates to the presence of *order* in creation, which includes the presence of natural laws that work, not just on earth, but throughout the creation. The reality that creation is good, along with the fact that creation is *not* God, was, as we have already registered, hugely important for the development of science. This is what enabled science to prosper in Christian cultures, and to be avoided as too sacred in many other cultures. Even though disasters happen in creation, from a human perspective, things like earthquakes, for example, the presence of the very tectonic plates that move to cause earthquakes, are absolutely necessary for a generally stable world and prove thus to be in line with the greater good and the goodness of God.

The fourth aspect of *being*, or the ontological aspects of the relationship between the Trinity and nonhuman creation, as discovered in science, is that of immensity.

Immensity

The mystery of the Trinity bespeaks the transcendence of a God whose size is infinite and beyond comprehension. The God of even the Christian church has often been too small and too predictable—as is evidenced in the costly way in which Copernicus, Giordano Bruno, and Galileo discovered empirically that the solar system was heliocentric. The dimensions up and down of creation support a God who is infinitely immense. The dimensions downwards into the microscopic and subatomic are a trace of the God who is also immanent. The transcendence of the God portrayed in the Bible provides a comforting backdrop for the immensity of the universe, which astronomy is still probing. Rather than inducing doubt about the existence of God, the immensity of God revealed in Scripture strengthens faith and evokes wonder and worship. "*Your God is too small*"[39] is an appropriate adage for scientism, and also for uninformed Christians who wish for a Santa Claus like God, rather than the God of the cosmos, who speaks eloquently through his creation: "the heavens declare the glory of God" (Ps 19:1). Of course, he is also a loving Father, and the coupling of immensity and immanence can only be achieved in the triune God who is at the same time Creator and Sustainer of the universe, in the Son, and by the Spirit, and the lover of our souls by the Spirit, who enables us to cry out, "Abba, Father," the One who numbers our hairs and holds us in the palm of his hands from conception to death.

The point is that there is a correspondence between what special Divine revelation has spoken concerning the ontology of God as infinitely immense, and tenderly and sometimes terrifyingly immanent, and what we know of the vastness of the universe, and the expressions of altruistic love among human beings as their best!

These then, are some of the traces of the triune coinherent God in creation as uncovered by science. These correspondences of ontology explain a common epistemology, and they support the proposal of theology and science as coinherent disciplines. In the following chapter we continue to investigate some further traces of the Trinity in creation.

---

39. This is a reference to the title of the book, Phillips, *Your God Is Too Small*.

Chapter 6

The Coinherent *Ontologies* of Theology and Science

The Being of God and the Being of Creation, Part Two

THE BEING, OR THE ontological aspects of the relationship between the Trinity and science, includes also the reality of *agency*. We begin with a discussion of agency in God, and then consider the corresponding trace of agency in the creation, and all its parts.

Agency

(i) Agency within the Trinity

One of the most profound realms of inquiry in a theology of creation is how God who is spirit can give rise to a creation that is material. How did God who is spirit create that which is matter? An important clue to that mystery is that he employed agency. Long after this mysterious act of creation, if we look at the incarnation and see God and humanity in one person, we may discover a clue to this. A crucial part of Trinitarian doctrine is that while the persons are in complete perichoretic communion, and participate together in the one Divine essence, these persons also are persons of differentiated and irreducible identity (the Son is not the Father even though the Son is in the Father). One aspect of that differentiation has to do with the generation of the persons. The Son is eternally generated by the Father, and the Father is filiated by the Son, and the Spirit proceeds from the Father (Eastern view) or from the Father and the Son (Western view), or from the Father through the Son (T. F. Torrance), and the Father (and the Son) are spirated by the Spirit. The tradition, as expressed through Athanasius, for example, is certain that the creation was not an extension of the Divine being (leading to notions of pantheism or monism). It was creation, not generation. Rather, the act of creation was an act of the Divine will, involving Divine agency, and as such it was an act of unnecessary and extravagant and contingent love. It is this which gives to creation itself its extravagant and contingent nature and whatever agency it has been given.

A further strand of thought in the tradition is that it was the agency of the distinct persons of the Son and the Spirit which was operative in creation, and that the Son was, in particular, eternally oriented toward incarnation, and therefore toward agency in this act of creation, and then in the reconciliation of creation, long before his incarnation on earth. Seventeenth-century Reformed theologians envisioned two phases in the life of the second person of the Trinity, the first as the unincarnate eternal Word (the *Logos asarkos*), who was the *object* of the Divine decree and as such, in time, would become the incarnate Word (the *Logos ensarkos*). He was eternally seen as *incarnandus* in the sense that he was destined to become incarnate in time, that is *incarnatus* (actually incarnate). This school of thought also acknowledged that the eternal Son must also have participated in the Divine council and Divine decree. Thus he was the *subject*, as well as the object of election. He did so, on this account, however, as the indeterminate *Logos asarkos*, that is, as one whose identity as the creating and reconciling agent, as the incarnate Word, in other words, had not yet been determined. His being and his existence as "toward being incarnate" is not yet determined when he makes this decision as participant in the Trinity. He is *incarnandus* only in an anticipated or proleptic sense, as a result of the decree for him to become incarnate. This is the point at which Karl Barth differed from his Reformed tradition and brought a much more radical insight to the understanding of the Son as the incarnate agent of creation. In light of the concreteness of the person of Jesus Christ, as the revealed Son, and the correspondence between the economic and immanent Trinity, Barth insists that it was as already the *Logos incarnandus* that he participated as the Subject of election in the decreeing council of the Trinity. He will thus, as Webster states, "deny to the *Logos* a mode or state of being above and prior to the decision to be incarnate in time." Barth will insist that "there is no *Logos* in and for himself in distinction from God's act of turning towards the world and humanity in predestination; the *Logos* is *incarnandus* in and for himself in eternity. For that move alone would make it clear that it is Jesus Christ who is the Subject of election and not an indeterminate (or 'absolute') *Logos Asarkos*."[1] His emphatic insistence on the eternally *incarnandus* identity of the Son is related to Barth's insistence that there is no God behind or back of the revealed God. He objected to the idea of a *Logos asarkos* and therefore "a God who can be known and whose Divine essence could be defined on some other basis than in and from the perception of his person and action as incarnate Word."[2] If God had ordained to be "for us," then the being of the *Logos* must be eternally toward-incarnation (*incarnandus*).

Karl Barth argues this point in his comments on the Johannine Prologue, where he demonstrates that there is no such thing as an unincarnate Word. Instead, he says we may speak only of a *Logos incarnandus*, that is, "a Word that will be incarnated."[3] The Apostle John does not speak of the eternal *Logos*, who is God in very essence (John 1:1), and who is also "with God," as differentiated person (1:1), and as coinherent agent (1:2), without speaking of his creating the world (1:3), and of his becoming flesh (1:14). For Barth, therefore, the Word has always been orientated toward being human and therefore he has always been orientated toward creating the creation and reconciling it. This has some justification also in texts like Revelation 13:8 which suggest that the Son was slain before the foundation of the world.[4] The Son who is spoken of as "the image of the invisible God" (Col 1:15), implying his incarnation, is also described as the firstborn or Lord over creation (1:15), and as such, has always, been the Crucified and Resurrected Jesus Christ (Col 1:20). Other texts bring the creation act of the Son into juxtaposition with his atoning work (1 Pet 1:18–19, cf. 29; Heb 1:1–3). Thus, Barth insists, if we imagine any *logos asarkos*, we must quickly speak of it only as a *logos incarnandus*. In a logical sense, Barth thus puts the incarnation before all creation and all history, rather than as merely a contingent historical datum.

This goes some way toward resolving the question of how a God who is spirit can create something material. The Son was God's mediatorial agent in this regard, because he was *incarnandus* from all eternity, oriented toward material creation and humanity, in pre-history, before he was incarnate in history. Crucial to our theme of agency in God and then in creation, Barth suggests that God, described most tellingly as the One who loves in

---

1. Webster, *Cambridge Companion*, 94–95.

2. Barth, *CD*, IV/1, 181.

3. See Barth's comments on the Johannine Prologue in *CD*, IV/2, 33–34.

4. The centrality of the cross in the eternal counsels of God helps toward offering at least one aspect of a theodicy (an explanation for the existence of evil and suffering in the world), that is, that in the Son, God suffers with us.

freedom, eternally generated the Son in freedom to become one with humanity, thus by creating in freedom and reconciling in freedom, to bring creation and humanity, by participation, into freedom.[5]

(ii) Agency in the Creation

The freedom and agency in the being of God (ontology) has a corresponding set of traces in the creation and its agency (derived ontology), which are observable, and have indeed been observed (epistemology) about the origins of the universe and of humanity. Creation is granted freedom in God's freedom. There are four principal views on how God relates to his creation. The first is deism, which entails the notion that God created the clock and wound it up, and is not now engaged with creation at all. The second, the polar opposite of deism, is occasionalism (Jonathan Edwards) in which God is the primary cause of absolutely everything. The third is the "secondary causation" view of Aquinas, in which God is thought of as the primary or ultimate cause of everything, whereas creation has been granted some degree of freedom and has its own secondary causations. The fourth is process theology,[6] in which, according to Charles Hartshorne, for example, creation is thought to be *in* God and indeed influences God, such that he suffers with it and grows in essence with it. Intrinsic to process theology is the idea that matter itself is not just matter, but that it has mental or psychic capacity of its own. The great Divine Mind is thought to be made up of mind present in all matter, and moves it along. What motivated process thought was the perceived insufficiency of natural selection as the driving force of evolution. The answer to the question as to why organisms evolve at all is not provided by natural selection in an intellectually satisfying way, especially considering the problems for entropy at the macro level and chaos at the micro level, which seem to mitigate against growing complexity. One

---

5. Barth, *CD*, vol. IV/3/1. See also *CD* IV/1, 42.

6. Process theology developed from the process philosophy of Alfred North Whitehead (1861–1947), though Hegel is an influence also. Charles Hartshorne (1897–2000) and John Cobb (b. 1925), as well as Pierre Teilhard de Chardin (1881–1955) are important proponents of process theology, which holds that God is "open" to the cosmos in the sense that he affects and is affected by temporal processes, and as such runs contrary to classical theism which affirms that God is in all respects nontemporal (eternal), unchanging (immutable), and unaffected by the world (impassible). Process theology does speak of God as in some respects eternal (he will never die), immutable (in the sense that God is unchangingly good), and impassible (in the sense that God's eternal aspect is unaffected by actuality), but its contradiction of the classical view lies in its insisting that God is in some respects temporal, mutable, and passible. It refers to all forms of theology that emphasize event, occurrence, or becoming over against substance.

can see why the idea of the psychic nature of matter might be appealing to process theologians, and why a God who draws the process along also might be an attractive idea. The challenge of process thought of this kind is that the distinctness between God and creation is blurred.

It seems to me that there is another alternative, an evangelical biblical modification . . . one in which freedom is given to the creation, such that matter can actually participate in the life of God in Christ, in a compatibilist way (that is, the agency of God and that of creation are compatible), but such that matter also actually participates in its own development. That is, the Son and the Spirit are present and providentially active in lovingly engaged ways, yet not with any confusion of the Divine and the elemental, and not in a manner that is coercive. On this view, that of asymmetric compatibilism, creation has a participatory freedom, but not one in which Divine and created existence are blurred in Neoplatonic ways. Human persons and matter are never more themselves that when they exist in the freedom of participation in the life of God.

An explanatory note is needed at this juncture. I am using the term "compatibilist" not in the deterministic manner that philosophical compatibilism might be understood. This is a *theological* compatibilism in which Divine foreknowledge and Divine sovereignty are somehow compatible with the libertarian freedom of humanity *and* creation, down to the first gluon. This is not causal determinism, which runs into the difficulty that it makes God the efficient cause of evil. It is a participational compatibilism in which there is affirmation of the providence of God and his ultimate sovereignty, but also the affirmation of space for human creatures who have sufficient agency such that they are responsible for their actions, and space for nonhuman creation which has a participational freedom also. The mechanisms by which this may be possible are beyond our scope here.[7] I am somewhat

---

7. It would seem irresponsible to invoke the term "mystery" at this point. It is mysterious in the sense that Scripture does not provide a mechanical solution as to how Divine sovereignty and human and creational freedom can be compatible. In a way that echoes what has been said about science, "mystery" does not, however, mean one cannot probe for answers, and must not be used to excuse good, hard thought. On this issue, I am to some extent content to admit that we don't yet know enough to decide how Divine sovereignty and human/creational freedom are compatible. I am intrigued by the work of philosophers who probe more deeply. This is a very brief summation of the ways in which philosophical theologians have sought to probe these mechanics, but not convinced there is a clear answer yet. The views include Theological Determinism (also called "compatibilism" in a philosophical sense), Molinism and Philosophical Arminianism. For a helpful presentation of the latter two views, see Rutledge, *Philosophical Arminianism*. I am offering asymmetric compatibilism as a solution which has degrees of freedom associated with it. Freedom for humans and substances is never absolutely free anyway. They have relative freedom, sufficient in the case of humans to

content to rest with a statement like that of seventeenth-century continental Reformed theologian, Francis Turretin, who proposed that careful study of Scripture leads to two indisputable conclusions, both of which may be affirmed and held in tension:

> that God on the one hand by his providence not only decreed, but most certainly secures, the event of all things, whether free or contingent; on the other hand, however, man is always free in acting and many effects are contingent. Although I cannot understand how these can be mutually connected together, yet (on account of ignorance of the mode) the thing itself is (which is certain from another source, i.e., from the Word) not either to be called in question or wholly denied.[8]

This accords with the Barthian viewpoint, established, as we shall shortly see, by examining the incarnation, and a model for Divine-human action. It avoids the pitfalls of open theism which challenges the aseity and sovereignty of God, and process thought which brings the further challenge of incipient monism.

Asymmetric compatibilism challenges the tendency we have even in modernity to think in binary and polarized ways, and it assists us inaccepting the possibility that God is at work, and his creation is at work too, in his work, and precisely in response to his work. In this compatibilism, God retains his providential sovereignty, and even suffers with the creation, not because in some fatalistic way he must, that is by way of necessity, but because in freedom he chooses to suffer. God has chosen in the freedom of his decree to create, and also to suffer. He knew that his creation would involve a cross that would be central to its existence and flourishing, for eternity, yet he created still. God has suffered and suffers explicitly in the Son. The Father suffers implicitly and mediately through the Son, in a way appropriate to his

---

incur responsibility for legitimate moral choices and actions. They have *relative* freedom as that freedom has been imparted to them by God. They *participate* in his freedom. And somehow, God will accomplish his own ends taking that relative freedom into account. I am content always to err on the side of letting God be God. The statement of how Divine providence and human freedom work in the Westminster Confession (sect. 3) seems to agree with the view I am expressing: "God from all eternity did by the most wise and holy counsel of his own will, freely and unchangeably ordain whatsoever comes to pass; yet so as thereby neither is God the author of sin; nor is violence offered to the will of creatures, nor is the liberty or contingency of second causes taken away, but rather established." This is apparently also in keeping with William Lane Craig's version of Molinism, which acknowledges the category of "middle knowledge," that is his knowledge of the counterfactuals of creaturely freedom. On Molinism, see Craig, *Only Wise God*.

8. Turretin, *Institutes of Elenctic Theology*, 512.

hypostatic uniqueness. Suffering is expressed in the eternal counsel of God as what the Lamb slain before the foundation of the world would undergo, and whatever creation and humans undergo, he is in solidarity and sympathy with them in this.

The compatibilism of the Divine freedom and that of created entities may be illustrated in two ways: first, by the relationship between the Divine and human natures of the Son of God, Jesus; and second, by the relationship between Divine and human action. In the first illustration, Christ as the Image of God expresses this compatibilism. In the second, the human person in the image of God expresses it. The application will then be made to creation which possesses a freedom in God's freedom. In this sense it exhibits freedom within God's freedom as the trace of his freedom. In all cases it will be evident that there is indeed a compatibilism between Divine and created freedom, but that it is always asymmetric, in the sense that Divine freedom is initial and in the sense that other freedoms are true only by participation in the Divine life and freedom.

1. *The two natures of Christ*:

    The two natures of Jesus, existing and working together in a compatible way, provide the first window into asymmetric compatibilism. This begins with the incarnation. In orthodox fashion the two natures of Christ operated in a compatible fashion that was true to the fully Divine and fully human natures of Christ. Barth insists that these were compatible even though the Divine nature has a logical priority. He draws upon insights from Cyril of Alexandria, that although the human nature of Jesus was fully human, there is a precedence to the Divine nature in that it is the Divine nature that assumes the human nature, and not the other way around. The Divine nature is the giver and the human the receiver. The Son remains Lord as he assumes humanity.[9] Thus, applying this to the freedom of creation and humanity,

---

9. These nuances of Barth's doctrine of the union of the two natures of Christ and of participation, are referenced by Adam Neder in his book *Participation in Christ*, 1–10, 58–92. The *participatio Christi* in Barth is the *unio hominus cum Christo*, that is the "mutual indwelling that occurs between the Word and human beings" is closely modeled on the unconfused and asymmetric nature of Barth's understanding of the relationship between the Divine and human natures of the incarnate Christ. Barth is firmly in the Reformed rather than Lutheran camp with respect to how the Divine and human natures relate in the God-Man Jesus. By this I mean first that Divine and human natures remain Divine and human, for Barth, as in Calvin. This is to say that the *communicatio idiomatum* as Luther (and the Orthodox) understood these, are rejected by Barth, or at least they are redefined in such a way as to ensure the natures are not confused and that they relate in an asymmetric fashion. That is, whereas the hypostatic union concept persists in Barth, and Alexandrian rather than Antiochene influences prevail, there is a

the precedence of Divine freedom or action is emphasized. Paradoxically, the human in this participation becomes more human for its being in communion with God.

Drawing upon this model, we might say similarly that creation is under the providential care and teleological supervision of God, and yet has its own distinct nature and degrees of freedom in its agency. In fact, it has its own idiosyncratic nature only as it is in the freedom of God. Further this Cyrilline and Barthian model of the incarnation in which there is an asymmetric compatibilism of the human and Divine natures, provides evidence that participation is unconfused: that is, that human and Divine natures can be in union in such a way that there is interpenetration or personality overlap, but without a confusion or mixture of natures. It is union but not synthesis or merger. That is, the human nature stays human, and the Divine nature stays Divine. By analogy, as an echo of this, the agency of God and creation are without confusion. The freedom of creation is real, and the freedom of creation to be itself is real, even though God is providentially at work.

Moving from the incarnation to the actual life of Jesus as the God-Man, it is evident that Jesus lived his life on earth in a relationship with the Father that further illustrates this theological asymmetric compatibilism. He does always those things that pleased the Father (John 8:29) and yet he does so in the full integrity of his own personhood. This is perhaps best illustrated by the anguished cry of Gethsemane, "*Father, if it be possible, let this cup pass from me; nevertheless, not my will but yours be done*" (Luke 22:42). This is a real Divine-human person in possession of his identity with integrity, wrestling with and being in compatibility with the Father. Throughout his life, Jesus acts as the most free human person that has ever lived, and at the same time, he is doing on what the Father does, fulfilling the Divine will and the Divine scriptural prophecies and types all the way through his journey as a man, and even in the passivity of his crucifixion. This is an illustration of feasibility of the *concept* of asymmetric compatibilism between God and creation, even though we recognize there is a significant difference

---

real union and there is a mutual influence of the Divine and human natures, but such that the Divine nature is the giver and the human nature the receiver, in this union. In other, words, Christ as Lord remains Lord of the union, and as such he ensures that it is the Divine nature that asymmetrically influences the human. This will facilitate for Barth his view of the assumption by the incarnate Son of a truly human nature as fallen, one which will by the influence of the Divine nature and the experiences of suffering be purified. This will enable also for Barth the assumption of humanity by the ascension of Christ, into the Godhead as humanity, *not* as a divinised humanity, which confuses the categories of divinity and humanity.

between a created entity such as an electron or a DNA molecule or a hominid, and the Divine-human person of Jesus, who is both fully God, coinherent with the Father and the Spirit, and fully human.

2. *Divine and human freedom within human action*:

The relationship between Divine and human action in the theology of Karl Barth actually mirrors his view of the hypostatic union of the Divine and human natures of Christ. For Barth, "where God acts, there we are seen to act—precisely in receiving."[10] In keeping with this, there is again both an assertion of the compatibilism of Divine and human action and the qualification that this compatibilism is asymmetric. With respect to how human activity works within Divine action in the Christian life, that is, the move from the indicative to the imperative, Barth stressed that this was "a perilous step."[11] Why so? Because when we raise the question of our own human activity, "we are only too readily inclined to turn things upside down . . . and to answer the question about the Christian life in a way that views the matter equilaterally: God has done something for us, now it is up to us to do something for him."[12] Barth's sketch of the Christian life is, in other words, shaped by a strong assertion that "the two sides in the relationship are not on [sic] an equality."[13] *But alongside this there is another affirmation: our non-equality to God does not signify our obliteration.* And so "the question about the Christian life as a question about what happens to us, about our little Ego, is a special one that very well deserves to be asked! In raising this question we are loyal and true."[14] And why is the question important? Because the Christian life has an eschatological setting, standing between achieved reconciliation and expected redemption. In fact, Barth's anthropology, linked as it is fundamentally to who the One true Human is, that is, his the-anthropology, does not reduce the rest of humanity to a epiphenomenon, as Balthasar suspected.[15] In fact, it is a glorious anthropology. Humanity is more human, and the human self most truly itself, in Christ. When

---

10. This is the description of Barth's thought in this regard by his disciple, Jüngel, "Gospel and Law," 105–26.

11. Barth, *Christian Life*, 16.

12. Ibid., 26.

13. Ibid.

14. Ibid., 20ff.

15. Balthasar averred that "Barth ends up talking about Christ so much as the true human being that it makes it seem as if all other human beings are mere epiphenomena." Balthasar, *Theology of Karl Barth*, 243.

understood correctly,[16] Barth will in fact be seen ironically to have a more lofty view of the human than that of others in the Reformed heritage. It is a vital view of man and spirituality determined appropriately by dogmatics, by Scripture and its derivative confessions, by the doctrine of God, by soteriology, by pneumatology, by the "ploddingly exegetical"[17] rather than by the insights of philosophy, the metaphysics of subjectivity, and general revelation; by a Christological bearing rather than an experiential one, a humanism of the Christian gospel rather than one gained by soul introspection with the predetermining paradigm of a Cartesian view of the human self.

Similarly, we may assume, creation as the trace of God, like humans in relation to God, has its own freedom, and yet is not crassly independent of God. It is imbued with Divine freedom and we may assume that it carries within it, by grace and in participation with Christ, its own identity and some creative power, derived and contingent though it may be. We turn our attention now to the agency and freedom of matter seen in this light.

How Divine and material agency works at the quantum level is a pressing issue. Quantum indeterminacy, that is the neutrality of particles like electrons, and gluons and quarks has been a source of interest for philosophers who value the real agency of creation, and therefore an open future, rather than a predetermined one. John Polkinghorne, for example, states that "the Copenhagen approach to quantum mechanics incorporates such a notion of indeterminacy, thus suggesting that divine agency can operate without detection, or interference in the autonomy of natural (particularly living) entities. God is thus the 'determiner of indeterminacies.'"[18] He also affirms that both chance and necessity are necessary for the universe to run

---

16. Misconceptions concerning Barth's anthropology can be discovered in the following works: Webster, *Barth's Moral Theology*; *Barth's Ethics of Reconciliation*; "Eschatology, Anthropology"; "Christian in Revolt"; "Rescuing the Subject," 49ff.; Mangina, *Karl Barth*. Krötke, "Karl Barth's Anthropology," 159–76.

17. Webster, "Rescuing the Subject," 68. This makes reference to this phrase borrowed from Milbank et al. (*Radical Orthodoxy*, 2). This refers to the Barthian methodology of determining theology, including anthropology, by the patient, deliberate study of the scriptural canon and, by derivation, the family of commentary traditions that Scripture, has evoked. An important text in discovering a relationship between Divine and human action is Phil 2:12–13: *Therefore, my dear friends, as you have always obeyed—not only in my presence, but now much more in my absence—continue to work out your salvation with fear and trembling, for it is God who works in you to will and to act in order to fulfill his good purpose.* The priority of the work of God in the life of the believer, and his Lordship, do not appear to lessen the force of the human command to work out one's salvation. He works and they work. Asymmetrically but compatibly.

18. Polkinghorne, *Quarks, Chaos*, 39.

in a manner that does not blur the Creator/creature distinction, as well as for doing science. He states,

> One of the reasons cosmologists can talk with such confidence about the early universe is because it is, in fact, a very uncomplicated system. However, this world, which started so simple, has, after fifteen billion years, become immensely rich and complicated. You and I are the most complicated known consequences of this fruitful history. A universe that, when it was a ten thousand millionth of a second old, was just a hot soup of elementary particles, has become the home of saints and scientists. Remember, this has only been possible because the universe has anthropic fine tuning built into its physical fabric. Such astonishing fertility doesn't look like a purposeless world of accident.[19]

Chance, on this account, is considered to be "a sign of freedom not blind purposelessness."[20] Polkinghorne also concludes from this that God has "created a world, able to make itself."[21] I might qualify that this is only true under the never-ceasing loving guidance, though not control, of the Creator in providence. Nevertheless, I *do* find this to be in keeping with the concept of asymmetric compatibilism as in Barth.

The precise mechanism by which Divine agency functions within a creation as discovered by science, including quantum science, and which has been granted freedom, is one which merits some detailed discussion. We will look at the ways in which some practitioners have approached this, beginning with John Polkinghorne.

Polkinghorne

With reference to the four views expressed above (deism, occasionalism, secondary causation, process), Polkinghorne found the predominant models for conceiving Divine action to have been unsatisfactory, and initially proposed a top-down informational view.

> Interventionism or supernaturalism is dismissed either because God is reduced to being just another actor in the world or because God's action in the world would be inconsistently intermittent; God acting only as creator of the world is too

---

19. Ibid.
20. Ibid., 43. See pp. 36–50 for a good discussion of this theme.
21. Ibid., 50.

deistic, leaving little if any room for ongoing divine action; the Thomistic doctrine of God as primary cause and creatures as secondary causes results in the bifurcation of one world into two ontological realms, the theological and the scientific; and process thought's doctrine of divine persuasive power is unable to sustain the eschatological promises of God as revealed in Scripture.[22]

Polkinghorne thus advocated for "a kind of 'top-down' or holistic model of divine causality, albeit through God's inputting of 'pure' or 'active' (as opposed to 'energetic') information at the level of non-linear or chaotic systems that are finely-tuned and extremely sensitive to initial conditions and are intrinsically open to the future."[23] He believed that this kind of "input of information does not violate the law of conservation of energy, and also avoids the criticism of the god-of-the-gaps since the 'gaps' are ontological rather than epistemological." He pointed to the laws of nature as "analogies of other top-down causal inputs of information" as well as "the interaction between the human mind and the processes of the brain, and quantum events." Divine action would, within this system, "be imperceptible to empirical inquiry"[24] and it appears thus to preserve the freedom of creation.

There was however, a discernible shift from 2000 onward in Polkinghorne's thinking which reflected his greater commitment to theology and to Trinitarian theological concerns in particular, especially as he discerned them in Jürgen Moltmann's work in particular.[25] He thus reconsidered his claim that God acts in the world only through the input of pure information, which involves absolutely no exchange of energy. He opted instead to draw upon an incarnational Trinitarian concept, that is, from kenotic theory, the self-emptying of the second person of the Trinity in the incarnation (Phil 2:5–8, where the Greek word for emptied is *ekenōsen*, v. 7).

Polkinghorne extrapolated the concept of kenosis in the Son to apply it to the possibility that, when God created the world, this was *in itself* a self-emptying act. By creating that which was "other" to him, and granting it space to be, and to fall, and to be reconciled by the costly act of the

22. Yong, "From Quantum Mechanics." Yong confirms Polkinghorne's belief, contra Bohm and others, that "epistemology models ontology." See Polkinghorne, *Belief in God*, 52–53; *Science and Theology*, 30–31; and *Quantum Theory*, 85–86.

23. Yong, "From Quantum Mechanics."

24. Ibid.

25. See Polkinghorne, "Kenotic Creation," 90–106. Yong notes that dialogue with the work of Jürgen Moltmann, a kenotic theology had already begun by the mid-1980s; see *Science and Creation*, ch. 4; cf. also *Faith, Science, and Understanding*, ch. 6.

self-giving of the Son, God did indeed empty himself in some sense when he created, not only by giving space to something other, but by enduring the consequences that would unfold in the creation. One could restrict even this creational kenosis to the person of the Son within the Godhead, since, as we have seen, he is the agent in creation, and seems to have been destined for self-emptying incarnation and death, from eternity, as *incarnandus*, to use Barth's term. One could then propose that the triune Godhead experienced this in a *mediated* and perichoretic way. Such an approach avoids the discussion of what may have happened to the attributes of God, as the whole triune God, in the act of creation.

Applying it *beyond* the Son, the idea is that God created by an act of the will, and in love, and so creation in itself was an act of costly love for the whole Godhead, even though the incarnation and death of Christ was the telos and climax of that cost and that act. Thus, on this account, the creating and ordering of the world is a kenotic act on God's part. This alternative does, of course, raise the issues of the attributes of God, and moves toward an open theist approach. According to Moltmann, a significant influence on Polkinghorne in this regard, it is not that God ceases to be omniscient but rather that he creates space for a creation from which he withdraws Divine omniscience and omnipotence. He does so "for the sake of conceding room to live to those who he has created."[26] This is then mirrored in the kenotic Christ who at times appears not to employ these Divine attributes. Other theologians are less concerned to preserve the attributes of omnipotence, omnipresence and omniscience and suggest that our understanding of these attributes need to be judged by what the incarnation reveals about how God holds his power and knowledge. As Sarah Coakley inquires, can they, in light of the full revelatory act of God in the incarnation, "really remain unimpaired?"[27] The possibility is that God himself as the triune God, in Coakley's words, always held his "power-in-vulnerability," and that the incarnation is only what most fully revealed this.[28]

Having explored the meaning of kenosis, we now return to Polkinghorne, who invoked kenosis to leave space for quanta and indeed for the whole creation, to have their own being, and a measure of freedom, albeit a contingent freedom which is always dependent on God, and under his providence. Four levels of Divine kenosis have been proposed. These are a kenosis of Divine power, Divine eternity, Divine omniscience, and one of participation in the causal nexus of creation. It is the last of these which

---

26. Moltmann, "God's Kenosis," 147. See also Moltmann, *God in Creation*.
27. Coakley, *Powers and Submissions*, 14.
28. Coakley, "Kenosis and Subversion," 5, *passim*.

especially has repercussions for explicating "divine action in general and [of] the causal joint between God and the world in particular."[29] The first three had led Polkinghorne to propose a Divine dipolarity akin to the process model, and a creaturely freedom, which together imply that God knows the future only in its modal status, rather than in its actuality. However, the fourth aspect of kenosis, that which has a causal status, led Polkinghorne to propose that Divine action should not be limited to the input of pure information, but rather that it would be analogous to creaturely activities which always involve a combination of energetic and informational causalities. God's activity in the world would then be considered as "divine special providence" which can "act as a cause among causes."[30] Polkinghorne's example of such Divine action is connected to the kenotic framework of the incarnation of God in Jesus Christ.

Certainly, Polkinghorne speaks to the tension of purpose and freedom in the creation, in Trinitarian terms. He speaks of the history of the universe beginning with the big bang, the "initial ball of energy" that "has become the home of saints and mathematicians."[31] The universe's history is envisaged as an evolving history, both on the cosmic scale and also on earth and in the evolving of biological life. Thus "the evolutionary process" involves "an interplay between chance and necessity," but not "blind" chance.[32] Chance, Polkinghorne deduces, is not capriciousness but "simply historical contingency, that this happens rather than that," that this rather than that "particular genetic mutation turns the stream of life in this particular direction," as opposed to another possibility with a different mutation. He concludes that "not everything that could happen has happened; history necessarily represents only a small selection from the range of cosmic possibility. Chance, therefore, is just a shuffling mechanism for exploring potentiality."[33] Very significantly, Polkinghorne affirms that chance precisely constitutes evidence of the freedom given to creatures, one given to them by the kenotic grace of God. In this sense, the creation, as we have contended, shows a trace of the freedom and agency of the coinherent God.

Polkinghorne references the development of the theory of evolution as an arena in which awareness of the freedom and agency of creation became apparent. In response to Darwin's *Origin of Species*, there were both negative and positive responses from church leaders. Two pastors who

29. Yong, "From Quantum Mechanics."
30. Polkinghorne, "Kenotic Creation and Divine Action," 104.
31. Polkinghorne, *Science and the Trinity*, 66.
32. Ibid., 66–67. Here Polkinghorne is referencing Jacques Monod.
33. Polkinghorne, *Science and the Trinity*, 66–67.

responded positively, Anglicans Charles Kingsley and Frederick Temple, "both gave an early welcome to Darwinian insight, seeing that evolution could be theologically understood as the way in which creatures have been allowed by their Creator 'to make themselves.'"[34] Polkinghorne concludes that "the God of love has not brought into being a world that is simply a divine puppet theatre, but rather the Creator has given creatures some due degree of creaturely independence."[35] I might perhaps qualify this in the spirit of Karl Barth and Torrance, that they are never more free and never more themselves than when they are in Christ, under the Spirit. Thus, they are themselves, and have freedom in his freedom, and though they act as he acts, they really act. Polkinghorne concludes that "Trinitarian theology does not need to see the history of the world as the performance of a fixed score, written by God from all eternity, but may properly understand it as the unfolding of a grand improvisation in which the Creator and creatures both participate."[36] I need to qualify that this does not and cannot imply that God does not work all things after the counsel of his will (Eph 1:11). It simply argues for a sovereignty that is not fatalism, and for an asymmetric compatibilism between Divine and human or creatorial agency.

Yong

A second author in the science/theology area, who has probed the issue of agency in creation, and how this relates to Divine agency, is Amos Yong. Yong has challenged Polkinghorne's vision of agency, suggesting that, while it emphasizes the incarnational, it lacks pneumatological weight, and is therefore not sufficiently trinitarian.[37] The Spirit in this new model is still associated only with input of pure information and thus "remains empirically veiled." He argues that a "more robustly trinitarian framework would not require abandonment of Polkinghorne's complementary model that includes both 'energetic transactions' and 'active information' inputs." "Rather," Yong argues, "divine action explicated pneumatologically could be explored at various levels: that of the indeterminacy of quantum events; that of chaos/dynamical systems which are extremely sensitive to initial conditions; that of 'top-down' or whole-part causation of wider (and wider) environments on their sub-systems; that of the input of pure information; and that of neurobiological, neuropsychological, and psychosociological processes."

---

34. Ibid., 67.
35. Ibid.
36. Polkinghorne, *Science and the Trinity*, 67–68.
37. Yong, "From Quantum Mechanics."

In summary, Yong contends that "once the possibility of divine action in energetic terms is granted by way of taking the incarnation seriously, then a theologically thick account of divine action must be pneumatologically informed as well." In fact, he suggests that Polkinghorne's method appears "to be a case of epistemological modelling upon a Trinitarian reality, rather than offering a Trinitarian *mechanism* to account for divine agency."[38]

Gunton

Another theologian who did add pneumatological weight to the doctrine of Divine and creational freedom is Colin Gunton, who asserted that freedom, or non-necessity, characterizes not only the inner life of the Trinity, but also the created world since it is the product of the free creating act of God. For Gunton, this has particularly to do with the work of the Spirit "who is the giver of freedom and the one who enables the created order to be itself: to become what it was created to be."[39] Another take on this matter of the harmonizing of Divine and creatorial agency has been offered by Steven D. Crain, in the context of evaluating Polkinghorne's work. He has suggested that since the transcendence of God makes Divine action metaphysical, rather than physical, in nature, this removes the need to find a "causal joint" between God and the world directly. It also makes Divine intervention in the salvation of humans from their sin both theologically and scientifically unobjectionable.[40] In light of the ongoing research in this area, Yong comments that "any theologically thick account cannot avoid either metaphysical assumptions (if not arguments) or the plausibility conditions of a scientifically informed worldview."[41]

---

38. Yong, "From Quantum Mechanics," emphasis added.

39. Gunton, *Triune Creator*, 86. Graham Buxton expounds ably on Gunton's pneumatology in *The Trinity, Creation and Pastoral*. He states: "The Spirit is therefore the eschatological 'perfecting' Spirit who holds the whole created order—animate and inanimate, human and non-human, personal and non-personal—in the freedom of divine love. Indeed, he is not only sustainer, but also, in a dynamic sense, the energising agent in what Gunton calls the 'forward movement of the cosmos': he is 'the divine energy releasing the energies of the world, enabling the world to realize its dynamic relatedness'" (127). Citations in singular quotes are from Gunton, *Triune Creator*, 161.

40. Crain, "Divine Action in a World Chaos," 41–61.

41. Yong, "From Quantum Mechanics," n25.

T. F. Torrance

The christological approach of theologian scientist T. F. Torrance, with respect to God's ontology or being as *sovereign*, or *Divine providence*, is precisely such a theologically thick account, albeit not the pneumatological one desired by Yong (though it does not exclude it). It is of particular interest both theologically and in terms of how it relates to the theory of the evolution of life and humanity, and genetic mutations and also to the quantum realm. In the realm of theology, the doctrine of providence as it relates to the inner being of God is built on the manifestation of Jesus Christ, once again on the assumption that God's being and activity is no different to the being and activity of the Son, Jesus Christ. The sovereignty of God is thus not some "impersonal and deterministic brute force"[42] but rather clothed in personal categories, and at work "in creaturely littleness and human weakness."[43] It is the reality of the cross of Christ by which the power and providence of God as love and "total self-sacrifice supreme over sin and guilt, evil and death, over anything and everything that might separate us from God," is most clearly seen, for Torrance. Providence is not seen "as the perpetuation of the original act of creation, but as God conserving the creation in a *covenantal co-existence* with himself, preserving creation by interacting positively toward and within it, and caring for creation out of limitless grace by the Word and through the Spirit."[44] Providence is thus a "redemptive ruling over history" that brings the creation to its redemptive end in the outpouring of God's love for it. Thus, Torrance does not see providence as exercised from afar in a dualistic separation from the world, but ,in Jesus Christ, and by the Spirit,[45] God is "personally and directly present and active in creation, even in its fallenness,"[46] not deistically abandoning it, but bearing its suffering, and "ruling over all things without detracting from

---

42. Colyer, *How to Read T. F. Torrance*, 165.

43. T. F. Torrance, *Christian Doctrine of God*, 221–22.

44. Colyer, *How to Read T. F. Torrance*, 165–66.

45. Space does not permit even a cursory view of the role of the Spirit in creation in Torrance's theology. He emphasizes the Spirit's creative activity but speaks of this in light of the character of God as Spirit. The creative role of the Spirit as Creator Spirit is described in the context of the Nicene Creed and the phrase "Lord and Giver of life." Significantly, Torrance speaks of the life-giving activity of the Spirit who is "able to sustain the creature in *open-ended* relation toward God without overwhelming or negating the reality and freedom of the creature." Colyer, *How to Read T. F. Torrance*, 217. The Spirit is in Torrance's understanding, the agent of providence, wooing and influencing the creature (electron or human being) to its true *telos* in relation to God.

46. Colyer, *How to Read T. F. Torrance*, 166, reflecting Torrance, *Christian Doctrine of God*, 221–22.

their reality or impairing their contingent nature, freedom or order, yet in such a way that in his absolute freedom he makes everything to serve his ultimate purpose of love and fellowship with himself."[47] Torrance is in fact "adamant that this providential power and activity cannot be construed in logical-causal or deterministic categories, but only in terms of the inexplicable power and activity of the immediate personal presence and operation of God."[48] It is the virgin birth and resurrection of Christ that must form our categories for understanding the working of God in creation. God, says Torrance, acts in freedom in the world "in innumerable multivariable ways while being consistently true to his own nature as Holy Love and consistently true to his creation of the world with a contingent rational order of its own."[49] How this works out *exactly* is "incomprehensible mystery," just as creation *ex nihilo* is mystery, comprehensible only as far as the revelation of the activity of God in Jesus Christ.[50] This resonates with the asymmetric compatibilism expressed above.

In the matter of putting the freedom of God together with the contingent freedom of his creation, in actual science scenarios, as we have suggested, mystery remains.[51] Much thought needs to still be applied to the

47. T. F. Torrance, *Christian Doctrine of God*, 224.
48. Colyer, *How to Read T. F. Torrance*, 166.
49. T. F. Torrance, *Christian Doctrine of God*, 222.
50. Ibid., 233.
51. Achtemeier challenges Torrance's assertions in *Divine and Contingent Order* that Einstein's theory of relativity does away with the deterministic nature of the universe inherent within a Newtonian worldview with its concept of matter as consisting of discrete particles operating under the classical laws of motion. Torrance welcomes "Einstein's reconception of the universe as a continuous space-time manifold described relationally in terms of field concepts" in that it represents the demise of determinism. While affirming that Einstein's theory does away with the particulate descriptions of Newtonian mechanics, Achtemeier's objection is that Einstein's theory is in fact still deterministic, in the sense that "the configuration of the relational space-time manifold evolves in rigidly defined patterns set by fixed and unchanging laws" (Achtemeier, "Natural Science," 295). He explains that "a physical system which assumes at some point a particular physical configuration A will evolve by fixed and unchanging laws toward a unique and rigidly determined successor configuration B" within the general theory of relativity, and it is thus deterministic. Beyond this technical point, however, Achtemeier states that his objection does not fatally compromise Torrance's general point that the overall "picture of the universe that modern science develops is *genuinely* nondeterministic and open when quantum mechanics, chaos theory, and developments in mathematical logic such as Gödel's theorem are added to the mix" (ibid., 296). Achtemeier also affirms, in more general terms, that Torrance's claims have validity if considered from a *psychological* viewpoint, that is with respect to our subjective "feel." That is, he was right that in Einstein's picture of the cosmos over against that of the Newtonian system, mathematics, for example, "has the 'feel' of a cognitive tool that provides entry into the mysteries of a universe that is deep and open, in stark contrast

ways in which the sovereignty of God and the particularity and freedom of molecules and subatomic particles and all matter in the cosmos may be understood. Some degrees of freedom seem to have been granted to even the first particle or sub-particles (quark?) or particles created *ex nihilo* by God, such that the big bang occurred and then over the next 14 billion years, the development of a habitable earth, and the evolution of plants and animals and humans. One side of the tradition has tended to emphasize the *methexis* participation of all matter in the life of God, thus explaining the directed or teleological nature of evolution. Torrance, with others, stresses that this is not *methexis* participation, but rather it is the work of the Son and the Holy Spirit in *koinōnia* relation to the creation. Either way, this participation allows for a teleological or guided evolution, rather than a dysteological evolution. The freedom of the discipline of evolutionary science need not be in conflict with the free discipline of Christian theology and its free disciplines, including the science and art of the proper interpretation of Scripture.

The Torrance-ian notion of providence creates a strong platform for seeking to come to terms with many aspects of science, both of origins and at the quantum level. God does not abandon the world to chance and necessity, and yet neither does he abrogate the contingent freedom and order of the genetic process or quantum particle movement and interaction.

This area of Torrance's theology also challenges the Aristotelian assumptions of medieval theology, and the Greek notions of impassibility and immutability which resulted from the influence of Aristotle's Unmoved Mover on the God of the Scriptures. Habet's treatment of Torrance's discussion of this sums up his thought concisely: "It is true that God is not moved by and is not changed by, anything outside the divine being, and that God is not affected by anything or does not suffer from anything beyond the divine being. But this simply affirms the biblical fact that God is transcendent and the one who created *ex nihilo*. The Fathers did not mean that God does not move Godself or that God is incapable of imparting motion to what God has made. . . . This is the God who was not always Creator but became Creator. This implies the notion that even in the life of God there is change. Nor was God eternally incarnate, for in Jesus Christ God became what God was not without ceasing to be what God was."[52]

Torrance drew on both Athanasius and on Karl Barth in this regard. The latter's assertions of the "being of God in God's act, and of the act of God in God's being, inseparably bound up with the transcendent freedom

---

to the Newtonian cosmos that is determined and enclosed by a rigid framework of eternal mathematical structures clamped down upon it 'from above'" (ibid.).

52. Habets, *Theology in Transposition*, 57.

The Coinherent Ontologies of Theology and Science   161

of God in God's love"[53] are central in Torrance's theological and scientific account. There is much to reflect on in these statements. The biblical witness is consistent in its assertions that God is unchanging, yet one must assume that these are references to the *character* of God. These assertions which challenge the Scholastic notions of the Godhead are grounded for Torrance in the incarnation, with its breathtaking implications. What is most important to note is that this area of discussion is a classic example of the ever-present influence of Christology in Torrance. He states that "patristic theology was tempted constantly by the thrust of Greek thought to change the concepts of impassibility and immutability in this direction, but it remained entrenched within the orbit of the Judeo-Christian doctrine of the living God who moves himself, who through his free love created the universe, imparting to its [sic] dynamic order, and who through the outgoing of his love moves outside of himself in the incarnation."[54]

In both creating and in becoming incarnate, God *became* what he had not previously been. With Torrance we must surely be guided in our theology proper by Christology, the factum that the agent in the creation of God the Father was God the Son, and the factum that God, in the Son, became human for us. The fact that God always possessed the power to create, that creation was in the mind of God before it came into being, and that God the Son was *incarnandus*, that is, oriented toward becoming human in eternity past prior to the incarnation . . . invoke areas of philosophical[55]

---

53. Habets, *Theology in Transposition*, 58; see T. F. Torrance, *Theological Science*, 343.

54. T. F. Torrance, *Ground and Grammar*, 65–66. In *The Christian Doctrine of God* (88–89), Torrance confirms that in his *ex nihilo* creation, God acted in an altogether new way, bringing into being entirely new events, for the creation of the world, *ex nihilo* is something new *even for God*.

55. The debate as to whether God is timeless or everlastingly temporal is evoked here, for one. The relation of God and time is certainly a complex one. The traditional view, which goes back to Augustine, is that God is timeless, that is he is outside of its realm and does not experience temporal succession. This is the *Divine timelessness* view (Stump and Kretzmann). The current trend among Christian philosophers is toward the view that although God is everlasting, that he never began and will never end, he is nevertheless temporal. He exists at each moment in time. This is the *Divine temporality* view. Among those who have taken a *via media* position are Padgett and DeWeese, who represent the "God as Relatively Timeless" position, and Lane Craig who preferred a "God as Timeless without Creation and Temporal with Creation." This latter view fits well with the incarnation narrative. Torrance took the temporalist position, though, as Mullins indicates, he "posits a distinction between the created time of the universe and the uncreated time of God." Mullins, "In Search of a Timeless God," 38. See Torrance, *Theological and Natural Science*, 50–51.

and theological[56] (the triune God as "being in act") debate which we cannot entertain here.

Most crucially what we can affirm by a *kataphysic* approach to theology which functions in an *a posteriori* way, is that through the personal revelation of the Son, and by the Spirit, God is revealed in himself to be an eternal self-giving communion. He is a God who does not require creation but creates and redeems creation as an outflow of that life of loving communion. The creation as therefore unnecessary, as extravagant, as requiring of individual attention in its particularity, as having contingent order and yet surprise, corresponds in all these ways to what science discovers it to be. But the consequence of the contingent nature of God's freedom and the consequent contingent nature of the universe is that both theology and science defy an *a priori* approach to knowledge. It can only be discovered empirically. For science this is obvious. The Greeks could not discover science for they considered matter not worth studying. As already noted, the presence of the Christian doctrine of creation in the medieval and Reformation period fostered and prospered the discovery of science.[57] Crucial to this was the belief that creation as good made it worth studying, and that its intelligibility made it amenable to study and systematization. Also important, however, was the Christian belief in the nature of the universe as contingent, which to some extent desacralized creation, thereby rendering investigative probings necessary and permissible. Theology also has been discovered by the church through its encounter with the incarnate Christ and the Holy Spirit, firsthand in the apostles and then as passed down and freshly experienced by the ecclesial community down through the ages. Theological realism is at the heart of this and the crucial notion of the incarnation and the Trinitarian concept of *homoousios* were, according to Torrance, vital to this.

In concluding this discussion of Divine and human agency, while not drawing the veil over further exploration to gain clarity, it seems to me that

56. What the act of God in the incarnation of Son means exactly for the essence of the triune God is a hotly debated topic among Barth scholars, and principally, Bruce McCormack and George Hunsinger. For an able summation of the controversy, see Cary, "Barth Wars."

57. See Achtemeier's discussion of "Overlapping Historical Development" in Achtemeier, "Natural Science," 281–92. Achtemeier largely affirms Torrance's view of the mutuality of the fields of theology and science with respect to the history of ideas: "Torrance narrates a sweeping intellectual history of the mutually influencing development of scientific and theological ideas in the West. While his account of the character of scientific knowing in both theology and the natural sciences gives a plausible account of their potential interactions, his particular historical claims for cross-fertilization between the disciplines are in certain instances difficult to evaluate" (Achtemeier, "Natural Science," 293–94). The reservations Achtemeier expresses with respect to this, mild as they are, are worthy of investigation.

what can be said is that there is an asymmetric compatibilism of a Barthian kind that is in operation between the freedom of God and the granted freedom given to creation. Searching the mechanism of this must include, as Yong rightly insists, biblical and thick and fully Trinitarian theology, and good science. In the pursuit, the parameters seem fairly clear . . . God is sovereign and sustains the universe in providential ways, by the Spirit and in the Son, but the creature, the quark, the electron, the mouse, the human, has some level of freedom grounded in their being which is always a grace-filled being-in-relation.

Another important parameter of this discussion is that it must give consideration to how it accounts for the origin and presence of evil in the world, and a theodicy that accounts for it. If humans and all creatures have no freedom, they cannot be held in any way accountable, and God as ruling despot must be directly responsible for sin and its consequences in the world, for every genetic accident and every tragedy.

While we can affirm that there was an *ex nihilo* creation of whatever the initial creation substances were, by Christ, this gave way to a creation that God permitted to evolve in its own way over fourteen billion years, or so it seems. If Christ made all things, he must have been involved in this process, watching over its development. Its creatures were also granted freedom (contingency and dependence). This is an important piece for a theodicy, that is, in the reconciling of the presence of evil and suffering within the creation of a good God. Creation, as we have noted, was in itself a kenotic act on God's behalf, before the incarnation was (perhaps both went together in the eternal purposes of God, given the seminal place of the incarnation and resurrection in the formation of the new creation from the old). As Polkinghorne has stated, "The existence of free creatures is a greater good than a world populated by perfectly behaving automata." However, with realism, Polkinghorne also notes, "that good has the cost of mortality and suffering."[58] This then leads him to speak of the transformation of the old creation into the new, the second stage of God's creation, that is its redemption and reconciliation by Christ, one that happens not by creation *ex nihilo*, but *ex vetere*. Why does this happen in this way? What is the purpose of this old creation? The answer lies in part in the freedom spoken of, and of the consequences that such freedom incurs. Another answer lies in the fact that somehow, in the providence of God, more glory is revealed of the God who redeems a contingent universe than one who creates perfect automata.

When viewed from a birds eye, the contingent freedom of creation which in an as yet mysterious way echoes the freedom of the God, who

---

58. Polkinghorne, *Science and the Trinity*, 165.

is the Father who generates the Son in freedom, and the triune God, who created the world in freedom through the Son, is evidence of a coinherent universe in which ontology is the ground of epistemology.

This discussion of freedom and agency anticipates another trace of the Trinity in creation, to which we will now turn.

Intrinsic fecundity or fruitfulness or productiveness . . . or the phenomenon of complexification

Evidence of both Divine providence and the agency of matter in the creation of the universe is offered by Polkinghorne in his reference to "the collection of scientific insights called the Anthropic Principle."[59] This principle which is evidence of fine-tuning in the universe, Polkinghorne states, "has led us to the surprising conclusion that a universe capable of evolving the complexity of life as we know it is a very special world indeed."[60] He continues:

> While life [after the Big Bang] did not appear until the universe was about ten billion years old, and self-conscious life when it was almost fourteen billion years old, there is a real sense in which the universe was pregnant with the possibility of carbon-based life almost from the moment of the Big Bang onwards. Its physical fabric was then of the exact form necessary to allow the eventual emergence of life.[61]

Two aspects of this anthropic principle serve to illustrate the point. If the exact details of the physical state of the earth had not been present, that is, if the universe was not fine-tuned, human life could not have emerged. That is, exposure of the earth to a steady source of energy like the sun, of a kind that enabled a process of the evolution of complex beings like humans, which takes three to four billion years, was necessary. The law of gravity, and the gravity constant, which governs how stars burn in a long-lived and reliable way had to be what it actually is, for the stars to be stable enough to provide energy over a long period of time. Second the role of the stars which in their internal nuclear furnaces produced elements necessary for life, that is carbon, oxygen and twenty or so others, was crucial to the presence of these elements on earth. These elements reached earth as stars burnt up and spread their stardust across the universe. "We are all creatures of stardust, formed from the ashes of dead stars," says Polkinghorne. He speaks

---

59. Ibid., 68.
60. Ibid.
61. Ibid.

of Fred Hoyle who was one of the scientists who "unravelled the delicate and beautiful chain of stellar nuclear reactions by which these elements were made," and who upon noticing that the nuclear forces had to be just what they were for the reactions to develop in this way, is reported to have said, "The universe is a put-up job."[62] There had to be an intelligent being behind it, was his conclusion. And yet it had some freedom of its own.

This seems unlikely just to be a happy accident. Admittedly this trace could be true for a deistic God, as much as a Trinitarian one, except that underlying the fecundity of the universe is its agency communicated as empowered by the loving Divine agency of the Son by the Spirit.

Particularity

The contingency of creation on God's part, gives to it also all the particularities of every created thing created and this is crucial in the development of science which involved the particularism of Scotus, which was necessary for the birth to science.[63] Scientists have to pay attention to particularity, to the "this-ness" of things. And they cannot know beforehand what they will discover. Their approach is empirical. It is full of surprises. Many of the greatest discoveries of science have been made serendipitously. When experiment confirms what expectations are, based on available data, the scientist gains a sense that what she has discovered and what she knows is reflective of what is actually there. This is a particular aspect of ontology that determines epistemology, creating the sense of realism that scientists avow. That is, their sense that what science is discovering is actually there, is actually what reality is.

T. F. Torrance was very much aware of the Franciscan tradition originating with St. Frances of Assisi himself, and Franciscan philosopher St. Bonaventure (1217–74), which offered a new kind of attention to the particulars of creation, as a seedbed for science. Their prodigy, Franciscan philosopher Duns Scotus (1265–1308), a careful thinker, dubbed the "subtle doctor" offered a defense of the centrality of the will (voluntarism) in God's creation, and challenged Aquinas by suggesting that both creation and the incarnation transcend reason and are evidence of "irrational love," or its extravagance. Scotus in affirming the univocity of being,[64] that is that we can indeed speak univocally of God with respect to our being (God exists and we exist) recognized the risk in the assertion that we don't exist

62. Ibid., 69.
63. Puhalo, *Evidence of Things Not Seen*, 14, 15ff.
64. *Opus Oxoniense* I iii 1–2, quoted in Grenz, *Named God*, 55.

by material participation and that our being is our own. The risk is that humans will take up their autonomy as independent of God, rather than in relational participation with God. Scotus avers that from the beginning God had willed to assume the consequences of human autonomy, by way of the cross. Thus creation was itself a kenotic act of God.

Whatever we think of Scotus, hero or a villain, he is to be credited with an awareness of the irreducible uniqueness and particularity of things, that is, the "thisness" (*haeccitas*) of things,[65] that encouraged the pursuit of science. His view also of "the primacy of Christ," of creation *for* incarnation, not vice versa, has something to contribute toward a theodicy.

Inter-relatedness or Mutuality

The final trace of the Trinity in the cosmos has to do with its interrelatedness. All substances in the universe contain elements from the same Periodic Table, albeit it expands as new elements are discovered, and all contain the same stuff of electrons and protons and neutrons and quarks. The movement of a bird's wings affects the energy on the other side of the cosmos. Plants and animals are involved in complex ecological systems. Both T. F. Torrance and Colin Gunton used the language of perichoresis as a helpful concept in their discussion of the dynamic interrelatedness of the cosmos, as a trace of the inner perichoretic life of God. Torrance spoke of the act of God as Creator being the result of a "dynamic three-way reciprocity" between Father, Son, and Spirit which he called "the perichoretic coactivity of the Holy Trinity,"[66] while Gunton suggested that the character of the universe may be expressed as a "perichoresis of interrelated systems."[67] Buxton comments that

> it is precisely because God embraces creation's "frail contingent reality within the everlasting power of his divine presence" that we should expect trinitarian theology to offer a cogent *analogia relationis* [analogy of relations] between the creator and his creation. God's own ecstatic perichoretic life finds expression in the creation that he has brought into being, the creation that he unchangeably and unconditionally loves and blesses. Creation is open precisely because God himself is open; it is free—in the contingent sense—precisely because God is free; alive and

---

65. Scotus, *Ordinatio* II, d. 3, p. 1. q. 2, n48.
66. T. F. Torrance, *Christian Doctrine of God*, 198.
67. Gunton, "Relation and Relativity," 106.

surprising because God is inexhaustibly living and creative in his inner being.[68]

In sum, we have highlighted some of the traces of the coinherent Trinity in the cosmos. The fact that they are just that, "traces," speaks both of the revealed-ness of God, but also of the hiddenness of God. He does not reveal himself in creation in obvious ways. This should not surprise us, for it has a certain correspondence to the character of his most overt revelation, that in the Son, the Word made flesh, whose regal glory was for the most part veiled as he lived among us. To the eye of faith, his deity and moral glory were abundantly evident, but mostly he lived among us as the Divine incognito. We have also reserved the right to say that not all of the traces have absolute clarity associated with them. That is, in the matter of agency, we have opted for an asymmetric compatibilist position which does not spell out exactly how God is sovereign and how matter has some degrees of freedom. This is in concordance with a time-honored strand of apophatic theology which honors the transcendence of God. It does not preclude the search for philosophical connections, but it recognizes that where Scripture is silent, we may not be able to fathom the depths of the working of a transcendent God. This kind of theological apophaticism is not a product of the "death of God" theology of the 1960s, nor of an eighteenth-century deistic avoidance of the interaction of theology with science or philosophy. In fact its roots go as far back as the Cappadocians of the 300s and Thomas Aquinas in the 1200s. Even more importantly, this apophatic stream which emphasizes the transcendence and hiddenness of God, is a theme in both the Old and New Testaments.[69]

The tension between the revelation and hiddenness of God, especially with respect to agency, has also been referenced recently by theologian scientist Nicola Hoggard Creegan. In her article "A Christian Theology of

---

68. Buxton, *Trinity, Creation and Pastoral*, 128; quoting T. F. Torrance, *Christian Doctrine of God*, 218. This reference to the openness of God is not necessarily an affirmation of open theism, but rather an affirmation of the relational openness of God to his creation, human, animate and inanimate.

69. For a helpful discussion on a grammatical approach to theological language which incorporates a certain kind of theological agnosticism, or negative approach to the knowledge of God, see Tanner, *God and Creation in Christian Theology*. According to Tanner, "Theologians seem to know that it is appropriate to say certain things about God without quite knowing what they mean by doing so. . . . Theologians may claim to know *that* their statements refer to God and are true of God's nature, but they do not claim to know in what way they refer or *how* they are true. . . . On this apophatic or agnostic reading, theological statements are not conveying information about God so much as they are suggesting how to talk in circumstances where we do not pretend to understand fully what we are saying." Tanner, *God and Creation*, 11–12.

Evolution and Participation,"[70] she bemoans the fact that often adherents to the evolutionary creation[71] model of creation "rarely examine" the matter of God's action "in the processes and order of the world because only secondary causes can be examined," thus leaving "antievolutionary perspectives to interpret and address the problem of seeing God in the world." To address this area of a theology of Divine action in light of evolution, in the midst of a discussion in which she invokes the Trinitarian nature of God, the incarnation and the hiddenness of God, she suggests realistically that "God's presence in the natural world will be discernible, but only within the natural processes, and thereby only in an obscured fashion."[72] Thus, as with Divine revelation in general, we may conclude with Polkinghorne that "God is neither totally hidden nor totally manifested in the works of creation."[73] I would simply add that both the revealed-ness of the coinherent God in creation and his hiddenness as Creator evoke an appropriate sense of wonder on behalf of his human creatures, just as the coinherent God of the cross, who is both deeply hidden and richly revealed, evokes our worshipful wonder. We may—without knowing every detail of how he has fashioned it and how his majestic voice holds it together—affirm with the songwriter the second person of the Trinity:

> You're the Word of the Father from before world began;
> Every star and every planet has been fashioned by your hand.
> All creation holds together by the power of your voice.
> Let the skies declare your glory, let the land and seas rejoice![74]

Moving beyond mere trace, then, we now turn our attention to humanity, made explicitly in the *image* of God, to look evidences of the triune God in anthropology, that is, for being-in-relationality, for freedom, for engraced capacity to receive intelligibility and to perceive beauty. This will give even greater evidence for an analogy of relations between the triune God and his creatures.

---

70. Creegan, "Christian Theology," 499–518.

71. Creegan uses the term "theistic evolution," whereas my own preference is for the term "evolutionary creation," which asserts that this is still a *creational* viewpoint.

72. Creegan, "Christian Theology," 499. She adds, "I also argue that newer understandings of evolutionary mechanisms are more consistent with theological appropriation than are strictly Darwinian ones."

73. Polkinghorne, *Science and the Trinity*, 61.

74. Stuart Towsnend, "Across the Lands" (Thankyou Music, 2002).

Chapter 7

The Coinherent *Ontologies* of Theology and Science

Humanity in the Image of God as *Intelligent, Personal and Relational, and Vocationally Significant*

"Praise the Lord, all his works, everywhere in his dominion."
PSALM 103:22

IN THIS CHAPTER, WE move from considering echoes of the coinherent God in Christ in nonhuman creation by way of trace, to a focused study of the echoes of that God in human persons who are expressly his *image*. The particular echoes derive from the three main ways in which the tradition has sought to understand the doctrine of the image of God: relationality (onto-relational), rationality (ontological, cognitive, volitional and emotive capacities) and vocation (functional, or work capacity). This chapter will reflect the conviction that the core of the concept is undoubtedly relational, and that the rationality and the vocation function best within that relationality, and toward that end. It will also reflect the ultimate and recapitulative christological fulfillment of the image in a manner consistent with the eschatological character of the book of Genesis. The particular attributes of the *triune* God which will be considered to be echoed in humanity in this chapter will be his goodness reflected in his relationality, intelligibility, beauty and in his creative and redemptive work.

Cognizant of the many significant ethical issues surrounding the doctrine of the image of God which we cannot engage here, it is important nevertheless to assert some convictions that will be unpacked further in the chapter. The first conviction is that *all* human persons from the moment of implantation to death, irrespective of the *degree* of their intelligence quota, sexual anatomy,[1] and vocational "success" or state of employment, are made in the non-degreed image of God, and must be treated with dignity and granted basic human rights.[2] It will also reflect the conviction that the fall marred, but did not destroy, the image. Sin defaced but did not erase it (Gen 9:6). Christians and non-Christians are made in his image. This is a matter of the core of its meaning, which is *relatedness* to the Creator. All human beings, having been created by God are in relatedness to him, which is not the same as being in *relationship* with him. A further conviction is that *Christ* is in an ultimate and representative sense, the image of the invisible God, the last Adam, *the* Man who as the full image, represents all humanity, and reigns with the new humanity united to him, bringing in a new creation. At the level of God's design, all human persons are intended to be restored to the fullness of the image of God in Christ (1 Tim 2:4). In this sense too, all human persons are in a non-degreed manner in the image of God, related to the matter of God's intended *telos* for them. They are all human, and therefore recipients of dignity and human rights. However, as human persons come into lived union with the living Christ by faith,

---

1. There is controversy in the tradition on whether the matter of anatomical sex (gender is a social construct and thus the term is avoided here) is intrinsic to the image of God or extrinsic to it. The words of Genesis 1:27, *"male and female created he them,"* seem very closely tied to the primary indicative statements, *"So God created mankind in his own image, in the image of God he created them . . ."* and this has led to the notion of sex as intrinsic to the image, and of the inclusion of sexuality of persons within their humanity. Sex is the only ontological descriptor which legitimately differentiates otherwise equal and equally human, human beings. Others have preferred the view that sex is extrinsic, and not definitive of human personhood, seeking to assure intersex persons for example, that they are fully validated as image bearers. The intrinsic and defining aspect of the image has, on this account, been the *telos* of all human persons in the eschaton as persons like Christ, *the* image in whom all participate by grace. The intrinsic view does not in and of itself preclude the embrace of all persons as image bearers. It allows for the fall in which *all* are broken and insists that the non-degreed core is the relatedness to God of all irrespective of the degree of brokenness. For further discussion, see Anderson and Guernsey, "Bonding Without Bondage," 85–104, and McKirland, "Image of God and Intersex Persons."

2. "Rights" is in quotation marks to signal a certain ambivalence toward "rights" language signaled by O'Donovan (see "Language of Rights, 193–207) related to the power connotations of the word.

they begin a journey toward the fullness of what was intended for them, by degree—from one degree of glory to another (2 Cor 3:18), which is the same as to say, toward being *fully* human. The scope of their recovery journey will include the use of cognitive and emotive faculties toward the development of shalom in their relationships and shalom with the creation, and a sense of significance in vocation related to the cultural mandate and participation in bringing in the new creation. For those who do not enter that redeeming union, relatedness remains, though not relationship, that is, human-ness, but something short of being fully human in all God's intentions for that. Matters of ontology such as degree of intelligence remain independent of being Christian or not. What is forfeited by lack of relationship with God is a sense of the ultimate significance of work and an orientation toward God and creation that provides a worshipful posture and a meaningful affect.

In the course of this discussion which is directed mainly toward the second objective of our project, that coinherence is seen in creation (here especially human creation), there will be occasion also to mention hints in the direction of the third objective, that image-bearing theologians and scientists and their vocations of theology and science are held together, each in the other, without loss of identity of the each, and even though the coinherence contains an asymmetry.

THE IMAGE OF GOD IN CONCEPT

In this chapter, then, themes in anthropology will be discussed under the wider theme of the image of God in humanity. If there are traces of the triune God in the nonhuman creation, we should expect that they will be revealed more fully in humanity made explicitly in his image. God as the one relational God Yahweh, who in the New Testament is more fully revealed as the God and Father of our Lord Jesus Christ in the fellowship of the Holy Spirit, has declared humanity to be his image (Gen 1:26–7), and in particular, and by way of recapitulation, that image has been fully expressed in his own Son (Col 1:15), who in the New Testament is called the image of the invisible God. The last Adam is the one who will bring to fulfillment all that was envisioned for humanity in the image of God, in what is called the cultural mandate, the command of God given to humanity to care for the creation, to live in families[3] (Gen 1:26, 28–31; 2:15–24), to work in areas

---

3. Ray Anderson argued that from its inception, "family" as the penultimate contingent relation to God has to do with the fulfillment of the core social paradigm, and therefore is a larger concept than the nuclear family. See Anderson, *Something Old, Something New*, 168–70. In the era of the new covenant, the family of God, the church,

that may be classified as agriculture, science and the arts (4:20–22). Christ is *the* regent, reigning now at the right hand of the Father, and all in Christ participate in the completing of the creation which in Genesis is depicted as "good," but not yet complete. The goodness yet incompleteness of creation assumes a place for human endeavor. There is an eschatological aspect to Genesis 1 and 2 that find their fulfillment in the One image bearer who by his incarnation and ministry and death and resurrection and ascension, brought about the *eschaton*, the end of all things. He is the one who fulfills perfectly all of the aspects of what the image of God means in Scripture, the ontological, the relational and the functional. And humanity in Christ participates with him in this kingdom reign.

Before investigating these aspects, it is important to note that there is, in light of the fact that it is the incarnate Son who really reflects the image of God in humanity, good reason for believing that it is an image not of a monadic God, but of the triune God of biblical revelation. The *imago Dei* (image of God) is indeed the *imago Trinitatis* (image of the triune God), for we know that the God-Man Jesus, the representative man, is man in hypostatic union with the Son, but he is also as Man imaging the God who is in the New Testament revealed to be the triune God.

As already suggested, the tradition speaks of the image of God in three different ways: as *relational*, in the sense that it is established by the initiative of God and in covenantal relationship with him, and in the sense that relationality is embedded in the first humans ("*male and female created he them*," Gen 1:27); as *structural* or ontological, which refers to cerebral, self-reflexive, emotional and volitional capacity and creativity; and as *functional*, in that the immediate command of God upon the first humans is to tend the garden and care for the earth. As noted also, a fourth, the eschatological view, has also been proposed as a way to ensure the non-degreed image of all humans. This is the idea that the intended *telos* in God's mind is the full Christ-likeness of all human persons.[4] I argue, however, that the non-degreed relatedness of God to all human beings which he has created is the foundational criteria, one which comes under the relational category, which includes relatedness and relationship. In reviewing this concept in the tradition, Jeremy Kidwell has wisely commented that "appreciation for the polyvalence of the doctrine allows for a composite meaning."[5] While this is true, the christological aspect of this doctrine of the image of God cannot

---

becomes the primary community of the Christian, though not to the exclusion of human families.

4. Anderson and Guernsey, "Bonding Without Bondage," 85–104, and McKirland, "Image of God and Intersex Persons."

5. Kidwell, "Elucidating the Image of God."

be neglected as a unifying theme, for without removing any of the aspects mentioned, it makes them possible. As suggested in Irenaeus, the image is recapitulated in Jesus, who by his representative actions from incarnation to resurrection and ascension, makes possible the restoration of the *imago*. The resurrection was the first day of the new creation, and as Oliver O'Donovan states, that resurrection of Christ is the reaffirmation of creation.[6] I would add that with this resurrection came the new community of humanity in Christ, who cannot but bear the image of the Trinity given they are in union with the incarnate Son and in communion with the triune God. As persons, and as a communion, the church, they image or are an icon of the Trinity (a concept well known in at least the Orthodox church). But in addition, as humans regenerated and restored into relationship and not mere relatedness to God, the vocational purpose of God for humanity becomes possible again. Human persons in relationship with God (theology) also fulfill the cultural mandate for earth-keeping (which includes science) in ways that are constructive, intellectually, and in actuality, for the good of the creation. Epistemology can thus reflect ontology.

Goodness and Reason or Intelligibility

The possibility that epistemology in science and in theology actually follows and reflects real reality, an important aspect of our thesis, is grounded in the reality or ontology of the *goodness* of the Creator. His goodness is seen most foundationally in his love, his profound eternal love as the Lover, Loved, and Love. This reflects his relationality as coinherent persons. How this is reflected in the image-bearing relationality and love of human persons will be considered below. His goodness is also implied in the perspicuity of his revelation to those he has created in love, both special and personal and general. They cannot be in relation with him without some capacity to receive revelation and respond to it with intelligible words and love. God's goodness undergirds the *intelligibility* of his revelation and the impartation of the contingent, engraced intelligence given to human beings to receive it. The first of the three patristic ideas mentioned by T. F. Torrance and referred to in the previous chapter, concerns the rational unity of the cosmos, grounded in the fact that the all-wise God through the agency of the Son, is the Creator of all. This ontology, who God is *in se*, revealed through the economic revelation of the Son, ensures that there is one pervading *taxis* or order in the universe. This not only ensures that the universe does not exist in some kind of perverse ontological dualism, but positively, it assures

---

6. O'Donovan, *Resurrection*, 14.

the seeker of truth that what she is discovering by way of empirical process corresponds to what really is.

The question as to whether there is an epistemology that mirrors a real ontology in God and in the cosmos, is primarily a *human* one. There are a number of biblical passages that suggest that inanimate, animal and plant creatures of God do sense the presence of a Creator and even praise it (e.g., Isa 55; Ps 103:22). The Apostle Paul also speaks of creation groaning in light of the fallen-ness of the creature God has assigned to be its regent (Rom 8:22). However, the matter of receptivity to the *intelligibility* of creation and of worship responsive to the intelligence or wisdom of the Creator, is principally a human concern, as far as we know. The question of the perception of beauty in the creation which reflects the *beauty* of the triune God, is also a human matter. That humanity can receive the information in an intelligible cosmos created by an intelligent triune God through his Son, who as the *Logos* is the repository of all the treasures of the wisdom and knowledge of God (Col 2:3), is evidence of the graced nature of humanity in Christ. Likewise, the fact that this humanity has the capacity to perceive beauty in creation, emanating from the glorious Supreme Harmony of All[7] who defines beauty, and then create beauty in artistic and scientific endeavors, is a mark also of endowed grace. It is hard to believe the idea that the fact that there is art, and that there are artists, is accidental.

One example of a particular kind of beauty found in creation is that of music which is discovered, more than made, by musicians. That there is music in the universe seems utterly unnecessary and extravagant. The Christian doctrine of creation would suggest that music is a particular manifestation of the general outflow of Divine triune love that issued in the creation. The thought of music as an analogy of the Trinity has a long history in the Christian tradition.[8] Bearing in mind cautions regarding analogies of the Trinity, the musical analogy seems more appropriate than visual representations. Music, like God, is invisible, for one thing. Music also involves sound waves and air in a way that reflects "the biblical ambiguity between wind and spirit" in both Hebrew (*ruach*) and Greek (*pneuma*). But third, music permits "a distinction in a shared space without conflict or compromise."[9] The question is posed by Trinitarian theologian of the arts Jeremy Begbie:

---

7. Edwards, *Miscellany*, 182.

8. See a detailed discussion of the place in this tradition of employing the major triad as an analogy of the Trinity in Broadhead, "Triune Triad," 23–33. See also these references contained in Broadhead's article: Fitzpatrick, "Trinity and Music," 143–52; Pelikan, *Bach among the Theologians*, 124–25; Bruhn, *Messiaen's*, 97–147.

9. I am grateful for these insights contained in Broadhead, "Triune Triad," 23.

What could be more apt than to speak of the Trinity as a three-note chord, a resonance of life; Father, Son, and Spirit mutually indwelling, without mutual exclusion, and yet without merger, each occupying the same space, "sounding through" one another, yet irreducibly distinct, reciprocally enhancing, and establishing one another *as* other?[10]

However, beyond analogy, the presence of music in the cosmos just seems to fit well with the idea of a Creator who is the Supreme Harmony in his triune relations, who *is* music, if you like, and who cannot but create with music in his handiwork, and who creates his image-bearing creatures with the capacity to hear and appreciate music, and then create it and voice it, so that it remanates back to him in worship.

These realities answer well to some of the themes in the theological anthropology of Karl Barth. The best news of the gospel for him is the election of the triune God to create and to be *for* humanity, to become one with humanity in Christ. The nature of humanity as defined first by this election, and *not merely evolutionary theory*, is what gives humanity the capacity to engage in scholarship and science and music as image bearers of the God of wisdom, knowledge, creativity, and beauty. What enables the human quest in these areas, including science, is the prior election of God to create, and to be *for* humanity. That he is for humanity is evident from his creation of it, and from his reconciliation of it in Christ, the Christ who became human, the elect Man for all humanity. The Christ, who as the *eschatos* Adam and the new Israel, stood in its place by his vicarious life, death, resurrection and ascension. Anthropology as it is determined first by Christ, the elect Man, and humanity in him, and not evolution, is the principal reason for the remarkable capacities of humanity, including the capacity to engage in science and the arts and learning in general.

The capacity of human persons for intelligent and creative thought and action by means of which they can relate to God and one another and creation is one aspect of the *image* of God in humanity.[11] This relates to the second objective of our project—to support the reality that human persons

---

10. Begbie, *Resounding*, 293.

11. *Imago* as inclusive of intellectual capacity must be kept in the context of relationality as the most critical and definitive aspect of the image. The capacity to love and be in relation is most crucial. Intellectual capacity clearly varies very widely within the human population, and persons who may have intellectual limitation due to congenital or idiopathic pathology are not considered any less image-bearing humans in the non-degreed sense. The intellectual knowledge and wisdom required for relationships does reflect the God of knowledge and wisdom, however, and progressive growth in loving God with the mind is growth into the image in a degreed sense.

image a coinherent God. However, this then becomes another evidence of the proposal that there is an echoed coinherence of the disciplines of theology and science from an *ontological perpective*. That is, these disciplines are practiced by the same species of person, persons made in the image of God, persons whose intelligence is derived from the same intelligent and intelligible God. Both theologians and scientists as human beings are, in their being as human persons, image bearers able receive and process intelligible truth and perceive beauty, and both reflect the *being* of the one intelligent and intelligible, and beautiful God. Their findings, one would imagine, cannot be other than coinherent.

Looking at this from another perspective, the wonder of the capacity for the *knowing* of information and beauty by humans (epistemology), reflected in their science and in their theology, is a reflection of their *being* as image bearers of God and in turn, most fundamentally, of God's being (ontology) as intelligible and glorious. Our capacity as made in the image of a relational and intelligible God (ontology), creates the possibility of human persons who can know and love (epistemology). What scientists often take for granted, that is, their remarkable capacity for understanding and perceiving, is from a theological perspective anything but a given, and anything but unremarkable. Polkinghorne makes the interesting observation that the

> development of modern science has shown us that our human ability to understand the universe far exceeds anything that could reasonably be considered as simply an evolutionary necessity, or as a happy spin-off from that necessity. The universe has proved to be astonishingly rationally transparent, and the human mind remarkably apt to the comprehension of its structure. We can penetrate the secrets of the subatomic realm of quarks and gluons, and we can make maps of cosmic curved spacetime, both regimes that have no direct practical impact upon us, and both exhibiting properties that are counterintuitive in relation to our ordinary habits of thought. Our understanding of the workings of the world greatly exceed anything that could simply be required for human survival. The assertion by a so-called evolutionary epistemology of the necessary validity of knowledge acquired in order to support such survival is only a partial insight, insufficient in itself to explain the success of science.[12]

It is a reality that evokes wonder that scientists are so gifted and privileged to be able to explore a universe "that is both rationally transparent

---

12. Polkinghorne, *Science and the Trinity*, 63.

and rationally beautiful in its deep and accessible order."[13] The naturalistic conclusion that discerns this simply to have been a "happy accident"[14] just doesn't seem rational.

Goodness and Relationality

The reality that human beings can by grace know and love creation and its God suggests also another aspect of human being perhaps even more remarkable than knowledge: this is that reality that human beings are *persons* and as such *persons in relation*. These realities of course reflect who the triune God is as persons in relation. This is the epitome of the reflection of Divine coinherence in human coinherence. The capacity to be human, to be persons, to be persons in community with God and our fellow human and creation, and as such to know and to love, all of these realities are wrapped up in the biblical doctrine of the image of God, and in particular as that doctrine is understood in light of Christ.

The crucial piece of information for considering *who* both scientists and theologians *are*, then, is that they are human persons, and image bearers, with yes, remarkable cranial capacity, with yes, ability to assess their own ideas, and yes, with profound creativity. *Their ontology creates the opportunity for intelligibility and thus epistemology.* However, the design of God for image bearers was to be and do these things in participational relationship with him. That is, they are to know and to love as human persons, which is to say, human persons in relation with him. When these capacities are exercised outside the core concept of relationality with God and the other human, the efforts of both theologians and scientists begin to be distorted and possibly destructive for creation, rather than constructive continuation of God's work in the world.

Emphatically, both theology and science are possible only because of the *graced* nature of human beings made in the image of God, and who are such only because of and in their relatedness and relationship to the One true image of the invisible God, the last or *eschatos* Adam. There is an echo of Divine coinherence in humanity related to capacity, that is, by way of what human persons made in the image of God and made recipients of the cultural mandate can do and are to do. They are, in relationship with God, to continue and complete the creation that God began. We have been made to be godlike creatures, and as such are characterized by curiosity and wonder and creativity and responsibility. Our ontology created in the being

13. Ibid., 64.
14. Ibid., 65.

and after the likeness of the intelligent, relational, free Creator is crucial for both theology and science, even though persons in these disciplines may not be aware of it.

The belonging together of knowledge and relational personhood is reflected in the early chapters of Genesis, which, as Barth has pointed out, have as their primary purpose, not providing information about science, but the unitedness of creation and covenant. In fact, in a real sense, Genesis is more about anticipation of the last Adam than it is about the first. In this vein, Karl Barth viewed God's prehistorical purpose for humanity in Christ (all of humanity) as all important, and like Irenaeus, he saw Christ's humanity as the recapitulation, indeed, first-intended nature, of God's purposes for the first Adam. It is really in participation with the last Adam, that the cultural mandate is fulfilled, and all that this means for the human pursuits of the sciences and the arts and theological scholarship.

Goodness and Vocation

Of crucial importance in humanity's fulfillment of all these covenant-partnering pursuits is that they are carried out in *participation* with God, in Christ and by the Spirit. Even in the prelapsarian state, humans were only capable of being humans by being human in relationship with God. Image-bearing may involve cerebral capacity, and it does involve the functions of earth-keeping and creation care and work, which, according to Genesis 4 includes things that seem to prefigure the arts (v. 21, "*Jubal; he was the father of all who play stringed instruments and pipes*") and the sciences (v. 22, "*Zillah also had a son, Tubal-Cain, who forged all kinds of tools out of bronze and iron*"—metallurgists, i.e., chemists), but all of this is contingent upon being in communion with and being guided by God, in Christ. John Calvin saw this clearly. Even in prelapsarian days, he insists that Adam participated in the life of the last Adam in the garden, for he was unfit for the Divine presence on his own, not because of sin, but because of the *metaphysical remove* between God and humanity. Christ was the mediator even then.[15]

---

15. Calvin recognized that "even if man had remained free from all stain, his condition would have been too lowly for him to reach God without a Mediator" (II.12.1). He insisted that it was Christ who was our Mediator even before the fall, by virtue of the fact that even from the beginning, "Christ was set over angels and men as their Head," as he was "'the first-born of all creation' [Col 1:15]" (II.12.4). "Hence, whatever excellence was engraved upon Adam [was] derived from the fact that he approached the glory of his Creator through the only-begotten Son" (II.12.6). Thus, only by way of participation in Christ was Adam a "mirror" of God's glory (II.12.6). Only by way of Adam's dynamic "union with Christ" did God behold himself (which is to say: did

The fall regrettably distances the cerebral and creative capacities of humanity from the relational participation. In Christ in whom all the treasures of wisdom and knowledge inhere, and who is in perfect relationship with the Father, as a Man, the *imago* is recapitulated. And all in union with him, are able to hold together their intellectual capacity with a profound humility and responsible administration of their theological or scientific knowledge. That is, the ideal posture of the scientist must be as a *theologian* scientist. Polkinghorne argues that the Holy Spirit as the Spirit of truth, who defines and reveals truth (John 15:26), "is at work in the truth-seeking community of scientists," even if they don't know it.

THE IMAGE OF GOD IN PRACTICE

With this introduction to the concept of the image of God, we now embark on an exploration of how each aspect, the rational, the relational, and the functional, correspond with various aspects of the reflection of the Trinity in human life, the arts, and in science in particular. The realistic note that humanity is fallen, and the consequences of this, will be sounded also. How the reconciling grace of God operates with respect to the image of God and human capacities, is both a celebrated and much debated matter in the tradition, and we will say something of the different manner in which the traditions have spoken of analogy of being (*analogia entis*) and analogy of faith or relations (*analogia fide/relationis/adventus*).

a. The Image as Cognitive or Rational: Intelligibility and Beauty

That the image of God includes various ontological aspects of human being, including the capacity to think, to self-perceive, to perceive order and to make structural connections, is perhaps rather obvious, given who the God we are imaging is. Nevertheless, this should not be downplayed. It serves to answer the big question—why is mankind so remarkably intelligent? This question, as we have seen, cannot be answered merely on the basis of evolutionary progress. Our intellectual capacity and pursuits are extravagant and beyond the mere requirements of survival. The contingent nature of the creation of God and its extravagant variety and beauty, are answered in the image-bearing capacities of humans reflected in quantum mechanics, in synthetic organic compounds, and in beautiful poetry and sculpture.

God "image" himself) in Adam. Adam and Eve were continually reminded that their very lives, their very ability to "image" God, was utterly dependent upon communion (κοινωνία) with God.

It is possible, on the other hand, to overplay this aspect of the Divine image. There has been a tendency to magnify this aspect by some in the Christian tradition, and with this came an isolating of reason from the relational core of the image. Rationality in human beings, once separated from covenantal relationship with God and the shalom he imparts, can appear as anything but rational. Since the fall, humanity has struggled with its own cognitive powers. The capacity to reason in the horizontal realm was not removed by the fall of humanity. The Christian human is not, by being Christian, given a higher IQ than others. The scientist who is Christian *will* by grace be blessed with a richer vocational awareness of their work as being a participation in God's work. They may also be blessed with the wisdom of putting scientific knowledge in wider aesthetic and ethical perspective, and with a priestly capacity to love and praise the Creator in response to what they know. When science is isolated from wider environmental and ethical concerns, and from aesthetics, the nature of the scientist and of humanity as human suffers. Evidences abound that the intelligence of scientists, for example, has often been put to less than rational use. The state of knowledge of science as a whole in the world has not prevented the trends that have led to global warming that threatens our existence. What science has created by way of technology is always a mixed blessing. It either enhances our being human, or distorts it. We celebrate the wonders of our advanced communications, on the one hand, but worry that the use of electronic devices and social media is impoverishing our relationships and altering the state of the deeper centers of our brains, and especially the creative capacity of their inner core.[16] The advent of modernity ushered in mainly by science is not all bad, then. I for one do not want to be premodern again as I enjoy the comforts and cleanliness of life in this age. I am glad of scientific advancement and medications and electric light and PowerPoint and Google . . . in every culture, including modernity, there is the good, the true, and the beautiful. There is also, however, that which is sinister and the advent of global warming is but one evidence of the imbalances of modern scientific humanity that is capable not only of great science but of destroying the whole earth (climate scientist Katherine Hayhoe recently made the comment that if the graphs continue as they are, by 2034 we will be in serious trouble[17]). Christians in science have great potential for being redemptive in this age, and for modeling the *shalom* of a priestly, humble approach to science.

16. See N.V., "The Internet Is Changing the Way You Think: The Difference Engine; Rewiring the Brain." *Economist*, Aug 6, 2010, http://www.economist.com/blogs/babbage/2010/08/internet_changing_way_you_think. See also Brockman, *Is the Internet*; Greenfield, *Mind Change*.

17. Regent College Conference on Creation Care, May 2015.

The Coinherent Ontologies of Theology and Science

All in all, the phenomenon of the cognitive powers of the human being which are reflected in intelligence and creativity, are a source of wonder. This not only images a God of infinite wisdom and his Son who personifies wisdom. It provides an ontology-underlying-epistemology link that seems self-consistent with the existence of a triune God.

Intelligible Universe, Intelligent Humans

The assumption that there is a bridge between ontology and epistemology relies on the presupposition of the goodness of God, and on the reality of the incarnate Logos who created and preserves the objective reality of creation, and mediates its accessibility to humans made in his image and who participate in his life and wisdom, so that what is there is intelligible in a perspicuous way.

This is a remarkable reality. Developing what he means when he affirms that the human capacity for scientific understanding by far exceeds the requirements of mundane evolutionary necessities, Polkinghorne speaks of perspectives from quantum physics. He states,

> There is the subatomic world of quantum physics, remote from direct impact upon our daily lives and requiring for its understanding modes of thought that are completely contrary to those of common sense. . . . In the quantum world entities can be in states which are an unpicturable mixture of "being here" and "being there." Light can sometimes display wave-like properties and sometimes behave as if it were a collection of tiny particles . . . there are the vast domains of cosmic curved space-time, whose geometrical properties are quite different from everyday Euclidean expectation. Yet these counterintuitive regimes have proved to be open to scientific exploration and understanding. The universe is astonishingly rationally transparent to us, exhibiting a remarkable degree of profound intelligibility.[18]

What is even more remarkable is that the unveiling of the secrets of these discoveries in physics is made employing the abstract discipline of mathematics. The Greeks, as we have noted, developed mathematics but not science, for they did not value the empirical. However, mathematics is hugely useful in illuminating what is going on in the sciences. At a very simple level, the progression in increments of 1 upwards in the elements of the Periodic Table, speaks of an intelligible God and our capacity for reading his intelligibility. At a much more sophisticated level, Polkinghorne speaks

18. Polkinghorne, "Trinity and Scientific Reality," in *Blackwell Companion*, 524.

of the wonder of the fact that the intelligibility of the universe is evident from mathematics, which is "the key for unlocking scientific secrets." The correspondence of reality to mathematical formulae arising from within the human mind is indeed remarkable. Polkinghorne states that in fundamental physics, mathematics is an actual technique of discovery. Equations that account for reality are actually sought out and looked for. He states, "Time and again we have found that it is only equations possessing economy and elegance of this kind that will prove to be the basis for theories whose long-term fruitfulness convinces us that they are indeed verisimilitudinous descriptions of physical reality." Then he cites Paul Dirac, whom he considered very highly, and one of the founding fathers of quantum theory, as having once said "that it was more important to have mathematical beauty in one's equation than to have them fit experiment."[19] Not that he undervalued empirical findings. Mathematics without empirics would take us all the way back to the sterile Greek view of science. But Dirac was just convinced that ugly equations could not answer to the reality of what was going on in matter, in creation. Metaphysics, mathematics, must fit the physics, and that usually means beauty.

Is all this "happy coincidence" again? Our point, as Polkinghorne expresses it, is that "theological insight can make cosmic intelligibility itself intelligible."[20] It is an attractive and coherent possibility that a Divine Mind is behind all this and indeed one that is revelatory and perspicuous. That Divine Mind, in accordance with the Augustinian Trinity may be thought of as the great *Logos, the eternal Word* who is the intellect of the Trinity.

Summing up, we may say that the nature of the universe as intelligible reflects on two great Trinitarian realities: (i) a triune God who in the *Logos*, the eternal and incarnate Word, has imparted a beautiful and rational order upon the creation, "without whom was not anything made that was made" (John 1:3), the Son who through creation and revelation speaks with perspicuity; (ii) humans created in the image of the triune God, who are given the capacity to discern order and structure and beauty. The brilliance and creativity of atheistic scientists in their science ironically provides evidence of an intelligent Creator. Their capacities, as we will argue, whether they know it or not, are given by grace and are not a given. They are exercised imperfectly and with varied consequences. At least in a formal sense, their capacities are available only by participation in Christ and by the discernment of the Holy Spirit, who is the Spirit of truth (John 15:26). Christ is in perfect relationship with the Father, as a Man, the *imago* recapitulated, so

---

19. Polkinghorne, *Science and the Trinity*, 63.
20. Polkinghorne, "Trinity and Scientific Reality," in *Blackwell Companion*, 524.

that scientists, in union with him, are able to hold together their intellectual capacity with a profound humility and responsible administration of their theological or scientific knowledge.

Another aspect, however, of the brain capacity of the human person, which is inseparable from intelligence, is the appreciation of beauty and then the expression of it.

Beautiful Universe, Humans Who can Appreciate It

Jonathan Edwards, the Protestant theologian best known for his theology of beauty and aesthetics, actually spoke of God as the "Supreme Harmony of All." He reflects a Trinitarian, relational conception of being. Beauty for Edwards was not an attribute attributed to God, so much as the very essence of the relational harmony of the three persons of the holy Godhead. He spoke of the beautiful society of the Trinity and the infinite consent of the persons to being, as equals.[21] Plurality and specifically "threeness" was not accidental in the Godhead for Edwards. He states, "One alone cannot be excellent" or beautiful. Ontologically, this is who God is. He *is* beauty. This is expressed in the worship of the Psalms: "*Worship the Lord in the beauty of his holiness*" (96:9). "*We beheld his glory*," is how John expresses this aesthetic appreciation of the Son of God in the New Testament (Jn 1:18). Beauty is thus communicated to creation in God's free creative act and by his redemptive work. Creation is an emanation of his glory that then returns to him by way of remanation, in the praise of the saints who see its beauty. The fact that we can as image bearers perceive by grace something of that beauty as we gaze on his matchless incarnate and ascended Son Jesus, and then see traces of that beauty in nature, and then even create beauty in the arts . . . this is an *epistemological* reality shaped by the *ontology*.

I have been privileged to see much beauty in surprising places, and in surprising people, in science. The lines between science and art have blurred when observing intricate organic and organometallic molecules, either natural products or molecules which have been synthesized, often by many steps requiring great creativity and great knowledge. The lines between scientist and artist have merged also when observing some of the great chemistry lecturers I have witnessed communicating with awe-inspiring ease the movement of electrons in ways that answered to their observed reactivities. One such lecturer in organic chemistry at the then University of Rhodesia, now Zimbabwe, was in fact lecturer by day and actor in the city's playhouse

---

21. Edwards, *Miscellany No. 117*, 283.

by night. This truly human person's teaching evoked for me the pinnacle of image-bearing, at least at one level.

b. The Image as Relational

The most fundamental meaning of the image of God, the one which governs the structural and functional dimensions, is that of relationality. Relationality may be understood in two related senses. The first is that God's gracious and covenantal relation to humanity is what stamps the image upon us. It is being in relation to God, the relational God, that constitutes the image. The second is, that, in stamping his image upon us by entering into relationship with us, God created humanity itself to be relational. That is, he created us to model himself, to be intrinsically relational persons who image him precisely as Trinity, that is, as persons-in-relation. This is emphatically symbolized in the creation of persons of opposite sex: "male and female created he them" (Gen 1:27). In this new entity of image-bearing humanity, "each" was equal to the "other," each was equally in the image, and each together were the image, and yet each was not like the other, differentiated with respect to embodied sex traits. In other words, the foundation of the prototypical human self is "the internalized response of the significant other," first the Divine "Other" and then the significant human "other."

Another way to express these two aspects of relationality is first to say that the primal foundation of the human self is the knowledge of God, that is, it is participational. This reflects the prevalent view throughout the history of scholarly Christian tradition that the image of God is a relational concept. This is the capacity given by God to humanity to be in relationship with him ("in the image of God created he them") in an intimate and covenantal way. T. F. Torrance interestingly notes that God is the primary actor when it comes to human beings bearing his image: "It is, fundamentally, God who does the beholding of the image. He images Himself in man."[22]

---

22. T. F. Torrance, *Calvin's Doctrine of Man*, 42, emphasis added. This image-making act by God in establishing of covenant relations does tend to make me lean toward a view that there was a coronation moment or event when *homo sapiens*, having evolved sufficiently to be able to bear the anatomical and physiological capacities required for image-bearing, could receive the image. Once endowed by this coronation event, the historical Adam becomes an image bearer. Other evolutionary creationists prefer the idea of humanity becoming the image of God by way of the evolutionary process. The event view helps to understand why death before the fall, which surely must have existed in animal life for it to evolve, was not a "sin" issue. The precursors to humans died, but this was a normal part of creation. It is only death for humans made in the image of God that is abnormal, and the consequence of sin. Image-bearing Adam and Eve were not intended to die. It is this holistic, including spiritual, death which the last Adam has,

The Coinherent Ontologies of Theology and Science 185

Because of this, second, and by God's grace, each person is a model of God, as a person in relation. That is, each human person is both personal and relational, able to be in relationship to God, and then in relationship with the fellow human, in a manner that reflects equality and otherness ("male and female created he them"), and to be in relationship with creation, as God's representatives in the temple of his creation. *Imago Dei*—or in light of all revelation, *imago Trinitatis*—is the communal nature of persons who are mutually loving and self-giving. The image, then, is the fundamental relational reality that human beings are persons-in-relation with God, each other, and creation. We are therefore an analogy of the relational and personal God. Thus we are remarkably unique persons, and at the same time, we are persons who are profoundly interpersonal. Though we cannot ever be completely mutually internal to one another, we are interdependent on one another. We know a measure of mutual interpenetration. We are able to inter-animate one another.

The importance of the concept and meaning of the term "person" may be measured by the comment of Joseph Ratzinger, who, upon narrating the history of the term *hypostasis* or *persona* through its challenging theological journey, in which it bore the weight of the theological battles toward establishing the doctrine of the hypostatic union and the Trinity, stated that ultimately the "passage from individual to person contains the whole span of the transition from antiquity to Christianity, from Platonism to faith."[23] Its importance lies in the reality that the heritage of the term persons as used for human persons, arises by way of the councils of the church from its usage for Divine persons and the incarnate person of Christ. The ontology that God is three interpenetrated persons, persons of irreducible identity, yet persons in a mutuality of communion, means that the ontology of image-bearing human persons is that we are persons-in-relation. We might therefore expect that our self-understanding as humans (epistemology) to be this: we are neither atomistic individuals, nor a collective of nondescript persons. Rather, we are genuine persons of unique and irreducible identity, with unique DNA and relational history, and yet persons who cannot be persons apart from community, from the moment of conception onward, yet without merger. Both personalism[24] and communion are critical to

---

by his death and resurrection, conquered.

23. Ratzinger, *Introduction to Christianity*, 160.

24. Personalism is a broad movement with many forms. Over against the de-personalizing philosophies of Enlightenment rationalism, Hegelian absolute idealism, as well as individualism and political collectivism, and evolutionary determinism, personalism has sought to vindicate the importance the human person. The contribution of Scottish philosopher John Macmurray (1891–1976) to a personalism that reflects the

defining humanity. The biblical and Christian tradition validates the nature and dignity of each human person, and requires personal response to God in salvation and worship. But equally, these traditions recognize the communal nature and orientation of the human person. From a biblical perspective, communal means first and foremost being communal in the community in Christ, that is ecclesial. However, given that all humanity is image-bearing, it is innately communal. We might expect that within the literature of anthropology and sociology and psychology, there might be theories that postulate a consonant view of the nature of the human person as a social self, or as an "interpersonal self." This is indeed the case.

The idea of an interpersonal self has been advocated in the field of psychology by Scottish psychologist Ronald Fairbairn, for example. Whereas Freud identified people in a subject's environment with the term "object"—e.g., to identify a person as the "object" of a drive, so that infants developed around these drives—Fairbairn posited that human infants were not seeking the satisfaction of drives, but rather actually seeking the satisfaction that comes in relation to real others. From birth, and even before it, we are formed by the other. Daniel Price has drawn an interesting correlation between Karl Barth's analogy of relations and the object relations theory of human development developed by Fairbairn.[25] Fairbairn challenges Freud's individualistic determinism, with respect to the psychological understanding of humanity, with the determinative impact of key human interactions with others in the development of the person.[26]

In the psychoanalytic tradition, Harry Stack Sullivan also proposed the idea of an interpersonal self,[27] and pastoral theologian David Switzer built on this. Switzer describes the development of the self in a growing child as she interrelates with her family and environment.[28] The proposal of the interpersonal self and attachment theory by John Bowlby,[29] reflects also an epistemology which could be undergirded by an ontology in God and humanity. Understanding who God is and therefore who we are, in the spirit of Calvin's double-knowledge, is crucial to an awareness of what human beings are.

Trinitarian tradition of persons in relation was considerable and has played a role in the resurgence of Trinitarian theology. See Macmurray, *Self as Agent*; *Persons in Relation*.

25. See Price, *Karl Barth's Anthropology*.
26. Price, "Issues Related to Human Nature," 170–80.
27. See Sullivan, *Interpersonal Theory*, vol. 1, ch. 1.
28. Switzer, *Dynamics of Grief*, 83.
29. Bowlby, *Attachment*; *Loss*; *Separation*; *Making and Breaking*; *Secure Base*.

The coinherent realities of the Trinity have been applied in pastoral counselling also, to describe a healthy relationship between pastor and counselee. David Cunningham's language of polyphony describes the coinherence of oneness and threeness within the Trinity as "simultaneous, non-excluding difference: that is, more than one note is played at a time, and none of these notes is so dominant that it renders another mute."[30] Thus, as opposed to a zero-sum game, Cunningham makes the observation that "a theological perspective informed by polyphony would challenge any view that claims that any two contrastive categories must necessarily work against each other."[31] Building on this and the relational ontology of Colin Gunton, Neil Pembroke[32] states that the "fundamental polyphonic categories are unity and difference."[33] He extrapolates this to refer to the "nearness and differentiation" in a pastoral relationship (which might equally be extended to all healthy relationships). He argues that "effective pastoral counseling involves both moving in close through empathy and acceptance, and creating appropriate distance through a process that Martin Buber refers to as confirmation." More precisely, Pembroke states that "effective pastoral caregivers know when and how to move in close, and when and how to create appropriate distance." He surmises that "a very important pastoral art . . . is managing the interpersonal space."[34] Drawing near is facilitated through empathy and acceptance; moving out facilitates confrontation.

Once again, care must be taken. The image is just that and no more. It is true by way of analogy and not univocity. The correspondence between God and humanity, though remarkable in a qualitative way, is not exact in a number of ways. The coinherence of Divine persons is such that the Son is omnipresent, because he is in the Father, and the Father is in him, whereas with human creatures, they are only to be found in separate determinate localities. Similarly, arguing that perichoresis refers to the reciprocal interiority of the Divine persons, Miroslav Volf rightly observes that, in a strict sense, "there can be no correspondence to the interiority of the divine persons at a human level. Another human self cannot be internal to my own self as subject of action. Human persons are always external to one another as subjects."[35] So the indwelling of other persons is an exclusive prerogative of God. However, in a constructive way, we maintain, with Volf, that

30. Cunningham, *These Three*, 128.
31. Ibid., 131.
32. Pembroke, "Space in the Trinity," 3.1–10.
33. Ibid., 3.2.
34. Ibid., 3.1.
35. Volf, *After Our Likeness*, 208–13.

perichoresis is reflected at the ecclesial level with respect to the interiority of personal characteristics. Bearing this distinction in mind, we can still, by way of an analogy of faith or relations (which we explain later), that is validated by the incarnation, retain the concept. As Graham Buxton has indicated, beyond the early christological appropriation of the word, the richness of the term perichoresis may be appreciated when we consider that, throughout the history of Christian thought, it "provides a way of attempting to express how unity and distinction are combined in the Trinity, in the incarnate Logos and in creation as reunited with God."[36]

All in all, in light of the relational nature of human persons, it seems safe to conclude that the sentiments expressed by DNA scientist Francis Crick in the assertion, "You are nothing but a pack of neurons,"[37] is patently reductionistic. If genes may be selfish in general, and this has been contested, as we have noted, what constitutes the fullness of a human person fully alive, is a person who loves, and who loves sacrificially in truly altruistic ways.

Relation as the Basis for the Imago?

The ordering of relationship and reason as definitive of the image of God has been the source of great controversy, in particular between the Catholic and Protestant traditions.

As signaled earlier, we need to address the issue of how sin or fallenness has affected the relational, rational and vocationally significant image of God. In what sense are we to understand the analogy between God and humanity expressed in the "image of God" concept, in light of both the metaphysical remove between deity and humanity, and the sinfulness of humanity?

The being of God and that of creation, including humanity with its capacity for reason, are not in the same category, since his being is of a transcendent order. This is what enables God to create matter without being compromised in his being. Creation is, of course, presupposed in the doctrine of the incarnation. In turn, historically speaking, the doctrine of the incarnation precipitated the doctrine of creation *ex nihilo* (the creation is distinct from the essence of God, and thus could not have been made out of his being, thus, of necessity, it must have been created out of nothing) in that it allows a distinction between God and creation in the act of God's creation, while insisting that the infinite and transcendent God can be immanent to creation without compromising his Divine essence. The imaging

---

36. Harrison, "Perichoresis in the Greek Fathers," 53–65.
37. Crick, *Astonishing Hypothesis*.

or the analogy between God and humanity must therefore come by way of the incarnation of Christ. How are we to understand the "being" of creation, and of humanity, if not in a univocal way, and how do humans know God? The incarnational answer just offered is, in sum, the distinctively Protestant one, sometimes called the analogy of faith or relations or *adventus*.

In Catholic theology, by contrast, this question was answered by the notion of analogy, and in particular, the *analogia entis* or analogy of being. Affirmed at the Fourth Lateran Council (AD 1215), it was then developed notably by Polish Jesuit Erich Pryzwara. In essence, this concept affirms an ontological correspondence between God and humanity which results in the noetic capacity of human persons to know God. It is a consequence of the person and work of Christ as *Logos* who grants reason (*logos*) to all human beings, who can in fact reason their way to God. These two components of the *analogia entis*, the ontic and the noetic, have, within the Thomist and Catholic tradition been located in the created state in the image of God. Thus our ontic correspondence to God in this original created state involved a noetic correspondence understood as reason, which remained intact after the fall. Humans are therefore considered to be free to think metaphysically from their creaturely state to God.

In Protestant theology, the analogy is stressed to be one of faith (*fidei*) or faithfulness or relations (*relationis*), rather than of being. To be more precise, however, it is not so much that an analogy of being is denied, but rather that the *source* of the analogy of being is different in the Protestant heritage. This tradition has considered the fall to be more radical, and has considered the analogy between God and humanity to be expressed in Christ alone, the one human for all humanity, in whom true correspondence exists between God and humanity, and through whom alone, believing humanity recovers the analogy. The real basis of analogy is Christ *the* human, not the old humanity which is fallen, and which merely anticipated the unfallen Adam.[38]

Thus, in contrast with the *analogia entis* school of thought, the Protestant Barth-Jüngel-Spencer[39] tradition looks to Christ first. The *entis* school of thought emphasizes *reason* as the core meaning of the image of God (*imago Dei*) in humanity in a manner that is abstracted from the *imago Christi*, that is Jesus Christ, the *eschatos* Adam, the prototypical man for humanity, who is the image of the invisible God, and who in grace confers this upon all in the believing covenantal community of faith.

---

38. The point has been made by David Congdon that the analogy of being was not needed to hold together the transcendence and immanence of God, or the mysticism and subjectivism that goes with each, because they are held together in Christ, Immanuel, God with us. Congdon, "Who's Afraid of the *Analogia Entis*?"

39. Spencer, *Analogy of Faith*.

It is easy to see then why another term for *analogia fidei* is *analogia relationis*. The latter term came originally from Bonhoeffer though it was Barth who developed it. As Barth scholar Bruce McCormack has noted,[40] Barth could understandably have reacted to the *analogia entis* once some of his theological colleagues embraced nationalist ideologies on the basis of this kind of understanding of human capacity. But Barth's corrective preceded this. The *analogia entis* was understood "as a given, created continuity between the being of God and the being of the creature, by virtue of which the creature could understand herself as 'open upward,' that is, as containing within herself an abiding revelation that made the knowledge of God a human possibility."[41] Barth as a Reformed theologian was against such a notion, and as McCormack has suggested he could have used the language of *entis* as *corrected* by the *analogia fidei*. "The true *analogia entis* is the consequence of a rightly ordered understanding of the *analogia fidei*,"[42] as McCormack noted, to emphasize the important reality that the *analogia fidei* does in fact have ontological implications. In fact, to avoid all misunderstanding, Barth chose to avoid the use of *entis* all together. As McCormack notes: "In the 1929 essay, Barth rejected Pryzwara's elaboration of the *analogia entis*. . . . Against Pryzwara's view, Barth held that human beings can know a great deal of themselves, but they cannot know that they are *creatures* in the strict theological sense of the term."[43] He cites Barth's *The Holy Spirit and the Christian Life* directly in support:

> If the creature is to be strictly understood as a reality willed and placed by God in distinction from God's own reality, that is to say, as the wonder of a reality which by the power of God's love, has a place and persistence alongside God's own reality, then the continuity between God and it (the true *analogia entis*, by virtue of which he, the uncreated Spirit, can be revealed to the created spirit)—this continuity cannot belong to the creature itself but only to the Creator *in his relation* to the creature.[44]

McCormack states in light of the stress Barth places on the Creator "in his relation" to the creature, that this "means that the true *analogia entis* must be understood to be the consequence of a dynamic relation of God to

---

40. McCormack, review of *The Holy Spirit and the Christian Life*, 312–14.
41. Ibid., 312.
42. Ibid.
43. Ibid.
44. Barth, *Holy Spirit and the Christian Life*, 5.

the creature, a relation that is never simply a given (a *datum*) but is always, in every moment, to be given (a *dandum*)."[45] Thus, he concludes,

> the true *analogia entis* is never a predicate of the creature but is rather a predicate of God's ongoing act of relating to the creature. It is a relationship of correspondence between the act in which God has his being (grace) and the act in which the creature has her being (obedience as the response to grace). Being, in this view, is a function of decision and act and not the other way around (as occurred in Catholic theology).[46]

As gestured by McCormack, the *basis* for the analogy is what is at stake. Barth insisted on the close relationship between God's creation and his covenant, and in this understanding, the analogy between God and humanity (and creation), between image (and the trace) is a gift, not a given. As Barth himself avowed, the knowledge of God is not in "Platonic fashion . . . a reminiscence, as Ancient Beauty."[47] Barth is referring critically here to Augustine's description of conversion as if it were the recalling of a memory from an innate knowledge of God. A rebuttal offered by the *entis* tradition has been that creation is itself a gift of grace. However the analogy is not innate, but is based on relationship initiated by God in his gracious covenant relations. "There is," as Barth says, "no original endowment in the human creature, but only . . . a second marvel of God's love, as the inconceivable, undeserved, divine bestowal on his creature."[48] This for Barth is an outflow of the deity and sovereignty of the Holy Spirit who creates the continuity between God and humanity, applying what has been accomplished in Christ for humanity, by the God who has thereby shown himself to be *for* humanity. Grace, says Barth, is "ever and in all relations God's *deed* and *act*."[49]

In this vein, another of Barth's disciples, Jüngel, radicalizing and yet correcting Barth at the same time (on the transcendence front), moves constructively to reorient the discussion by way of what he called the *analogia adventus*.[50] That, is, he made the advent of Jesus Christ the norm for understanding God's being and human being, and the nature of the God-human relation. The analogy must really find its center in the one mediator between God and the one true man, the man Christ Jesus. It is first the *analogia*

45. McCormack, review of *The Holy Spirit and the Christian Life*, 313.
46. Ibid.
47. Barth, *Holy Spirit and the Christian Life*, 5.
48. Ibid.
49. Ibid.
50. For a full treatment of the work of Jüngel and Barth with respect to the analogy of being and the analogy of faith, see Spencer, *Analogy of Faith*.

Christi, in other words, not first the analogy of general humanity. It does however become the *analogia entis* for humans in Christ, that is, for those who believe (*analogia fidei*), that is those in union with Christ, who are in correspondence with Christ and with God.

Another crucial issue in this debate has to do with mediation, the Protestant critique being that the "analogy of being" viewpoint seems to foster a mediator other than the one mediator, Christ Jesus, who alone created and reconciled humanity to God and brings those who exercise faith into ontological correspondence with God. In this vein, as Congdon states, we are "not free to reason our way to God apart from the way, the truth and the life." His "role of mediation encompasses our reason but not apart from our need for a redeemer . . . in Christ alone there exists an analogy."[51] Or to say this another way, any analogy between God and humanity/creation that does not need the incarnation is suspect. What Barth and those who came under his influence objected to was the failure of the *entis* viewpoint to understand humanity in light of the person of the one man for humanity, Jesus Christ. Thus the Barthian school of thought expressed as *analogia fidei* insisted that ontic and noetic correspondence to God is found in Christ alone, or, to put it another way, our being in the image of God is found in Christ alone. As Congdon has provocatively stated, "the *imago Dei* is not a mediator between God and humanity apart from the sole image of God, Jesus Christ." Scholars who favor the *analogia entis* object at this point that the *analogia entis* was never believed to be salvific, and that multiple mediations are a misunderstanding of this position. The *analogia entis* is "not a rival but a complement to Christ set up by Christ that anticipates Christ and is meaningless without Christ."[52] Nevertheless, the *analogia adventus fidei* expresses with greater clarity that we are, as Congdon avers, "in the *imago Dei* only insofar as we conform to the *imago Christi*, and thus we exist in analogical correspondence to God in that God existentially conforms our being in correspondence to Christ."[53] He continues by insisting that "the doctrine of the analogy in light of this Christological reformulation affirms our true humanity and our certain knowledge of God in light of God's self-revelation in Jesus Christ." He concludes appropriately that the "doctrine of analogy is thus a correlate of Christology."[54]

In sum, the faith in reason of the *analogia entis* viewpoint, grounded in Aristotelian and Thomistic logic, stands over against the Protestant *analogia*

---

51. Congdon, "Who's Afraid of the *Analogia Entis*?"
52. Milliner, "Who's Afraid of the Analogia Entis?"
53. Congdon, "Who's Afraid of the *Analogia Entis*?"
54. Ibid.

adventus fidei viewpoint which has as its starting point not reason, but the revelation of God in Christ. But a number of questions arise from these deliberations for scientists and for the practice of science and its relationship to theology.

What then shall we make of humanity and specifically scientists, who are not Christian? If only those of the covenantal faith community are in correspondence with God and reflect his image, what are we to do with the reality that scientists manifest a brilliance of reason irrespective of whether they have Christian faith or not? And how is the Christian to engage in a public square where Christian convictions are not welcome, and make sense of their Christian ethics around science or in general, to their fellow human? Would not this appear to favor the *analogia entis* position? Would it not make sense to appeal to reason, on the grounds that all humans can reason their way to God, and by some understanding of natural law, arrive at Christian ethics, or a Christian way of seeing science?

In the Calvinist tradition, it has always since Calvin been believed that the image of God was not totally destroyed by the fall. It was effaced in its material sense, not erased. Emil Brunner made a distinction between the *formal* capacity all humans have by nature to receive revelation and to have a sense of "oughtness," and the *material* capacity which they do not have, apart from grace. Barth's concern was that to acknowledge even a formal capacity was to pave the way for natural theologies including the Nazi nationalistic one. Trevor Hart's resolution that both could have agreed that humans apart from grace have the "capacity to receive the capacity" for receiving revelation by grace is helpful. In fact, what is so surprising about this Barth-Brunner debate is that while Barth is adamant that nature and all purely human philosophies and religion have come under the sentence of death in Christ crucified, he does in fact affirm the universality of grace through God's redeeming action in Christ. Thus in fact by means of the analogy of relations (*analogia relationis*), that is, by the constant outpouring of grace from God to humanity which is in relation to God in Christ, (rather than the Catholic notion of the analogy of being), Barth can in fact affirm that which is good in human culture, even if human nature cannot save itself.

What is also ironic in this debate is that Barth, along with Bonhoeffer, was anxious that the church speak out and engage ethically in the public and political arena. On what basis could he hope for that to have any influence if there was no capacity for the population to hear? For Barth the incarnation of Christ played a critical role in theology, including anthropology. Barth's confidence to engage his culture was not based so much on creational grounds, or on the basis of any capacity related to natural law, but rather on the basis of the reaffirmation of creation by the incarnation and resurrection of Jesus. It was on the basis, not of nature, but the gospel of the incarnation of the Son, who alone was the true human *imago Dei* and who by grace has brought all humanity into the Godhead in a formal and representativesense. God has become a neighbor to humanity in that his Son has become fully human. It is on the basis of the "ethic of neighbor" that Barth can engage the world. It was the "neighbor concept" in Barth which for him meant that Christians could engage in the public arena. As Ray Anderson states: "One implication of Barth's theological ethics is that Christians can and ought to be able to participate in the setting of moral agendas and even in morally committed actions that affect the social and public lives of human beings, side by side with those committed to a different theology of the church and with a different ideological view of political and economic structure."[55]

Barth was in fact, no despiser of human culture. His love of the music of Mozart is well known.[56] It was his custom to listen to Mozart most days prior to setting about his theological writing and the form of his magisterial *Church Dogmatics* reflects the stylistic patterns of Mozart's music. However, it was on a christological and gospel basis that he could affirm what was positive in human culture, including the practice and findings of science. We may affirm the positive aspects of culture as remnants of the *imago Dei* imparted by God to all humanity and not erased by the fall, as in Brunner, or, we may do so as in Barth, on the basis of the grace of God granted to humanity as a consequence of the entering into humanity of his Son in his incarnation, and by virtue of the formal justification of humanity in his vicarious humanity. The consequences are the same. We affirm the positive dynamics in the arts and the sciences, but, along with Barth, we must also be fully aware of the darker side of humanity and of its particular manifestations in science. It has to be conceded that Barth's overly pessimistic evaluation of the image of God in humanity may have hindered his interest in science. His aversion to natural theology did not negate his rich doctrine of creation and the incarnation, but as we have noted, it took T. F. Torrance to build a bridge to science and a robust theology/science relation that Barth did not cross. Torrance did this precisely by means of the incarnation.

---

55. Anderson, *Shape of Practical Theology*, 153–54.

56. "There is one aspect of Barth's personality that is reflected in his writing. He was very fond of music, a performer of sorts on the violin, and a passionate devotee of the music of Mozart. He began every day by listening to a piece by Mozart on his hi-fi, and when he went to his desk to work on the *Church Dogmatics*, the effect carried over; for often, especially in the later volumes, the thesis at the head of the section is treated as a theme, and the exposition consists of a series of variations on it, rather than a demonstration of it by discursive reasoning." Hendry, review of *Karl Barth, His Life*.

The Coinherent Ontologies of Theology and Science 195

What then of *reason* in particular? A point of relevance for science here is that the followers of *analogia fidei* (and then *entis*) are not saying that reason is not involved in the image of God reality. As expressed, the understanding of the nature of the *imago* is polyvalent and includes relationality (ontological) as primary, and then reason (ontological) and image-bearing functions like work, in the context and as guided by relationality. The *fidei* position simply stresses that the notion of relationality with God is crucial if reason is to work within the covenantal framework, and if reason expressed in science and technology is to bring shalom to the creation. The history of the human race since the discovery of science is very much a mixed bag in this regard. The reason which remains post-fall is not always tempered by the covenantal relations expressed by God at the inception of image-bearing human life. We as a human race must confess that the wonders of modern medicine and the technology that sends rovers to Mars, reflective of image-bearing as they are, must be seen alongside the atomic bombs of Hiroshima and Nagasaki, and the depletion of the ozone layer and global warming that now threatens the planet. The reason deficit in very smart humanity is not with respect to IQ, but it has to do rather with alienation from God, and with participating in his work of new creation, in such a way that the planet as a whole flourishes. The *analogia fidei* tradition wishes to emphasize this. And scientists who are non-Christian or even anti-Christian, can by virtue of the fact that they bear the image in a formal and ontological manner often have a concern for the shalom of creation or "nature" as they may prefer, and be as environmentally and socially conscious as any Christian. So what difference does it make to be a person of faith, in covenantal relationship, receiving the fullness of the image of God, or acting out the *analogia adventus fidei*? The Christian has a profound awareness that, as Hanby has shown, science is much more than the facticity that naturalism or scientism assumes it to be. It reveals act and it evokes wonder as a result. The scientist who is a thoughtful Christian sees more. And science is more than mere knowledge. It reflects the wisdom of the Creator Christ. The Christian has an orientation to shalom that is primary in their contextualizing of the science they are engaged in. The Christian has a humble orientation toward her discoveries, for she knows whose wisdom and beauty is being revealed in her fields of study. The Christian has a priestly orientation, recognizing that humanity has been charged by God, with Christ, through the Spirit, with knowing creation in order to steward it, and to offer her work back to God as a priestly offering. And, above all, the Christian in science, as a priest who, in the words of Loren Wilkinson, gives creation a voice, offers worship to the God who created and sustains his creation.

c. The Image as Functional—Vocation

There is a third aspect of the meaning of the image of God that is expressed in the early chapters of Genesis which then becomes implicit in the whole canon of Scripture. This is the functional dimension, which has to do with the created human's work and its significance. This is a theology of work, echoing the work of the Creator. Work in relationship with him, and in relationship with fellow humanity and the whole creation. No sooner are the image-imparting words out of the Divine endower uttered than he is instructing the first human persons about their vocation to continue the work of creation he had begun: "*God blessed them and said to them, 'Be fruitful and increase in number; fill the earth and subdue it. Rule over the fish in the sea and the birds in the sky and over every living creature that moves on the ground'*" (Gen 1:28).

The functional builds on the structural or intellectual aspect, or the capacity of the human image bearer for self-reflection. It is what enables him and her to function, and to evaluate as to the goodness of the work. The joy in the carrying out of the functional and the shalom that accrues in its outcome is also very much dependent on the relational dimension of the image. In relationship, in participation with God, work would bring glory to God, joy and a sense of significance to the worker, and it would result in the flourishing of the fellow human and the creation. This in essence is the core of the Christian theology of work, including scientific work. It is instructive that an integral part of human being is human doing, just as the being and act of God cannot be separated. There is a popular ideal that one sometimes hears preached in churches by well-meaning preachers, that we simply need to focus on being, or on who we are, or who we are in Christ. Don't derive your worth from what you do, but from who you are! These are well-meant words. Being probably comes before doing and must infuse it. And undue reliance on our work to make us feel significant is problematic and usually underlies workaholism. But it is important to emphasize that there is no such thing as being without doing. Work is a vital aspect of human being that reflects a Creator who worked and who marked the human calendar with a six-day work and one-day Sabbath rest pattern. The undue emphasis on being that neglects the doing is actually a modern form of Gnosticism. One of the reasons unemployment and firings hurt so much is that a crucial piece of the human make-up that reflects our triune Creator and Redeemer and Consummator is the ability to work.

Implicit in the functional or vocational aspect of the *imago* is the fact that the creation described in Genesis 1 was good, even very good, but that it was not yet perfected, not yet complete. The descriptor "good" did not mean that creation arrived at its "final destination," because God in fact chose to build change into its very fabric.[57] Thus, human beings, created into God's image as his coworkers, were called to transform untamed nature into a flourishing social environment.[58] God thus created a role for humanity *in participation with himself* in its management and perfection. That is, there is a required role of image-bearing humans as receivers of the baton in creation, and the role of science comes within this, as we have already indicated. The eschatological fulfillment of creation is of course in a primary sense found in Christ, but as humans in Christ, the image is recapitulated. It is thus entirely fitting that Christians, those in Christ, might take their place as priests of creation, pursuing its understanding, utilizing its resources, and managing it within the wider creation. This is an enterprise most fitting for human persons fully alive! There is a Christian theology of vocation which I believe is crucial for the healthy functioning of scientists. They are participating in God's work in the world in their endeavors. Scientific research can be brutally difficult, lonely and fraught with doubting with respect to its significance. Scientists need a sense of vocation, a sense that they are doing what it is humans are intended to do—to participate in creation, to do so by seeking to understand it. Their work itself is missional. There is still a need for the overcoming of dualism in the church with respect to the clergy-laity distinction. Theology gives a sense of vocation to the scientist and it is a lofty one. To be priests of Christ's creation. *To reflect the under-the-iceberg vocation of God in our above-the-iceberg work in creation.*

Much has been made in recent biblical/theological scholarship of the importance of *history* in the outworking of the gospel. Thus, the gospel narrative according to a Kuyperian way of speaking, follows the events of creation, the fall, redemption or reconciliation of creation, and consummation of creation. Along with this has come an emphasis on valuing *creation* and keeping the creation and redemption of humanity and the cosmos together. The gospel is not a gospel of evacuation. The gospel entails a doctrine of creation in which *creation matters*. It matters because it is the product of God's creating action; it matters because it has been pronounced good by the Divine Creator; it matters because it has been entered into in the incarnation of the Son, and because by his resurrection, Christ has reaffirmed the creation. The *creatio ex nihilo* and the *creatio continua* (continuing creative activity) have led through the advent of the Christ of creation to the *creatio ex vetere* (transformation of the old creation) in which humanity, in Christ, the last Adam, can participate. The Christian faith, in light of God's

---

57. Provan, *Seriously Dangerous*, 283.
58. Mouw, *When the Kings Come Marching*, 35.

estimation of and purpose for creation, should foster the pursuit of science with the care of creation in mind. Furthermore, the cultural mandate by which God passed on the baton of creating to his image bearers (for it was good but not perfect), positively urges the Christian in the journey towards being restored and redeemed in order to become more fully human, to do so according to particular vocations. This includes being scientists committed to understanding creation, to being priests of creation, giving creation a voice; to be the artists who in their painting and sculpting take their cue from the God of triune beauty who has created a beautiful world; to be the musicians in particular emanating sound that reflects the "Supreme Harmony of All."

However, in addition to these in vogue *historical* and *creational* commitments of the Christian faith, in order to give perspective to the value of human work, I want to focus on what happens in pre-history and pre-creation. For this is where the gospel begins. It begins in the eternal love of the triune Godhead, it begins in the electing of God to create, to create humanity, and to be *for* humanity, in fact for *sinful* humanity. I am not referring to a secret decretive act of God, by means of which some individuals are chosen for salvation and some for perdition. I speak rather of the electing of God in eternity past, within the covenanting purpose of God, to choose the Son to become human, and to act vicariously for that humanity. In the premundane election by God (in which the Son participated, as God) God the Son was elected and elected specifically to enter into sinful humanity, to enter into the forsakenness of the Divine "No" of humanity's sinfulness on the cross, and then into the Divine "Yes" of the resurrection in which humanity finds its reality and function as image-bearing persons, scientists and artists and economists. The good news is that because of the incarnation and resurrection, we can be assured that God has elected to be for humanity. Because the One really real Human, Jesus Christ, is in fact the last Adam, and because his covenant people with him are together with him that communal last Adam, humanity in Christ has not only been redeemed and reconciled, but participates together in the human pursuit given to image-bearers of Yahweh. In the present time they are to care for creation, to probe its secrets, to be creative as God is creative, and to participate in the *creatio ex vetere*, perceiving the prods of the Spirit toward the consummation.

All of this is as graced humans, humans elect in Christ, in participation with Christ, who can only study any of these disciplines as humans *engraced*, and with the ideal that each pursues their vocation in gratitude. The two acts of God, election and revelation, work to establish humanity in the reality of grace, which creates the possibility of human reciprocity in gratitude. Humanity thus is *ontologically grounded* in the realities of Divine grace and the truly human response of gratitude. This act of gratitude is a uniquely human reality. It can be uniquely directed to God in both disciplines, science and theology. In this way, the encounter of grace opens the door for human freedom and human responsibility. These two realities, lived in obedience to the Word of God—as a result of God's invocation—form the very basis of an ontological description of humanity that is true to our reality as created by the Creator God. This ontological description is not the sum of human self-understanding but the beginning of it. This is what humanity is without separating humanity from creation or the Creator.

Karl Barth freely admitted that many forms of anthropological understanding derived from sociology, psychology, biology, existential philosophy, naturalism and evolutionary science hold some significance for "in their limits they may well be accurate and important."[59] They all describe humanity in its uniqueness, based on the unique methodological features of each field of study. These descriptions can be helpful, useful and accurate, but they cannot fully describe humanity, he insisted. For they are "all bracketed, and no decisive enlightenment about man is to be expected from within these brackets, but only from a source outside. This source is God."[60] True humanity cannot be understood apart from God. To remove the Creator from the definition of humanity, means to remove the foundation of what humanity is. Barth suggests that if "we think of man in isolation from and independence of God, we are no longer thinking about real man."[61] For Barth humanity exists because of the election of God and only in relationship with God. Outside of this relationship humanity ceases to be human. The significance of this relationship means that it "is not peripheral but central, not incidental but essential to that which makes him a real man, himself."[62] Evolutionary understandings of humanity that pay particular attention to humanity's environment are no doubt helpful in understanding humanity. But, as Barth states, "if man does not know himself already, long before his attention is directed to these phenomena, he will be blind even though he sees. In face and in spite of these phenomena he will always look on the wrong side. He will always think with the animal and the rest of creation generally."[63] The created and reaffirmed nature of the human person as made in the Divine image answers the "who" question and it is crucial to all humble scholarship, be it scientific of theological. The *subject* in the

59. Barth, *CD* III/2, 122.
60. Ibid.
61. Ibid., 123.
62. Ibid.
63. Ibid., 90.

disciplines is the same, image-bearing humanity with divinely endowed capacities and hopefully, relationship with the Creator that forms the character that bears the capacities, and guides their use. I reiterate, scientists themselves with all their brilliance and creativity strike me as anthropological evidence of the God they sometimes deny.

THE IMAGE-BEARING, PRIESTLY, COINHERENT VOCATION OF THE SCIENTIST AND THE THEOLOGIAN

It is perhaps easier to imagine that theologians might be image-bearing, priestly and coinherent persons in their vocation. T. F. Torrance spoke of theology in coinherent terms. He stated that it is "as our communion with God the Father through Christ and in the Spirit is founded in and shares in the inner Trinitarian consubstantial or homoousial communion of the Father, Son and Holy Spirit, that the subjectively-given pole of conceptuality is constantly purified and refined under the searching light and quickening power of the objectively-given pole of divine revelation." It was within this communion and that polarity that "Christian theology becomes what essentially is and ought always to be, *logike latreia*, rational worship of God."[64] But given that science is coinherent within theology, and contributes to an encyclopedic theology, Torrance had no difficulty in saying that correspondingly, and in accordance with its own peculiar subject matter and techniques and levels, scientists in each science too can become participants in the rational priestly worship of God, by means of his Son by whom and through whom all things are made, and in whom, all priestliness is recapitulated, through the work of the Holy Spirit.

The value and dignity of a scientist is remarkable. The vocation of the scientist is a coinherent one, in more than one way. Every Christian ought to be a scientist, if only as an amateur. It is part of the mission of the whole people of God not only to make disciples, as in the Great Commission, and to love God and the near and distant neighbor as in the Great Commandment, but to love creation, to be curious about it, and to work within it for the good of neighbor and creation. Even more so, as image bearer, the professional scientist functions in participation with God and his ongoing work in the world for humanity, just as the triune God is for humanity, and for creation's good, just as God made creation good. The scientist echoes the triune God as she participates in the life and work of Christ, the last Adam, in her work. She echoes his intelligence, his industry, his creativity. And as part of the human race entrusted with knowing the secrets of

---

64. T. F. Torrance, "Theological Realism," 193.

creation's structures and functions, the scientist acts on behalf of a creation that cannot speak, and becomes the voice for the voiceless creation. She gives creation a voice.

To affirm that equal validity and honor of the theologian and the scientist is not to say that all subject material is of equal stature. Building on Einstein and Polanyi, Torrance considered hierarchical structures to be crucial for knowledge of being, or the ontology beneath the epistemology. For Einstein, the hierarchical structure which could be applied to each science was made up of the physical, the theoretical and the meta-theoretical. Polanyi went further and proposed a hierarchy of sciences, with higher level sciences having influence over those at lower level, a principle which Torrance called "coherent integration from above." This stood in contrast with the Newtonian manner of a mechanistic reading of the lower levels up to the higher. Interestingly, in this regard, Einstein, Polanyi and Torrance all reflected the methodological insights of Duns Scotus and Kurt Gödel.[65] Applying this to theology as the theological science, Torrance claimed for theology the highest level of knowing in light of its object of study, the triune God, and thus, in a modern era, recapitulated a defense of theology as the queen of the sciences.

This stratification which reveals objective structures, or "the back-side of reality,"[66] within theological science itself entailed three categories or levels: (i) the evangelical and doxological level or "experiential apprehension" level whose focal point is the encounter with Jesus Christ, both personally and in the church's worship and life, its *kerygma* and *didache*—this apprehension of the *evangelical Trinity* is a largely intuitive apprehension of God's self-revelation (an incipient theology)[67] . . . it is the essential foundation for all theological reflection that will follow it; (ii) the theological level in which the *economic Trinity* is encountered and explored, the heuristic device connecting the first and second levels being the *homoousion*; and (iii) the higher theological level, the *ontological Trinity*, which is the decisive point for theological science for Torrance, where the "objective structures of reality"[68] exist. By means of what we know of the Father, Son and Holy Spirit in the economy, Torrance states that "we seek to formulate in forms of thought and speech the hypostatic, *homoousial*, perichoretic relations in the eternal, dynamic Communion in loving and being loved of the three Divine

---

65. T. F. Torrance, "Intuitive and Abstractive," 291–305, and *Space, Time*, 86–90.
66. T. F. Torrance, "Stratification of Truth," 147.
67. T. F. Torrance, *Christian Doctrine of God*, 89.
68. T. F. Torrance, *Reality and Scientific Theology*, 144–47.

Persons which God is."[69] We may conclude that the personal freedom and the relational communion of humanity echo loudly the coinherent relationship of the three Divine persons-in-communion of the Trinity, as illustrated through the primary categories that define the image of God: reason, relationality and creative vocation. We may also gesture toward the concomitant likelihood that the common image-bearing nature of theologians and scientists with their received intelligence, the common source of all revelation (general and special) in the One God in Christ, and the common participation in God of both theologians and scientists, all point toward the conclusion that theology and science as disciplines may be coinherent. It is particularly the christological fulfillment of the *imago Dei* as *imago Trinitatis* for those who participate in Christ, God become human, which points firmly toward the coinherence of science within theology, for such humans are by the gospel enabled to participate in his reign over all creation, which includes knowing it in order to manage it. Christ, the eternal Creator as God, has as God become man in order to become the image of God, reigning for God and in union with the triune God (theology) so that humanity in him might be all it was intended to be, which includes earth-keeping and therefore science. The human who participates in Christ participates in the life of God, which includes the life of the mind. This is theology. Equally, the human who participates in Christ participates in his rule of the earth, which requires attentiveness to creation and knowledge of it, in science. And such a human in Christ brings all she discovers of the life of God (theology) to bear on all she learns of life with the image-bearing Christ as earth-keeper (in science), and all she learns of the latter she brings to bear on the former.

---

69. T. F. Torrance, *Christian Doctrine of God*, 109.

Chapter 8

Trinitarian Theology as the "Theory of Everything" and Its Practice

Bringing Epistemology and Ontology Together

Wherefore with my utmost art, I will sing Thee,
And the cream of all my heart I will bring Thee...
Sev'n whole days, not one in sev'n I will praise thee;
In my heart, though not in heav'n, I can raise Thee.
Small it is, in this poor sort to enrol Thee:
E'en eternity's too short to extol Thee.

GEORGE HERBERT (1593–1633)

IN THIS CHAPTER WE pull together what we have learned about the coinherence of the triune God and the coinherence of the Divine nature of the incarnate Christ with created humanity, as these have manifested themselves in the tradition; what we have learned also of the echoes of coinherence in humanity as image, and in nonhuman creation, as trace, thus leading to our proposal concerning the coinherence of Trinitarian theology and science with respect to the history of ideas, epistemology and ontology. In light of this we offer support for the audacious claim made by Polkinghorne that "a deeply satisfying intellectual candidate for the title of a true 'Theory of Everything' is in fact provided by Trinitarian theology," especially with the qualification that we are not inferring the Trinity from nature. Rather, with Polkinghorne we affirm "that there are aspects of our scientific understanding of the universe that become more deeply intelligible to us if they are viewed in a Trinitarian perspective."[1] Before offering justification of such a claim, it is important to emphasize that the coinherence proposal is not to be understood as strictly speaking a "model" to improve upon other models, say the conflict, independence or integration models. It stands over against the very essence of "model" which is in many ways a product of modernity. What draws us to consider coinherence is its unfathomable depth. It is better called a mystery, one large and deep enough to be plumbed endlessly. Mysteries are lived into. Coinherence concerns the mystery of being. It is not a mechanical model for control, nor can it be controlled. Rather it invites us into the depth of who God in Christ is and what his creation is.[2]

There are a number of reasons why it is not as audacious as it might first appear to be to consider coinherence and Trinitarian theology as a "theory of everything." Granted that this does require a faith perspective. But as we have noted, this is not unique to theological or scientific claims given that faith is a real dynamic in all knowing, no matter the discipline. The issue is, does this faith claim to universality have merit? In the spirit of critical realism, does it fit the data reasonably well, and is it self-consistent? Is it reasonably clear that the epistemology seems to reflect ontology, as best we can determine this? The following are some of the reasons why and how Trinitarian theology is a good candidate for a "theory of everything."

1. The most obvious reason that Trinitarian theology is a theory of everything is that a theory of *everything* must include *God* in the everything, given the evidence from the revelation he has given us of himself in creation and supremely in Christ. It must include not just a monadic or generic concept of God, however, but the *concrete reality of the triune coinherent God*, seen in history in the person of Jesus of Nazareth, in the presence of the Holy Spirit in the history of Israel, and in the history of Jesus, and in his outpouring upon the church.

2. Trinitarian theology fits as a theory of everything, secondly, because, as has been demonstrated, there are correspondences between the coinherent triune God as the ultimate author of everything and the creation as revealed by science. That is, there are traces of his coinherent nature in creation, and his chosen image, humanity, reflects these especially. These correspondences have been noted, not by looking for

---

1. Polkinghorne, *Science and the Trinity*, 61.
2. Gabriel Marcel exposes the influence of modernity on our obsession with models in *The Mystery of Being* and *Being and Having*.

inane evidences of three-ness or triplicity, but by looking for core concepts that reflect God as Trinity in his creation and humanity—things like freedom, agency, personhood in relationality, fecundity, intelligibility and beauty.

3. Trinitarian, coinherent theology fits as a theory of everything, thirdly, because it exhibits a way of knowing that is common to all fields of knowledge. In both creedal theology and science, a faith-seeking-understanding epistemology that may be summarized as critical realism, pertains. This is to say that the moderate aim of self-consistency is what is hoped for in both discourses.

   An example of the role of faith and imagination in all knowing is present in the work of Alister McGrath, who has insisted that the question of the psychology of human perception involves not just reason, but affective response and enactive interaction. His appeal to contemporary psychological theories of perception to discover how human beings made sense of things required McGrath to move beyond the Enlightenment way of understanding perception as a "sense-making exercise" to a heuristic framework grounded in the "Platonic triad" of truth, beauty and goodness, which "takes account of the rational, aesthetic, and moral dimensions of the human engagement with nature."[3] In his 2009 Gifford lectures,[4] McGrath developed this approach by presenting a case study in this brand of natural theology, by focusing on the "anthropic phenomena" and cosmic "fine-tuning." McGrath summarizes his point in this way: "The fundamental argument is that the capacity of the Christian faith to accommodate such phenomena must be regarded as an indication of its truth, though not constituting a deductive 'proof' of God's existence."[5]

4. Trinitarian, coinherent theology fits as a theory of everything because it is a theology grand enough in scope that all reality is acknowledged, and in which all disciplines may be seen to be coinherent. A vision of the triune God of the Bible is one in which God is Lord, infinitely transcendent, and yet minutely immanent. He is conveyed as triune Creator of all of creation, in a narrative in which he is Redeemer of the cosmos, and Lord of history. All knowledge is revealed through him and is to be found in him. This is what leads us from a faith perspective to say that all disciplines will be coinherent within an encyclopedic theology. And, in a way that reflects both the personhood and

---

3. McGrath, *Science and Religion*, 228.
4. Published as McGrath, *Fine-Tuned Universe*.
5. McGrath, *Science and Religion*, 228.

the relations or communion and co-essential nature of the Trinity, in which each lives eternally in hypostatic freedom, and in infinite mutuality, each of the disciplines will have its own identity and freedom to be itself and yet be interdisciplinary. Science will be free to be itself and yet will be the richer for its awareness of theology, and vice versa. Practitioners of science will be the richer also for the meaning and sense of vocation imparted by thoughtful theology.

5. Trinitarian theology fits as the theory of everything because it is nuanced enough to depict order and levels within knowledge, starting with the asymmetry of all disciplines, including science, with respect to conciliar theology. In that the object of its study transcends all objects, being transcendent (and yet, as Trinity, also immanent), theology must be considered as the queen of the sciences and arts. This accords with the reality that within the coinherent Trinity in both the Eastern Orthodox and the Western tradition, there is a functional primacy granted to the Father as the font of the Trinity (this is not subordinationism, but a functional mutual submission). Trinitarian theology as the theory of everything will thus bring theology to the discussion in a way that shapes the agenda and gives it meaning and boundaries. That is, to hear the science as science very clearly, and yet to consider this interface in a manner that truly honors God as Creator and Redeemer, and that gives due primacy to the knowledge (*scientia*) of God as the principal field of knowledge granted by grace to human beings in the person of his Son, Christ Jesus, and by his Holy Spirit, and as that field of knowledge which subsumes all others.

In other words, we wish to give primacy to confessional or conciliar theology in that it is the culminative revelation of God *in* and *through* and *as* Jesus Christ, received by the church and discerned in the conciliar expressions of the church. By this means, humanity has received the primary truths that are necessary for doctrine and life. To borrow from Jamie Smith's classification of theology, this is the theology[1] level, if you like. Its content has been received by the church in response to real historical events, as recorded in Scripture, the final authority of Christians in all matters of faith and practice. Even first-order theology, as T. F. Torrance has shown, is a scientific theology, or theological science. The conviction that this confessional theology, though it may be enriched and nuanced by science and what other disciplines reveal about God, will not change in its essence, is an act of faith, though it is grounded in a reasoned way on historically experiential testimony. As science develops, however, a theology associated with science also develops, and this second-order theology is taken up into what may be termed a second-order-theology theology,² also called a second-order theological science.⁶ The insistence on the primacy of the creedal or conciliar approach is crucial for the unity of the body of Christ as it dialogues on these issues of theology and science, in the second-order realm, and therefore for scientists of various opinions about origins, for example. The creed states flatly *that* God as Creator created all things. All Christians, including all Christians who are scientists, can agree on this and dialogue respectfully on the ground of this extant unity of the faith, while pursuing mature unity in all matters of the faith, recognizing that there will be disagreements on secondary issues until the fullness of the *eschaton*. The creed says nothing about *how* God created all things. For knowledge of that we have to turn appropriately to science and to Scripture *as properly interpreted*. The Scriptures pertaining to origins do play a significant role in discussing the *how* questions. The intent of the author of these sections must be born in mind (what question do these texts answer?), as well as good scholarship regarding the genre and form of these texts, as well as the history of interpretation of these texts. The question "what kind of text is this that I am reading" is of primary importance.

In advocating for the primacy of theological science, that is, Trinitarian theology, there is, of course, a double-edged sword to be aware of. Such a proposition is *not* one which ignores science in any way. It is not to be confused with concordism. It is not to be equated with the contentions of those who for example, simply advocate a literalist interpretation of Genesis 1 in the face of overwhelming evidence from science that the world could not have been created four or even ten thousand years ago. There are apparently those within this literalist camp who even admit that the science runs counter to the literalistic view, but who are prepared to go with their literalist interpretation and hold this in some kind of tension with the science they admit contradicts this view. This obscurantist approach fails to give any credence to the science and fails to recognize science as at least a part of general revelation. The viewpoint being advocated, first of all takes the literary genre of Genesis 1 and 2 seriously, but, to the point at hand, it takes the findings of evolutionary science seriously and seeks integration of the Scripture and the science, recognizing of course, that the Bible is not and was never intended to be a scientific textbook, a

---

6. Smith, *Introducing Radical Orthodoxy*, 90.

matter even Calvin asserts.[7] The gesture toward the recovery of theology as the queen of the sciences is not evoked by a desire for theology to override the sciences or to control the research that goes on in the sciences and their results. Nor is it suggesting that theology is queen because it prescribes answers to all of the questions discussed in the sciences. Rather, it is queen because it must take up into itself all of the well-researched and well-reasoned answers of science in order to enrich our understanding of conciliar theology and in order to be an encyclopedic theology (at the secondary level), that is, a theology that takes into account all of reality and does not hide from it.

Crucially, coinherence, though it involves mutual holding of the each in the other, does not necessarily imply that each of the "eaches" always have the same honor. In the case of the Trinity, equality is indeed the case for the three persons, as far as *essence* is concerned, as well as ultimate *honor* or glory received in the economy of redemption.[8] There are, however, acts of the triune God in which there is a mutual submissiveness of the one to the other, the case of the incarnate Son on earth in his obedience to the Father being the most obvious. He expressly came to do the will of the Father and bring glory to his name. In these instances we have a somewhat asymmetric coinherence. Analogously, science, though a discrete entity of its own, serves ultimately through its findings to reveal the glory of God. The relationship of the Divine and human natures of the incarnate Son, Jesus, provide another example of an asymmetric coinherence. Karl Barth, following a Cyrilline Christology, was anxious to say that the hypostatic union is a union of

---

7. Calvin, *Commentary on Genesis*. "For it appears opposed to common sense, and quite incredible, that there should be waters above the heaven. Hence some resort to allegory, and philosophize concerning angels; but quite beside the purpose. For, to my mind, this is a certain principle, that nothing is here treated of but the visible form of the world. He who would learn astronomy, [60] and other recondite arts, let him go elsewhere. Here the Spirit of God would teach all men without exception; and therefore what Gregory declares falsely and in vain respecting statues and pictures is truly applicable to the history of the creation, namely, that it is the book of the unlearned... The things, therefore, which he relates, serve as the garniture of that theater which he places before our eyes. Whence I conclude, that the waters here meant are such as the rude and unlearned may perceive. The assertion of some, that they embrace by faith what they have read concerning the waters above the heavens, notwithstanding their ignorance respecting them, is not in accordance with the design of Moses."

8. Jonathan Edwards had a particular concern that in his own theological heritage the Spirit was not assigned equal honor in the work of the economic Trinity, because the Spirit was sometimes thought of as merely the applier of the salvation accomplished by Christ. Edwards corrected this by making it clear that the Spirit was not merely the applier, but the Gift, the goal or aim of the atonement. For more on this, see Hastings, *Life of God*.

asymmetric compatibilism. That is, it was one in which the divinity has influential preference, since the Divine Son took on humanity and not the other way around. This did not lessen the reality of the humanity, which was (and is) still of a fully human kind. This is the appropriate model of coinherence for theology and science. They belong together in a perichoretic manner in which theology has ultimate preference, in a way that reflects the perichoretic relationship between the Divine and human natures of Christ, while still preserving the true identity of both the theology and the science. In one of his earlier books, *Science and Creation*, John Polkinghorne expresses the relationship between the knowledge areas of theology and science well: "Theology's regal status lies in its commitment to seek the deepest possible level of understanding. In the course of that endeavor it needs to take into account all other forms of knowledge, while in no way attempting to assert a hegemony over them. A theological view of the world is a total view of the world."[9] Another way to express this is to say that biblical theology must be about covenant and not just about creation.

The primacy of God or of theology as it attempts to describe God and his person and works, need not be an oppressive primacy. It is true that the biblical description of God is that he is the God of unrivalled sovereignty who called the being of the universe into existence and sustains and guides it. He is also good, essentially good, defined by love in three interpenetrated and interanimated yet distinct persons, each giving space for the other. When theology is spoken of as the regal science, one way to understand that is to see the remarkable communicable ontological realities of God that we have written about as being bequeathed to the creation providing space for matter to be, and to be what it is, thus providing science with categories and context that give it meaning. What mathematician Eric Priest depicts as a way to see the integration of the sciences and the humanities, one could just as easily see as the integration, or as I prefer, coinherence, of theology which gives these categories to the arts, and the sciences. The diagram I am referring to shows an inner circle containing the names of all the sciences, and an outer circle which bounds the sciences, with the following descriptors: creativity, community, wonder, reason, meaning, beauty.[10] These reflect a remarkably close similarity to the theological, ontological categories I have outlined as being reflected in science.

---

9. Polkinghorne, *Science and Creation*, 1.
10. Priest, *Reason and Wonder*, 5.

These are not oppressive categories held over science, but those which lovingly move it forward and give it significance.

In sum, in this relationship between theology and science which may be termed "asymmetric compatibilism," there will be a mutuality about science and theology, indeed, an "in-ness" of one in the other, even if the theology is the partner that has the preeminence for revelatory and doxological reasons, the one that makes it asymmetric. In such a relationship, the scientist will be looking for evidences within creation of a Creator who is triune, who is majestically beautiful, who is infinitely wise and ordered, while at the same time, who is contingent and extravagant in his creating. The move that makes theology primal in the dialogue with science is most definitely and admittedly, a *faith* perspective that says that everything in science brings glory to God, and nothing that science discovers can contradict the doctrines of the faith discovered from the revelation of God in Jesus Christ, which are expressed throughout Scripture as properly interpreted by the great tradition of the church, and expressed in the councils and creeds of the church. This a matter of prioritizing the forms of revelation given to us by a gracious God. It is to say that the personal revelation of God in Christ by the Spirit, and the special revelation of that revelation in the Bible, trumps general revelation or natural theology. This is not to say that nothing new can be said about first-order theology as a result of new scientific discoveries, and in that sense, conciliar theology is dynamic and not static. However, faith in the same Creator-Redeemer God who both created the universe and sent his Son, ensures that no major tenet of the faith can ever be altered by a scientific discovery. A conciliar truth may be refined and more deeply understood, but it cannot be abrogated or disproved by science.

6. Trinitarian theology fits as a theory of everything, because it contains and promotes a profound connectedness to creation and therefore to science. The doctrine of creation by a good God, and the coming into creation of the Son of God at the incarnation, encourage, indeed necessitate, the embodied existence of human creatures and their engagement in creation and care of it. Christians who grasp these realities will, of all people, be fearless in their approach to science and its discoveries. Christians, in light of their triune, coinherent God, will be *science-affirming people*, inquisitive, curious, and worshipful. Of course, they will be discerning, too. They will thoughtfully interpret Scripture according to normal interpretation, which excludes its use as a science text, and unnecessary concordism. They will adjust its

interpretations where nonessentials are concerned. They will find ways to incorporate the findings of quantum and chaos and string theory, and all theory that passes the rigorous scientific review processes that exist in science. Trinitarian theology gives that space.

Another way to say this is that coinherent Trinitarian theology as a theory of everything does have an appropriate, and appropriately nuanced *natural theology* tradition. In other words, Christian theology which is creation affirming, can and must therefore be connected to the realities in science if it is true to its doctrine of creation and the cultural mandate.

The history of natural theology is a somewhat troubled one, especially in the Protestant world, and we need therefore to understand some of the difficulties and solutions. Karl Barth, for good reasons, expressed concern over the concept of natural theology, if by it the revelation of God in Jesus Christ was subverted in any way. Naturally, he eschewed nationalist ideologies which were justified by such a theology, along with their inherent assumptions about the human capacity for self-salvation. Theologian scientists in the Protestant tradition sought to affirm these instincts in Barth and yet have sought to find a way to make the relationship between disciplines like science and theology more explicit. John Polkinghorne[11] and Alister McGrath,[12] for example, have cordoned off a nuanced place for natural theology in their understanding of the relationship between theology and science. Each of these theologians, however, though they express their own nuances, owe a debt to T. F. Torrance in this regard.[13] We will consider his work on this which enabled his theology to have a nuanced natural theology and greater interaction with science than did Barth.

The properly mutual relations between theology and science, which provide nuance to the coinherent relationship of theology and

---

11. Polkinghorne, *Science and Creation*, 2–3. Polkinghorne defines natural theology as "the search for the knowledge of God by the exercise of reason and the inspection of the world." This must, however, be seen within the context of his affirmation of conciliar theology as having regal status. If "theism is true," says Polkinghorne, "the world is not just a neutral theatre in which these individual revelatory acts take place" . . . but it is "the creation of God and so potentially a vehicle also for his self-disclosure." This is to say what Scripture itself says about the creation and its revelatory function in places in the Scriptures like Ps 19:1, "The heavens declare the glory of God."

12. McGrath's three-volume *Scientific Theology* (2001–3) "explore how the working methods and assumptions of the natural sciences could enrich and sustain a systematic Christian theology." This is McGrath's own summation of these volumes in McGrath, *Science and Religion*, 225.

13. See T. F. Torrance, "Problem of Natural Theology," 121–35.

science, thereby providing some justification for the "theory of everything," which are[14]

i. This is a natural theology which preserved the *distinction between theology and religion*. Many treatments of the subject of the interrelatedness of science and these disciplines make no distinction between Christian theology and religion, but there is an important distinction to be made. In this regard, Torrance follows his principal teacher Karl Barth in that "religion" concerns human consciousness and behavior rather than knowledge of God received by revelation. Torrance states,

> Theology is the unique science devoted to knowledge of God, differing from other sciences by the uniqueness of its object which can be apprehended only on its own terms and from within the actual situation it has created in our existence in making itself known.[15]

Torrance, on the one hand, therefore, speaks pejoratively of natural theology of this kind, like Barth. The kind of natural theology that is understood to be a compiling of conclusions from the *sensus divinitatis* in all human communities, for example, is not what Torrance affirms (for it is not the *sensus Dei*). Neither is it the kind of theology which cordons off reason and faith from each other. The two great periods of the flourishing of natural theology were also the periods of strongly dualistic thought in the world. First, this was true in the Middle Ages when a dualism of "the sensible world of brute perception and the intelligible world of spiritual apprehension" gave rise to "the line between nature and supernature."[16] It was in this era in which Anselm developed his ontological argument, and Aquinas presented his *Five Ways*[17] (so called "proofs" of the existence of God). Second, in the eigh-

---

14. His most important works in this area were *Theological Science* and *Reality and Scientific Theology: Theology and Science at the Frontiers of Knowledge*.

15. T. F. Torrance, *Theological Science*, 281.

16. Torrance is summarized here by Polkinghorne, *Science and Creation*, 13–14.

17. Aquinas, *Summae Theologiae*, I.2.3. These were five natural arguments for the existence of God. They were (i) the existence of change which implies there has to be an originator of change; (ii) the existence of causation which implies there must be a first cause; (iii) the existence of coming to be and ceasing to be, implying the existence of an unchanging ground of its existence; (iv) the existence of gradations of qualities in creational things which implies the existence of one in whom all these qualities are full and perfect, and from which they flow to all creatures; and (v) the existence of purpose in the world which implies an intelligence directing and giving it purpose.

Trinitarian Theology as the "Theory of Everything"

teenth century when natural theology resurged, a dualism of a different kind arose. This was "the division between the extended substance of matter and the thinking substance of mind, whilst the Deists sharply differentiated a detached God from the world that he had launched upon its way."[18] In both of these eras with their differing dualisms, natural theology found its appeal in that it provided a logical bridge between these divides, in a manner illustrated throughout the *Summa* of Aquinas, for example.

ii. This is a natural theology in which theology and the natural sciences could be understood to be in dialogue because both *belong under the same philosophical category of critical realism*. That is, each is determined by the reality of the object which is seeking to be apprehended. Theology "arises from the actual knowledge of God given in and with concrete happenings in space and time. It concerns knowledge of the God who actively meets us and gives himself to be known in Jesus Christ." Torrance adds, we "do not therefore begin with ourselves or our questions, nor indeed can we choose where to begin; we can only begin with the facts prescribed for us by the actuality of the subject positively known."[19] In other words, both theology and science respond in an *a posteriori* manner "to the way things are," and "are committed to some form of realism."[20] They deal with reality as it is, prior to seeking to apprehend it. Torrance states,

> We are concerned in the development of scientific theories to penetrate into the comprehensibility of reality and grasp it in its mathematical harmonies or symmetries or its invariant structures, which hold good independently of our perceiving: we apprehend the real world as it forces itself upon us through the theories it calls forth from us. . . . This is the inescapable "dogmatic realism" or a science pursued and elaborated under the compelling claims and constraints of reality.[21]

If the natural order is the reality which the natural sciences encounter, it is the reality of Christian revelation which theology encounters. Torrance states, again:

---

18. Polkinghorne, *Science and Creation*, 14, summarizing Torrance.
19. McGrath, *Science and Religion*, 199, summarizing Torrance.
20. Ibid.
21. T. F. Torrance, *Reality and Scientific Theology*, 54–55.

> The basic convictions and fundamental ideas with which our knowledge of God is built up arise on the ground of evangelical and liturgical experience in the life of the church, in response to the way God has actually taken in making himself known to mankind through historical dialogue with Israel and the Incarnation of his Son in Jesus Christ and continues to reveal himself to us through the Holy Scriptures. Scientific theology or theological science, strictly speaking, can never be more than a refinement and extension of the knowledge informed by those basic convictions and fundamental ideas, and it would be both empty of material content and empirically irrelevant if it were cut adrift from them.[22]

As McGrath underlines, God's self-revelation is viewed by Torrance as an objective reality, independent of human rational activity, and that in this, Torrance again follows Barth. One can see that this approach would not be acceptable to those who view religion as reflection on human experience, or who take an extreme postmodern stance in which no objective reality is granted. But this leads to a third point about Torrance's approach, in which he differentiates himself from Barth:

iii. This is a natural theology which is not just a prior preparation for the receiving of revealed theology, but rather, is integral to the whole theological endeavor. Torrance thus transcended Barth in that he allowed for and encouraged a friendly and helpful and mutual dialogue between the natural sciences and theology, whereas Barth was dismissive of any such dialogue. Torrance argued for a role for the natural sciences within systematic theology, which McGrath sees as analogous to Einstein's use of geometry.[23] "If we reject a deistic disjunction between God and the world," says Torrance, "which we are bound to do, natural theology cannot be pursued in its traditional abstractive form, as a prior conceptual system on its own, but must be brought within the body of positive theology and be pursued in indissoluble unity with it." As intrinsic rather than extrinsic to the knowledge of God, Torrance saw it as functioning "as a necessary *infra-structure* of theological science."[24]

---

22. Ibid., 85.
23 McGrath, *Science and Religion*, 200.
24. T. F. Torrance, *Reality and Scientific Theology*, 40.

Natural theology is thus the "epistemological geometry" of revealed theology. Polkinghorne surmises that Torrance, in using the term "geometry," may have had "in mind the analogy of the integration of geometry and mechanics which Einstein's General Theory of Relativity brought about." Whereas in classical Newtonian physics, geometry was *a priori* to physics in that "space was the given container in which particles of matter executed their mechanical interactions," in general relativity, "space and matter, geometry and physics, impinge upon each other. What we think of as the force of gravity is due to the curvature of space, which is itself due to the distribution of matter."[25] The focus of attention may at times be on the geometry and at other times on the matter, but they always form an integrated whole. This is precisely how Torrance saw the relationship between natural theology and revealed theology. There are two consequences of such a relationship: *fullness*, fullness or wholeness of knowledge meaning that there is a unity of knowledge, not a dualism, and interpenetration. That is, theology must therefore "take account of all that we know about the world in the course of its inquiry."[26] It must be encyclopedic. Knowledge that is the result of an interpenetration or mutuality of natural and revealed theology, even if the latter takes precedence.

Another way to say this is that to build a revealed theology (first-order theology) without reference to natural theology (which includes science), and to build an encyclopedic second-order theology without natural theology, is to reverse the hypostatic union of the two natures of Christ. Theology and science belong together in a perichoretic manner that reflects the perichoretic relationship between the Divine and human natures of Christ. And as mentioned above, Cyrilline Christology depicts a union of asymmetric compatibilism (understood not as determinism but as 'being compatible'), one in which the divinity which took on humanity, has influential preference, even while the humanity is of a fully human kind.

7. Trinitarian theology is fitting as a theory of everything in that it permits no dualism with respect to matter and Divine knowledge. John Polkinghorne notes that the church in its history became prone to this dualism, but that this was not always its *modus operandi*. He points

---

25. Polkinghorne, *Science and Creation*, 14.
26. Polkinghorne, *Science and Creation*, 15.

to the *Logos* theology of the Greek Fathers in the second century to resolve the mystery of a "changeless self-contained being" who was "at the same time the active Creator God," the mystery of the dialectic of being and becoming. The incarnation was the answer to this, and this was a theology "from above," in a descending movement, in contrast to the ascending flow of natural theology. Polkinghorne contends that the incarnation and the *Logos* theology, with its active "wisdom" roots in the Hebrew Scriptures, and the more static Stoic notion of rational order (deed and word together, process and pattern together, becoming and being together), began to fade out of later patristic thought, to its detriment, particularly through Augustine in the West, of whom he is quite critical.[27] His judgment of Augustine aside, knowledge of God and knowledge of matter are brought together by an incarnational Trinitarian theology.

8. Trinitarian theology fits as a theory of everything in that it acknowledges the freedom of the triune Creator and the freedom of creation to be creation. The Christian doctrine of creation does exactly this. It worships a God who created contingently, in freedom, not necessity, according to his will and in love, not out of his essence. This God also created a creation that is granted degrees of the freedom, such that its integrity as creation is preserved, as is the "Godness" of God.

The most appropriate analogy for this dialectic of Divine and human freedom is the dialectic of Divine grace and human response in human salvation. The descriptions of Paul and then of Karl Barth in interpreting Paul are helpful in this regard. In Philippians 2:12–13, for example, Paul says, "Continue to work out your salvation with fear and trembling, for it is God who works in you to will and to act in order to fulfill his good purpose." The preservation of human freedom within Divine freedom is in some way possible in Paul's theological mind, though he does not press for more clarity than to say that each is true. Scholars of Karl Barth suggest this is Barth's approach also[28]—the acknowledgment of both Divine freedom and of human freedom by way of the analogy of relations,[29] with respect for both the mystery of the way in which they are related, and also for the mystery of divine free-

---

27. Augustine, *Commentary on John*, 7–8.
28. See Barth, *CD* III/2, 193–95; III/3, 188–89; and IV/2, 356.
29. The basic train of thought behind this Barthian compatibilism is that Barth acknowledges the analogy between Divine and human freedom as this is grounded in the correspondence between the being and act of the inner being of God, and the incarnate person of Jesus Christ (*analogia relationis*), and therefore with humanity.

dom itself—which because it is the determinative and original freedom, has precedence and preeminence—hence the asymmetry.[30] The asymmetry is apparent in the noted phrase Barth uses for human freedom: "Being a slave of Christ means being free."[31] And yet the freedom for the created to be what it has been created to be, which is analogous to the freedom of God to be who he is, is real. It is a real freedom even though it is bestowed by God, and it is a "being in activity in line with God's own goodness,"[32] reflecting his own triune being in activity. This articulation of the relationship between God and creation is crucial to the avoidance of pantheism on the one hand, or even participation of a *methexis* variety, and, on the other hand, the avoidance of notions of the freedom of created matter or beings in a way that implies their independence or "self-initiated self-making."[33] In analogous fashion, Christian theology of the core, conciliar kind is in relationship with science in a way that suggests also an asymmetric compatibilism. This in no way diminishes the freedom of science to be science and to ask its own questions. But the prior and preeminent nature of revealed theology makes for an asymmetric relationship. And the assumption of all knowledge from science into an encyclopedic theology fits the analogy of the Divine-human compatibilism of the incarnation. This could be construed as a vengeful correction of the imbalance of the Enlightenment in which reason triumphed over faith. Indeed, a discipline of science which was originally spawned by the Christian faith and then, in Modernity, became the rebellious teenager. Be that as it may. What I am definitely *not* suggesting is some form of fideistic dualism. The truth is that the two are deeply intertwined in every exercise of both the scientific and theological disciplines.

---

30. See, e.g., Webster, *Barth's Moral Theology*, 91–92, 101–2; and Hunsinger, *How to Read Karl Barth*, 197–98. Jesse Couenhoven has attempted to clarify this relationship and the concepts of divine and human freedom. See Couenhoven, "Karl Barth's Conception(s)," 239–55. Couenhoven, while being careful to avoid saying Barth was a philosophical compatibilist, for anachronistic reasons, and because of Barth's dislike of a philosophical approach to freedom, nevertheless affirms, first that Barth is *not* incompatibilist with respect to divine and human freedoms, and second, positively, the "plausibility of a compatibilist reading of some of Barth's key terms in his discussion of divine and human freedom" (254). Couenhoven goes on to say that "a final attraction of reading Barth in a compatibilist light is that it places him in continuity with a venerable host of theologians who defend related views including Augustine, Aquinas and Calvin" (255).

31. Godsey, *Karl Barth's Table Talk*, 37.

32. Couenhoven, "Karl Barth's Conception(s)," 248.

33. Ibid.

9. Trinitarian theology fits as the theory of everything because it means something on the ground, in everything and everywhere. Not just in the church, but in the laboratory, in the school, in the real estate office, in Wall Street and 10 Downing Street, on the football field and the opera. Life in the triune God must be able to be practiced, and Trinitarian theology can be, in the whole of life, everywhere. It is a biblical theology which will enable its followers to demonstrate a holistic biblical *spirituality* that is grounded in earthiness and will have as its aim human persons being human, living in relationship with God, each other and creation, and bringing shalom to the world. That is, it will urge people away from dualisms and it will foster the pursuit of being human, not superhuman. It will encourage an embodied existence not a disembodied one. Every truly biblical Christian living under the Trinitarian theory of everything will be an amateur scientist, being concerned about all of God's good creatures and his good creation. While valuing the uniqueness of human beings as image bearers, adherents of this theory of everything will, by having a natural theology of the kind outlined above, not be narrowly anthropocentric.[34] Thus the incarnational Trinitarian will be very concerned with the welfare of animals and plants and the air quality in God's good creation, assuming the role given in Adam and recapitulated in the last Adam. Such a Christian will be conscious that in their work they are participating in the ongoing story of the Bible toward the new creation. This will be true of the scientist also. Concern for the globe and the cosmos, and being an amateur scientist is the human vocation of every person, but to know some aspect of the nature of the cosmos in detail, is the particular vocation of the scientist.[35] This understanding of Trinitarian theology is, I believe, wide enough and deep enough to give the scientist a framework within which to hold knowledge of God and knowledge of his creation, in an interrelated way; in an interpenetrated way, yet in a manner that preserves the distinctness of each; and in an interanimated way, such that each enhances the other, and in

---

34. Reflecting on the late chapters of the book of Job, and the references to the mythic hippopotamus and crocodile, Polkinghorne comments that it "is characteristic of natural theology that it delivers us from a narrow anthropocentricity." Polkinghorne, *Science and Creation*, 5. Moltmann, in this regard, states: "No theological doctrine of creation must be allowed to reduce the understanding of belief in creation to the existential self-understanding of the person. If God is not creator of the world, he cannot be my creator either." Moltmann, *God in Creation*, 36.

35. Andy Crouch, with reference to the science career of his wife, Catherine, offers a wonderful tribute to the vocation of the scientist, with realism about its pleasures and its pain in Haarsma and Hoezee, *Delight in Creation*, 16–31.

such a way that evokes for the scientist personal value, a sense of wonder and worship, and a rich and nuanced evangelical ethic to guide the course and outcomes of science. Every member of reconciled humanity is called in a general sense to be a king-priest of God's creation. But the scientist has a very particular calling as a king-priest. To help in the stewarding of God's good creation by knowing it well. To give creation a voice. To lead creation's universal anthem of praise of the glory of the triune God who is the source and end of all creation. This involves contemplative appreciation of beauty in both our theology and in our science (Edwards, von Balthasar). A sense of curiosity and wonder which is transformative. Part of this is the acknowledging of mystery, and the limitation of human knowledge in both disciplines. In response to Trinitarian theology as the theory of everything, it will be appropriate to end this book by encouraging a doxological orientation in both theology and in science.

The theology and praxis of the Orthodox tradition, steeped in a Trinitarian orientation has much to teach us in this doxological orientation. Theology for the Orthodox was always the journey of purification through *theoria* (theology), that is experiential knowledge of God, and on to *theosis*, that is, becoming like Christ. The wonder of creation as discovered in science is therefore part of this *theoria* or theology, by its very definition. Innate to this for the Orthodox was a posture of wonder and silence rather than achieving mastery of the reality we encounter by our words and concepts. In science this is to acknowledge the difference between *models of creation* and *creation itself*, which, in turn, parallels the difference between what we call "theology" and who God really is in himself. So many conflicts between science and theology have been between "models of creation" which were mistaken for creation itself, or between science and models of God understood using our provisional theological language. The language we use for science and that for theology is limited, as Orthodox priest-scientist Puhalo confirms by his assertion that "lingusitically based assumptions are derived from the presumption of visualizability." Thus, when we use language for the unseen which has been developed from the matrix of what is visible and is "a developed system of imitation of, and metaphor for, things heard and seen," idolatry is the inevitable result. This is precisely what Cappadocian father "St Gregory the Theologian warns us against when he says, '*Every concept of God is merely a simulacrum, a false likeness, an idol: it cannot reveal God Himself.*' (*Against*

Eunomius, Discourse 3)."³⁶ The tragedy of the distancing of theology and science through scholasticism, from Puhalo's perspective, was the depriving of the "Christian community of its primary vocation to love God's creation as God loves it. It deprives us of the world itself." Historical and scientific "facts," artificially grounded "in ideology and philosophical theories" displace an "empirical regard for nature, which science may deepen our appreciation of."³⁷ Scholasticism, which all traditions have been influenced by, has also reduced spirituality to a cognitive dimension. This is the point at which Puhalo venerates his own tradition which has been protected from this idolatry by the concept of *apophatic* or negative theology, that is, the acknowledgment that we cannot really describe or define anything that God is, but "only circumscribe our understanding of Him by saying what He is not."³⁸ Fascinatingly, this sounds quite similar to Popper's falsification methodology which we encountered earlier, with regard to scientific findings. It is not to say that nothing positive can be affirmed, but it is to acknowledge when no more can be said. On this account, even though God has been revealed in Christ, and we can know him by his energies, when it comes to his Divine *essence*, say the Orthodox, we cannot still either describe or even visualize it (although I humbly insist that we do know it is triune!). It leaves us speechless. Another Orthodox theologian, Vladimir Lossky, has expressed the goal to which such apophatic theology takes us, "if, indeed, we may speak of a goal or ending when it is a question of an ascent toward the infinite—this infinite goal is not a nature or an essence, nor is it a person; it is something which transcends all notions both of nature and of person: it is the Trinity."³⁹

What then of theology in this tradition? As mathematics is to science so theology is to the reality of God. It is an attempt at description. But, fascinatingly, Puhalo speaks of mathematical formalisms in quantum mechanics as "an expression of speechlessness."⁴⁰ There is a real coinherence between theology and science here at this point. One of the things which brings about the speechlessness in the science world is beauty. I am often stunned into silence by the beauty and symmetry of molecules I have studied. I have also often been in awe of organic synthetic chemistry for the artistry beyond science in its synthetic pathways and molecular stereochemistry.

36. Puhalo, *Evidence of Things Not Seen*, 72.
37. Ibid., 42.
38. Ibid., 72.
39. Lossky, *Mystical Theology*, 44.
40. Puhalo, *Evidence of Things Not Seen*, 76.

But the beauty of both the micro and the macro evoke wonder, and after silence comes the language of praise. Gerard Manley Hopkins expressed this inimitably.

> God's Grandeur:
>
> THE WORLD is charged with the grandeur of God.
> It will flame out, like shining from shook foil;
> It gathers to a greatness, like the ooze of oil
> Crushed. Why do men then now not reck his rod?
> Generations have trod, have trod, have trod;   5
> And all is seared with trade; bleared, smeared with toil;
> And wears man's smudge and shares man's smell: the soil
> Is bare now, nor can foot feel, being shod.
>
> And for all this, nature is never spent;
> There lives the dearest freshness deep down things;   10
> And though the last lights off the black West went
> Oh, morning, at the brown brink eastward, springs—
> Because the Holy Ghost over the bent
> World broods with warm breast and with ah! bright wings.[41]

The common doxological aim is what makes both theological and scientific vocations one. And this is what makes the sheer hard work in both worthwhile. It is the reality that the kingdom of God has already broken into history in Christ, which brings with it a doxological orientation in both theology and in science. Christ has come to recapitulate old Adam's orientation. There are two stages within the redemption of humanity and God's creation. The first is in this present age. The kingdom *has* come with the first advent of Christ and the coming of the Spirit. There are signs of that redemption in the church and humanity under the influence of the kingdom of God. Wherever people in Christ live the lives of persons alive in Christ, and in the fullness of their humanity work for the glory of God and steward his creation wisely, there the new creation is visible. When scientists of intellectual humility discover new realities in creation, giving creation a voice, and praise the name of triune Creator, the kingdom has come. The church especially as it feeds on the physical created elements of bread and wine is a sacrament of a reconciled cosmos. But the fullness of the *eschaton* will however reveal a new creation in its more fully developed stage. The kingdom then will be fully come. Whereas in this old creation, the creation reveals something of the nature and glory of God (Ps 19:1),

---

41. Hopkins, "God's Grandeur."

the relationship between the Creator and his creation is somewhat veiled. There are some evidences of the sacramental nature of all creation—that is, signs of his presence and glory in creation. However, when the kingdom has fully come, when creation is fully reconciled, even though it will still be distinct from God ontologically speaking, all of creation will be sacramental. Thus whereas the old creation has functioned with a veil over God's presence, then the veil will be removed. The revelation of the glory of Christ and with that, the revelation of the reflected glory of the church, will usher in the freedom of creation and its every aspect will be fully and obviously iridescent with the glory of God. Scientists in the "now" get glimpses of glory in creation. I wonder to myself if in the new creation they, more than others, will appreciate what creation reveals of the Divine glory of the triune God. Just by the way, this eschatological view of creation is possible only by closely linking Christ and creation. It is Trinitarian.

This doxological orientation also relates to a "going back to the future." The vocation of the first human persons depicted in the garden of Eden was a doxological orientation to creation. These persons were called to see, to know, to name, and to delight in creation (Robert Farrar Capon).[42] They were also called to offer or oblate (Loren Wilkinson).[43] For Alexander Schmemann, to name it was to bless it for it revealed the very essence of the thing as gift given by the Creator. So everything that exists does so as a gift of God, and it exists to make God known to man, to enable his life to be one of communion with God. "O taste and see that the Lord is good" is the summation of the gospel. God blesses all that he creates. It is in love that God made food for humanity, for example. As Schmemann says, "Behind all the hunger of our life is God. All desire is finally a desire for him."[44] This removes all dualism from life with God. The task of naming and blessing the creation was not a religious or cultic act, but a way of life, an earthy spirituality. The idea of eating and drinking in communion with God, being for the life of the world, is not an encouragement to escape the earthy, physical realm for a spiritual mysticism, or evacuation theology; nor is being for the life of the world, on the other hand, a crass activism distanced from contemplation and communion. *Homo sapiens* we may be, but we are not first that or just that, in Yahweh's eyes. Rather we are *homo adorans*. Man is first defined as a priest. The *imago* in its very essence is man in relationship to God, and as such, a mediator of God's love to creation and a thankful consumer and blesser to God on behalf of creation. He receives the world from

---

42. Capon, *Supper of the Lamb*.
43. Wilkinson, lecture in Christian Thought and Culture class.
44. Schmemann, *For the Life*, 14.

God for his hunger, and he offers it back to God as a blesser, as an offerer of Eucharist. As Schmemann says, "The first, the basic definition of man is that he is *the priest*. He stands in the center of the world and unifies it in his act of blessing God, of both receiving the world from God and offering it to God—and by filling the world with this eucharist, he transforms his life, the one that he receives from the world, into life in God, into communion with him. The world was created as the 'matter,' the material of one all-embracing eucharist, and man was created as the priest of this cosmic sacrament."[45]

This is the posture of the scientist, and of the theologian, in the Trinitarian theory of everything.

---

45. Ibid., 15.

Bibliography

Achtemeier, Mark T. "Natural Science and Christian Faith in the Thought of T. F. Torrance." In *The Promise of Trinitarian Theology: Theologians in Dialogue with T. F. Torrance*, edited by Elmer M. Colyer, 269-302. Lanham, MD: Rowman & Littlefield, 2001.
Alexander, Denis. *Can We Be Sure about Anything? Science, Faith and Postmodernism*. Leicester, UK: Apollos, 2005.
———. *Creation or Evolution: Do We Have to Choose?* Oxford: Monarch, 2008.
———. *Rebuilding the Matrix: Science and Faith in the 21st Century*. Oxford: Lion, 2002.
———. *Rebuilding the Matrix: Science and Faith in the 21st Century*. Grand Rapids: Zondervan, 2003.
Anderson, Ray S. *Something Old, Something New: Marriage and Family Ministry in a Postmodern World*. Eugene, OR: Wipf & Stock, 2007.
Anderson, Ray S., and Dennis B. Guernsey. "Bonding without Bondage." In *On Being Family: A Social Theology of the Family*, 85-104. Pasadena, CA: Fuller Seminary Press, 1985.
Andrews, E. H. *God, Science & Evolution*. Welwyn, UK: Evangelical, 1980.
———. *Who Made God? Searching for a Theory of Everything*. Darlington, UK: EP, 2009.
Aquinas, Thomas. *Summa Theologiae: Latin Text and English Translation, Introductions, Notes, Appendices, and Glossaries*. Cambridge: Blackfriars, 1964.
Augustine. *De Trinitate*. Edited by W. J. Mountain, with assistance from Fr. Glorie. 2 vols. Corpus Christianorum Series Latina 50. Turnhout: Brepols, 1968.
———. *The Literal Meaning of Genesis*. Vol. 1. Translated and annotated by John Hammond Taylor. Ancient Christian Writers 41. New York: Paulist, 1982.
Badger, Steve, and Mike Tennesen. "Does the Spirit Create through Evolutionary Processes? Pentecostals and Biological Evolution." In *Science and the Spirit: A Pentecostal Engagement with the Sciences*, edited by Amos Yong and James K. A. Smith, 92-116. Bloomington, IN: Indiana University Press, 2010.
Baik, Chung-Hyun. *The Holy Trinity—God for God and God for Us: Seven Positions on the Immanent-Economic Trinity Relation in Contemporary Trinitarian Theology*. Eugene, OR: Pickwick, 2011.
Balthasar, Hans Urs von. *Cosmic Liturgy: The Universe According to Maximus Confessor*. Translated by B. E. Daley. San Francisco: Ignatius, 1988.
Barbour, Ian G. *Religion in an Age of Science*. San Francisco: Harper & Row, 1990.

———. *Religion and Science: Historical and Contemporary Issues.* San Francisco: HarperSanFrancisco, 1997.
Barth, Karl. *The Christian Life.* Translated by J. Strathearn McNab. London: SCM, 1930.
———. *Church Dogmatics.* Vols. 1–4. Edited by T. F. Torrance and G. W. Bromiley. Reprint. London: T. & T. Clark, 2009.
———. *The Holy Spirit and the Christian Life: The Theological Basis of Ethics.* Introduction by Robin Lovin. Philadelphia: Westminster John Knox, 1993.
Bauckham, Richard. *Jesus and the Eyewitnesses: The Gospels as Eyewitness Testimony.* Grand Rapids: Eerdmans, 2006.
Begbie, Jeremy. *Resounding Truth: Christian Wisdom in the World of Music.* Grand Rapids: Baker Academic, 2007.
Behe, M. *Darwin's Black Box.* New York: Free, 2006.
———. *The Edge of Evolution.* New York: Free, 2008.
Berry, R. J. *Real Scientists, Real Faith.* Oxford: Monarch, 2009.
Blackwell, Richard J. *Galileo, Bellarmine, and the Bible.* Notre Dame: University of Notre Dame Press, 1991.
Bowlby John. *Attachment.* Vol. 1 of *Attachment and Loss.* 2nd ed. New York: Basic, 1999.
———. *Loss: Sadness & Depression.* Vol. 3 of *Attachment and Loss.* International Psycho-Analytical Library 109. London: Hogarth, 1980.
———. *The Making and Breaking of Affectional Bonds.* London: Tavistock, 1979.
———. *A Secure Base: Parent-Child Attachment and Healthy Human Development.* Tavistock Professional Book. London: Routledge, 1988.
———. *Separation: Anxiety & Anger.* Vol. 2 of *Attachment and Loss.* International Psycho-Analytical Library 95. London: Hogarth, 1973.
Bowler, Peter J. *Monkey Trials and Gorilla Sermons: Evolution and Christianity from Darwin to Intelligent Design.* Cambridge: Harvard University Press, 2007.
Broadhead, Bradley K. "The Triune Triad: A Musical Analogy Concerning the Trinity and Humanity." *Imaginatio et Ratio, A Journal of Theology and the Arts* 3 (2014) 23–33.
Brockman, John, ed. *Is the Internet Changing the Way You Think? The Net's Impact on Our Minds and Future.* New York: HarperCollins, 2011.
Brooke, John Hedley. *Heterodoxy in Early Modern Science and Religion.* Oxford: Oxford University Press, 2005.
———. *Science and Religion: Some Historical Perspectives.* Cambridge: Cambridge University Press, 1991.
Brooke, John Hedley, and G. N. Cantor. *Reconstructing Nature: The Engagement of Science and Religion.* New York: Oxford University Press, 2000.
Brown, W. S., and B. D. Strawn. *The Physical Nature of Christian Life: Neuroscience, Psychology and the Church.* New York: Cambridge University Press, 2012.
Brueggemann, Walter. *Genesis.* New Interpreter's Bible. Louisville: John Knox, 1982.
Bruhn, Siglind. *Messiaen's Interpretations of Holiness and Trinity: Echoes of Medieval Theology in the Oratorio, Organ Meditations, and Opera, Dimension & Diversity* Hillsdale, NY: Pendragon, 2008.
Buxton, Graham. *The Trinity, Creation and Pastoral Ministry: Imaging the Perichoretic God.* Paternoster Theological Monographs. Eugene, OR: Wipf & Stock, 2007.
Calvin, John. *Calvin's Commentaries.* 22 vols. Edited by John King et al. Translated by Calvin Translation Society. Grand Rapids: Baker, 1981.

———. *Commentary on Genesis*. Vol. 1. Translated by John King. Christian Classics Ethereal Library. Grand Rapids: Eerdmans, 2005. https://www.ccel.org/ccel/calvin/calcom01.html.

Canlis, Julie. *Calvin's Ladder: A Spiritual Theology of Ascent and Ascension*. Grand Rapids: Eerdmans, 2010.

Capon, Robert Farrar. *The Supper of the Lamb: A Culinary Reflection*. New York: Random House, 1969. Reprint, 2002.

Carlson, Richard F. *Science & Christianity: Four Views*. Downers Grove, IL: InterVarsity, 2000.

Cary, Phillip. "Barth Wars: A Review of Reading Barth with Charity." *First Things*, April 2015. https://www.firstthings.com/article/2015/04/barth-wars.

Chapp, Larry S. *The God of Covenant and Creation: Scientific Naturalism and Its Challenge to the Christian Faith*. London: T. & T. Clark, 2011.

Chepkwony, Adam K. Arap. *Dialogue in Religion and Science: An African Perspective*. Eldoret, Kenya: Moi University Press, 2009.

Coakley, Sarah. *Powers and Submissions: Spirituality, Gender and Philosophy*. Malden, MA: Wiley-Blackwell, 2002.

Cochrane, Arthur C., ed. *Reformed Confessions of the 16th Century*. 2nd ed. Philadelphia: Westminster John Knox, 2007.

Collins, Francis S. *The Language of God: A Scientist Presents Evidence for Belief*. New York: Free Press, 2006.

Colyer, Elmer M. *How to Read T. F. Torrance: Understanding His Trinitarian and Scientific Theology*. Downers Grove, IL: InterVarsity, 2001.

———. "A Scientific Theological Method." Chapter 9 of *The Promise of Trinitarian Theology: Theologians in Dialogue with T. F. Torrance*, edited by Elmer M. Colyer. Lanham, MD: Rowman & Littlefield, 2001.

Congdon, David W. "Who's Afraid of the *Analogia Entis*?" *The Fire and the Rose*. Congdon's blog. December 30, 2006. https://fireandrose.blogspot.com/2006/12/whos-afraid-of-analogia-entis_30.html.

Connor, Daniel, and Francis Oakley. *Creation: The Impact of an Idea*. New York: Scribner, 1969.

Couenhoven, Jesse. "Karl Barth's Conception(s) of Human and Divine Freedom(s)." In *Commanding Grace: Studies in Karl Barth's Ethics*, edited by Daniel L. Migliore, 239–55. Grand Rapids: Eerdmans, 2010.

Craig, William Lane. *The Only Wise God: The Compatibility of Divine Foreknowledge and Human Freedom*. Grand Rapids: Baker, 1987.

Craig, William Lane, and Quentin Smith. *Theism, Atheism and Big Bang Cosmology*. Oxford: Oxford University Press, 1995.

Crain, Steven D. "Divine Action in a World Chaos: An Evaluation of John Polkinghorne's Model of Special Divine Action." *Faith and Philosophy* 14 (1997) 41–61.

Creegan, Nicola Hoggard. "A Christian Theology of Evolution and Participation." *Zygon: Journal of Religion and Science* 42 (2007) 499–518.

Crick, Francis. *The Astonishing Hypothesis*. New York: Simon and Schuster, 1994.

Crisp, Oliver D. "On Original Sin." *International Journal of Systematic Theology* 17 (2015) 252–66.

———. "Problems with Perichoresis." *Tyndale Bulletin* 56 (2005) 119–40.

Cross, F. L., and E. A. Livingstone, eds. "Circumincession." In *The Oxford Dictionary of the Christian Church*, 357. 3rd ed. Oxford: Oxford University Press, 1974.

Cunningham, Conor. *Darwin's Pious Idea: Why the Ultra-Darwinists and Creationists Both Get It Wrong.* Grand Rapids: Eerdmans, 2010.

Cunningham, David. *These Three Are One: The Practice of Trinitarian Theology.* Malden, MA: Wiley-Blackwell, 1998.

Danaher, William J., Jr. *The Trinitarian Ethics of Jonathan Edwards.* Columbia Series in Reformed Theology. Louisville: Westminster John Knox, 2004.

Danielson, Dennis Richard. *The Book of the Cosmos: Imagining the Universe from Heraclitus to Hawking.* Cambridge, MA: Perseus, 2000.

Davis, Edward B. "The Motivated Belief of John Polkinghorne." *First Things*, July 2009. https://www.firstthings.com/web-exclusives/2009/07/the-motivated-belief-of-john-polkinghorne.

Davis, Martin. "T. F. Torrance: Scientific Theology and Critical Realism." *God For Us!* (blog). January 2, 2010. http://martinmdavis.blogspot.ca/2010/01/t-f-torrance-scientific-theology-and.html.

Dawkins, Richard. *The Greatest Show on Earth.* New York: Free, 2010.

———. *River Out of Eden.* New York: Basic, 1996.

Del Re, Giuseppe. *The Cosmic Dance: Science Discovers the Mysterious Harmony of the Universe.* Radnor, PA: Templeton, 2000.

Dillenberger, John. *Protestant Thought and Natural Science: A Historical Interpretation.* Notre Dame: University of Notre Dame Press, 1960.

Draper, John. *History of the Conflict Between Science and Religion.* Charleston, SC: CreateSpace, 2014.

Dupré, Louis. *Passage to Modernity: An Essay in the Hermenuetics of Nature and Culture.* New Haven: Yale University Press, 2011.

Edwards, Denis. *Breath of Life: A Theology of the Creator Spirit.* Maryknoll: Orbis, 2004.

———. *The God of Evolution: A Trinitarian Theology.* New York: Paulist, 1999.

Edwards, Jonathan. "Miscellany No. 117." In *The Works of Jonathan Edwards*, edited by Thomas A. Schafer, 13:283. New Haven: Yale University Press, 1994.

———. *The Works of Jonathan Edwards.* Vol. 16. Edited by George S. Claghorn. New Haven: Yale University Press, 1998.

Eiseley, Loren C. *The Firmament of Time.* New York: Atheneum, 1960.

Evans, Craig A., et al., eds. *The Book of Genesis: Composition, Reception, and Interpretation.* Leiden: Brill, 2012.

Fackre, Gabriel. *The Doctrine of Revelation: A Narrative Interpretation.* Grand Rapids: Eerdmans, 1997.

Fergusson, David A. S. *The Cosmos and the Creator: An Introduction to the Theology of Creation.* London: SPCK, 1998.

Ferngren, Gary B. *The History of Science and Religion in the Western Tradition: An Encyclopedia.* New York: Garland, 2000.

Fitzpatrick, Kathleen. "Trinity and Music: Intonations of the Triune God." In *Trinity and Salvation: Theological, Spiritual, and Aesthetic Perspectives*, edited by Declan Marmion and Gesa Elsbeth Thiessen, 143–52. Studies in Theology, Society and Culture. Oxford: Lang, 2009.

Foster, Michael B. "The Christian Doctrine of Creation and the Rise of Modern Natural Science." *Mind* 43 (1934) 446–68.

———. "Man's Idea of Nature." *Christian Scholar* 41 (1958) 361–66.

Gadamer, Hans-George. *Truth and Method.* Rev. ed. Translated by Joel Weinsheimer and Donald G. Marshall. New York: Continuum, 1989.

Giberson, Karl, and Donald A. Yerxa. *Species of Origins: America's Search for a Creation Story.* Lanham, MD: Rowman & Littlefield, 2002.

Giberson, Karl, and Mariano Artigas. *Oracles of Science: Celebrity Scientists versus God and Religion.* Oxford: Oxford University Press, 2007.

Giberson, Karl, and Francis S. Collins. *The Language of Science and Faith: Straight Answers to Genuine Questions.* Downers Grove, IL: InterVarsity, 2011.

Gilkey, Langdon. *Naming the Whirlwind: The Renewal of God-language.* Indianapolis: Bobbs-Merrill, 1969.

Godsey, John, ed. *Karl Barth's Table Talk.* Richmond, VA: John Knox, 1963.

Gould, Stephen Jay. "Impeaching a Self-Appointed Judge." *Scientific American* 267 (1992) 118–21.

Green, Joel, and Stuart Palmer. *In Search of the Soul: Four Views of the Mind-Body Problem.* Downers Grove, IL: InterVarsity, 2005.

Greenblatt, Stephen. *The Swerve: How the World Became Modern.* New York: Norton, 2011.

Greene, John C. *Science, Ideology, and World View: Essays in the History of Evolutionary Ideas.* Berkeley: University of California Press, 1981.

Greenfield, Susan. *Mind Change: How Digital Technologies Are Leaving Their Mark on Our Brains.* New York: Random House, 2015.

Gregory of Nazianzus. "To Cledonius the Priest against Apollinarius." Epistle 101. http://biblehub.com/library/cyril/select_letters_of_saint_gregory_nazianzen/to_cledonius_the_priest_against.htm.

Gregory of Nyssa. "On 'Not Three Gods': To Ablabium." In *Nicene and Post-Nicene Fathers* (2nd ser.) 5:331–36. Translated by H. A. Wilson. New York: Christian Literature, 1893.

Grenz Stanley J., and Roger E. Olson. *20th-Century Theology: God and the World in a Transitional Age.* Downers Grove, IL: InterVarsity, 1992.

Gunton, Colin E. *Christ and Creation: The Didsbury Lectures, 1990.* Eugene, OR: Wipf & Stock, 2005.

———. *Father, Son, and Holy Spirit: Essays Towards a Fully Trinitarian Theology.* London: T. & T. Clark, 2003. See especially chapter 7.

———. *The One, the Three and the Many: God, Creation and the Culture of Modernity.* Cambridge: Cambridge University Press, 1993.

———. *The Promise of Trinitarian Theology.* London: T. & T. Clark, 1997.

———. *The Triune Creator: A Historical and Systematic Study.* Grand Rapids: Eerdmans, 1998.

Haarsma, Deborah B., and Loren D. Haarsma. *Origins: Christian Perspectives on Creation, Evolution, and Intelligent Design.* Grand Rapids: Faith Alive, 2011.

Haarsma, Deborah B., and Scott Hoezee. *Delight in Creation: Scientists Share Their Work with the Church.* Grand Rapids: Center for Excellence in Preaching, 2012.

Habets, Myk. *Theology in Transposition: A Constructive Appraisal of T. F. Torrance.* Minneapolis: Fortress, 2013.

Hanby, Michael. *No God, No Science: Theology, Cosmology, Biology.* Oxford: Wiley-Blackwell, 2013.

Harrison, Peter. *The Bible, Protestantism, and the Rise of Natural Science.* Cambridge: Cambridge University Press, 1998.

———. *The Territories of Science and Religion.* Chicago: University of Chicago Press, 2015.

Harrison, Verna. "Perichoresis in the Greek Fathers." *St. Vladimir's Theological Quarterly* 35 (1991) 53–65.

Hart, David Bentley. *The Beauty of the Infinite: The Aesthetic of Christian Truth*. Grand Rapids: Eerdmans, 2003.

———. *The Experience of God: Being, Consciousness, Bliss*. New Haven: Yale University Press, 2013.

Hastings, W. Ross. *Jonathan Edwards and the Life of God: Towards an Evangelical Theology of Participation*. Minneapolis: Fortress, 2015.

———. *Missional God, Missional Church: Hope for Re-evangelizing the West*. Downers Grove, IL: IVP Academic, 2012.

Hefling, Charles, ed. *Charles Williams: Essential Writings in Spirituality and Theology*. Cambridge, MA: Cowley, 1993.

Hefner, Philip. "Religion and Science: Separateness or Co-inherence." *Zygon, Journal of Religion and Science* 41 (2006) 781–84.

Heisenberg, Werner. *Philosophie. Le manuscrit de 1942*. Translated with introduction by Catherine Chevalley. Paris: Seuil, 1998.

Hendry. George S. Review of *Karl Barth, His Life from Letters and Autobiographical Texts*, by Eberhard Busch. *Theology Today* 34 (1977) 194–98.

Henry, Carl F. H. *Horizons of Science: Christian Scholars Speak Out*. San Francisco: Harper & Row, 1978.

Hindmarsh, Bruce. *The Spirit of Early Evangelicalism: The Quest for True Religion in the Modern World*. New York: Oxford University Press, forthcoming 2018.

Hodge, Charles. "Princeton College and the General Assembly." *Nassau Literary Magazine* (1893) 137–38.

Hodge, Charles, and Mark A. Noll. *What Is Darwinism? And Other Writings on Science and Religion*. Grand Rapids: Baker, 1994.

Holmes, Stephen R. "Triune Creativity: Trinity, Creation, Art and Science." In *Trinitarian Soundings in Systematic Theology*, edited by Paul Louis Metzger, 73–85. London: T. & T. Clark, 2005.

Holmes, Stephen R., et al. *Two Views of the Doctrine of the Trinity*. Edited by Jason S. Sexton. Grand Rapids: Zondervan, 2014.

Honner, John. "A New Ontology: Incarnation, Eucharist, Resurrection and Physics." *Pacifica* 4 (1991) 15–50.

Hooykaas, Reijer. *Religion and the Rise of Modern Science*. Grand Rapids: Eerdmans, 1972.

Hopkins, Gerard Manley. "God's Grandeur." 1877. http://www.sparknotes.com/poetry/hopkins/section1.rhtml.

Howell, Kenneth J. *God's Two Books: Copernican Cosmology and Biblical Interpretation in Early Modern Science*. Notre Dame: University of Notre Dame Press, 2002.

Houston, James. *I Believe in the Creator*. Grand Rapids: Eerdmans, 1980.

Huxley, Julian. "The Evolutionary Vision." In *Evolution after Darwin*, vol. 3, *Issues in Evolution*, edited by Sol Tax and Charles Callender, 252–53. Oxford: University of Chicago Press, 1960.

Irenaeus. *Against Heresies*. http://www.newadvent.org/fathers/0103506.htm.

Jaeger, Werner, and Edward S. Robinson. *The Theology of the Early Greek Philosophers*. Oxford: Clarendon, 1947.

Jastrow, Robert. *God and the Astronomers*. New York: Norton, 1978.

Jeeves, Malcolm. *Human Nature: Reflections on the Integration of Psychology and Christianity*. Radnor, PA: Templeton, 2006.

———, ed. *Rethinking Human Nature: A Multidisciplinary Approach*. Grand Rapids: Eerdmans, 2011.

Jenson, Robert W. "Does God Have Time? The Doctrine of the Trinity and the Concept of Time in the Physical Sciences." *CTNS Bulletin* 11 (1991) 1–6.

John of Damascus. *An Exposition of the Orthodox Faith*. Translated by E. W. Watson and L. Pullan. Nicene and Post-Nicene Fathers, 2nd. ser., 9. Buffalo, NY: Christian Literature, 1899. Revised and edited for New Advent by Kevin Knight. http://www.newadvent.org/fathers/3304.htm.

———. *The Three Treatises on the Divine Images*. Translated by Andrew Louth. Yonkers, NY: St Vladimir's Seminary Press, 2003.

Judge, Edwin. "Commentary on Karl Popper." http://www.gospelconversations.com/who-are-we/edwin-judge.

Jüngel, Eberhard. *Karl Barth: A Theological Legacy*. Translated by G. E. Paul. Philadelphia: Westminster, 1986.

Kaiser, Christoper P. *Creation and the History of Science*. Grand Rapids: Eerdmans, 1991.

———. *Creational Theology and the History of Physical Science: The Creationist Tradition from Basil to Bohr*. Leiden: Brill, 1997.

———. *The Doctrine of God*. Eugene, OR: Wipf & Stock, 2001.

———. *Toward a Theology of Scientific Endeavour: The Descent of Science*. Aldershot, UK: Ashgate, 2007.

Keeton, William T., and James L. Gould. *Biological Science*. New York: Norton, 1993.

Kidner, Derek. *Genesis*. Tyndale Old Testament Commentaries 1. Downers Grove, IL: InterVarsity, 1967.

Kidwell, Jeremy. "Elucidating the Image of God: An Analysis of the Imago Dei in the Work of Colin E. Gunton and John Zizioulas." MCS thesis, Regent College, 2009.

Knight, Christopher C. *The God of Nature: Incarnation and Contemporary Science*. Minneapolis: Fortress, 2007.

Krötke, W. "Karl Barth's Anthropology." In *The Cambridge Companion to Karl Barth*, edited by John Webster, 159–76. Cambridge: Cambridge University Press, 2000.

Lamoureux, Denis O. *Evolutionary Creation: A Christian Approach to Evolution*. Eugene, OR: Wipf & Stock, 2008.

———. *I Love Jesus and I Accept Evolution*. Eugene, OR: Wipf & Stock, 2009.

Larsen, Duane H. *Times of the Trinity: A Proposal for Theistic Cosmology*. Worcester Polytechnic Institute Studies in Science, Technology and Culture. New York: Lang, 1995.

Larson, Edward J. *Summer for the Gods: The Scopes Trial and America's Continuing Debate over Science and Religion*. New York: Basic, 1997.

Lennox, John C. *God and Stephen Hawking: Whose Design Is It Anyway?* Oxford: Lion, 2010.

———. *God's Undertaker: Has Science Buried God?* Updated ed. Oxford: Lion, 2009.

———. *Seven Days That Divide the World: The Beginning according to Genesis and Science*. Grand Rapids: Zondervan, 2011.

Lindberg, David C. *The Beginnings of Western Science: The European Scientific Tradition in Philosophical, Religious, and Institutional Context, Prehistory to A.D. 1450*. 2nd ed. Chicago: University of Chicago Press, 2007.

———. *God and Nature: Historical Essays on the Encounter between Christianity and Science*. Berkeley: University of California Press, 1986.

———. *Reappraisals of the Scientific Revolution*. Cambridge: Cambridge University Press, 1990.

———. *When Science & Christianity Meet*. Chicago: University of Chicago Press, 2003.

Livingstone, David N. *Adam's Ancestors: Race, Religion, and the Politics of Human Origins*. Baltimore: Johns Hopkins University Press, 2008.

———. *Darwin's Forgotten Defenders: The Encounter between Evangelical Theology and Evolutionary Thought*. Grand Rapids: Eerdmans, 1987.

———. *Putting Science in Its Place Geographies of Scientific Knowledge*. Chicago: University of Chicago Press, 2003.

Livingstone, David N., and Mark A. Noll. "A Biblical Inerrantist as Evolutionist." *Isis* 91 (2000) 283–304.

Loder, James E., and W. Jim Neidhardt. *The Knight's Move: The Relational Logic of the Spirit in Theology and Science*. Colorado Springs: Helmers and Howard, 1992.

Lohdahl, Michael. *God of Nature and God of Grace: Reading the World in a Wesleyan Way*. Nashville: Kingswood, 2003.

Long, V. Philips. "Narrative and History: Stories about the Past." In *A Biblical History of Israel*, by Iain Provan et al., 75–97. Louisville: Westminster John Knox, 2003.

Longman, Tremper. *How to Read Genesis*. Downers Grove, IL: InterVarsity, 2005.

Lorenz, Edward N. "Deterministic Nonperiodic Flow." *Journal of the Atmospheric Sciences* 20 (1963) 130–41.

Lossky, Vladimir. *The Mystical Theology of the Eastern Church*. Cambridge: James Clark, 1957.

MacKay, Donald MacCrimmon. *Brains, Machines, and Persons*. Grand Rapids: Eerdmans, 1980.

Macmurray, John. *Persons in Relation*. Gifford Lectures, 1954. London: Faber & Faber, 1961.

———. *Science and the Quest for Meaning*. Grand Rapids: Eerdmans, 1982.

———. *The Self as Agent*. Gifford Lectures, 1953. London: Faber & Faber, 1957.

Madueme, Hans. "Adam and Eve: An Evangelical Impasse?—A Review Essay." *Christian Scholar's Review* 45 (2016) 165–83.

Mangina, Joseph L. *Karl Barth on the Christian Life: The Practical Knowledge of God*. Issues in Systematic Theology 8. New York: Lang, 2001.

Marcel, Gabriel. *Being and Having*. Milton Keynes: Andesite, 2015.

———. *The Mystery of Being*. Translated by G. S. Fraser. South Bend, IN: St. Augustine, 2001.

Markham, Paul N. *Rewired: Exploring Religious Conversion*. Eugene, OR: Pickwick, 2007.

McCormack, Bruce L. Review of *The Holy Spirit and the Christian Life: The Theological Basis of Ethics*, by Karl Barth. *Princeton Seminary Bulletin* 15 (1994) 312–14.

McFadyen, Alistair. *Call to Personhood: A Christian Theory of the Individual in Social Relationships*. Cambridge: Cambridge University Press, 1990.

———. "Trinity and Human Individuality: The Conditions for Relevance." *Theology* 95 (1992) 10–18.

McGilchrist, Iain. *The Master and His Emissary: The Divided Brain and the Making of the Western World*. New Haven: Yale University Press, 2012.

McGrath, Alister E. *Dawkins' God*. Malden, MA: Wiley-Blackwell, 2004.

———. *Dawkins' God: Genes, Memes, and the Meaning of Life*. Malden, MA: Blackwell, 2005.

———. *A Fine-Tuned Universe: Science, Theology and the Quest for God*. Gifford Lectures, 2009. Philadelphia: Westminster John Knox, 2009.

———. *A Fine-Tuned Universe: The Quest for God in Science and Theology*. Lousiville: Westminster John Knox, 2004. See especially chapter 6.

———. *The Foundations of Dialogue in Science and Religion*. Malden, MA: Blackwell, 1998.

———. *The Re-enchantment of Nature: Science, Religion and the Human Sense of Wonder*. London: Hodder & Stoughton, 2003.

———. *Science and Religion: A New Introduction*. 2nd ed. Malden, MA: Wiley-Blackwell, 2010.

———. *Science & Religion: A New Introduction*. Hoboken, NJ: Wiley, 2011.

———. *Science & Religion: An Introduction*. Oxford: Blackwell, 1999.

———. *The Science of God: An Introduction to Scientific Theology*. Grand Rapids: Eerdmans, 2004.

———. *A Scientific Theology*. Vol. 1, *Nature*. Vol. 2, *Reality*. Vol. 3, *Theory*. Grand Rapids: Eerdmans, 2001.

———. *T. F. Torrance: An Intellectual Biography*. Edinburgh: T. & T. Clark, 1999.

McGrath, Alister E., and Joanna Collicutt McGrath. *The Dawkins Delusion: Atheist Fundamentalism and the Denial of the Divine*. Downers Grove, IL: InterVarsity, 2007.

McKirland, Christa L. "The Image of God and Intersex Persons." Paper presented at the Logos Institute, St. Mary's College, University of St. Andrews, October 12, 2016.

Meyer, Stephen. *Darwin's Doubt*. New York: HarperOne, 2013.

———. *The Signature of the Cell*. New York: HarperOne, 2010.

Milliner, Matthew J. "Who's Afraid of the Analogia Entis?" Millinerd.com (Milliner's blog). December 16, 2006. http://www.millinerd.com/2006/12/whos-afraid-of-analogia-entis.html.

Moltmann, Jürgen. *God in Creation: A New Theology of Creation and the Spirit of God*. Minneapolis: Fortress, 1993.

———. "God's Kenosis in the Creation and Consummation of the World." In *The Work of Love: Creation as Kenosis*, edited by John Polkinghorne, 137–51. Grand Rapids: Eerdmans, 2001.

———. "Perichoresis: An Old Magic Word for a New Trinitarian Theology." In *Trinity, Community and Power: Mapping Trajectories in Wesleyan Theology*, edited by Douglas M. Meeks, 111–25. Nashville: Kingswood, 2000.

Moore, James R. *The Post-Darwinian Controversies: A Study of the Protestant Struggle to Come to Terms with Darwin in Great Britain and America, 1870–1900*. Cambridge: Cambridge University Press, 1981.

Mouw, Richard. *When the Kings Come Marching In: Isaiah and the New Jerusalem*. Rev. ed. Grand Rapids: Eerdmans, 2002.

Mullins, Ryan. "In Search of a Timeless God." Thesis submitted for the degree of PhD at the University of St Andrews, 2013.

Murphy, George L. *The Cosmos in the Light of the Cross*. Harrisburg, PA: Trinity, 2003.

———. *Pulpit Science Fiction*. Lima, OH: CSS, 2005.

———. "The Third Article in the Science-Theology Dialogue." *Perspectives on Science and Christian Faith* 45 (1993) 162–68.

Murphy, Nancey. *Bodies and Souls, or Spirited Bodies?* New York: Cambridge University Press, 2006.

Murphy, N., and W. S. Brown. *Did My Neurons Make Me Do It? Philosophical and Neurobiological Perspectives on Moral Responsibility and Free Will.* Oxford: Clarendon, 2007.

Nagel, Thomas. *Mind and Cosmos: Why the Materialist Neo-Darwinian Conception of Nature Is Almost Certainly False.* New York: Oxford University Press, 2012.

Neder, Adam. *Participation in Christ: An Entry into Karl Barth's Church Dogmatics.* Louisville: Westminster John Knox, 2009.

Neidhardt, W. Jim. "Biblical Humanism: The Tacit Grounding of James Clerk Maxwell's Creativity." *Perspectives on Science and Christian Faith* 41 (1989) 137–42.

———. Introduction to *The Christian Frame of Mind: Reason, Order and Openness in Theology and Natural Science*, by T. F. Torrance. Eugene, OR: Wipf & Stock, 2010.

Nesteruk, Alexei V. "Design in the Universe and the Logos of Creation: Patristic Synthesis and Modern Cosmology." In *Design and Disorder: Perspectives from Science and Theology*, edited by Niels Henrik Gregersen and Ulf Görman, 171–202. London: T. & T. Clark, 2002.

———. *Light from the East: Theology, Science and the Eastern Orthodox Tradition.* Minneapolis: Fortress, 2003.

Newbigin, Lesslie. *Proper Confidence: Faith, Doubt, and Certainty in Christian Discipleship.* Grand Rapids: Eerdmans, 1995.

Nicolescu, Basarab. "The Idea of Levels of Reality: Its Relevance for Non-Reduction and Personhood." *Transdisciplinarity in Science and Religion* 4 (2008) 11–25.

Nichols, Terence L. *The Sacred Cosmos: Christian Faith and the Challenge of Naturalism.* Grand Rapids: Brazos, 2003.

Noll, Mark. *The Princeton Theology.* Grand Rapids: Baker, 1983.

———. *The Scandal of the Evangelical Mind.* Grand Rapids: Eerdmans, 1994.

Numbers, Ronald L. *Science and Christianity in Pulpit and Pew.* Oxford: Oxford University Press, 2007.

O'Donovan, Oliver. "The Language of Rights and Conceptual History." *Journal of Religious Ethics* 37 (2009) 193–207.

———. *Resurrection and the Moral Order: An Outline for Evangelical Ethics.* Grand Rapids: Eerdmans, 1986.

Olson, Roger. "Wolfhart Pannenberg's Doctrine of the Trinity." *Scottish Journal of Theology* 43 (1990) 175–206.

Oord, Thomas Jay, ed. *Divine Grace and Emerging Creation: Wesleyan Forays in Science and Theology of Creation.* Eugene, OR: Pickwick, 2009.

Osborn, Robert T. *Freedom in Modern Theology.* Philadelphia: Westminster, 1967.

Ott, Ludwig. *Manual de Teología Dogmática.* Barcelona: Herder, 1969.

Otto, Randall E. "The Use and Abuse of Perichoresis in Recent Theology." *Scottish Journal of Theology* 54 (2001) 366–84.

Padgett, Alan G. *Science and the Study of God: A Mutuality Model for Theology and Science.* Grand Rapids: Eerdmans, 2003.

Pannenberg, Wolfhart. *The Historicity of Nature: Essays on Science and Theology.* Edited by Niels Henrik Gregersen. West Conshohocken, PA: Templeton, 2008.

———. "The Question of God." In *Basic Questions in Theology*, translated by G. H. Kehm, 2:228–32. London: SCM Press, 1971.

———. *Systematic Theology*. Translated by Geoffrey W. Bromiley. 3 vols. Grand Rapids: Eerdmans, 1991–94. For Spirit agency, see I:383 and II:83–84.
Peacocke, A. R. *Paths from Science towards God: The End of All Our Exploring*. Oxford: Oneworld, 2001.
Pelikan, Jaroslav. *Bach among the Theologians*. Philadelphia: Fortress, 1986.
Pembroke, Neil. "Space in the Trinity and Pastoral Care." *Journal of Pastoral Care and Counselling* 65 (2011) 3.1–10.
Peters, Ted. "The Trinity In and Beyond Time." In *Quantum Cosmology and the Laws of Nature: Scientific Perspectives on Divine Action*, edited by Robert John Russell et al., 263–89. 1993. Reprint. Vatican City and Berkeley: Vatican Observatory and the Center for Theology and the Natural Sciences, 1999.
Phillips, J. B. *Your God Is Too Small: A Guide for Believers and Skeptics Alike*. New York: Touchstone, 1952.
Pinnock, Clark. "The Other Hand of God: God's Spirit in an Age of Scientific Cosmology." *Stone-Campbell Journal* 9 (2006) 205–30.
Placher, William Carl. *Unapologetic Theology: A Christian Voice in a Pluralistic Conversation*. Louisville: Westminster John Know, 1989.
Poe, Harry Lee, and Jimmy H. Davis. *God and the Cosmos: Divine Activity in Space, Time, and History*. Downers Grove, IL: IVP Academic, 2012.
Polanyi, Michael. *Personal Knowledge: Towards a Post-Critical Philosophy*. Enlarged ed. Chicago: University of Chicago Press, 2015.
Polanyi, Michael, and Amartya Sen. *The Tacit Dimension*. Chicago: University of Chicago Press, 2009.
Polkinghorne, John C. *Belief in God in an Age of Science*. New Haven: Yale University Press, 1998.
———. *Exploring Reality: The Intertwining of Science and Religion* New Haven: Yale University Press, 2005.
———. *Faith, Science and Understanding*. New Haven: Yale University Press, 2000.
———. "Kenotic Creation and Divine Action." In *The Work of Love: Creation as Kenosis*, edited by John Polkinghorne, 90–106. Grand Rapids: Eerdmans, 2001.
———. *One World: The Interaction of Science and Theology*. London: SPCK, 1986. Repr., Princeton University Press, 1987.
———. *One World: The Interaction of Science and Theology*. Philadelphia: Templeton Foundation, 2007.
———. *Quantum Physics and Theology: An Unexpected Kinship*. New Haven: Yale University Press, 2007.
———. *Quarks, Chaos & Christianity: Questions to Science and Religion*. New York: Crossroad, 1996.
———. *Reason and Reality: The Relationship between Science and Theology*. Philadelphia: Trinity, 1991.
———. *Science and Creation: The Search for Understanding*. Boston: Shambhala / New Science Library, 1989.
———. *Science and Providence: God's Interaction with the World*. Boston: Shambhala / New Science Library, 1989.
———. *Science and Religion in Quest of Truth*. New Haven: Yale University Press, 2012.
———. *Science and the Trinity: The Christian Encounter with Reality*. New Haven: Yale University Press, 2004.
———. *Science and Theology: An Introduction*. Minneapolis: Fortress, 1998.

———. *Scientists as Theologians: A Comparison of the Writings of Ian Barbour, Arthur Peacocke and John Polkinghorne*. London: SPCK, 1996.

———. *Serious Talk: Science and Religion in Dialogue*. Valley Forge: Trinity, 1995.

———. *Theology in the Context of Science*. New Haven: Yale University Press, 2009.

———. *Traffic in Truth: Exchanges between Science and Theology*. Norwich, UK: Canterbury, 2000. Repr., Minneapolis: Fortress, 2002.

———. *The Trinity and an Entangled World: Relationality in Physical Science and Theology*. Grand Rapids: Eerdmans, 2010.

———. "The Trinity and Scientific Reality." In *The Blackwell Companion to Science and Christianity*, edited by J. B. Stump and Alan G. Padgett, 523–32. Malden, MA: Wiley-Blackwell, 2012.

———. *The Way the World Is: The Christian Perspective of a Scientist*. Grand Rapids: Eerdmans, 1983.

Popper, Karl. *Conjectures and Refutations: The Growth of Scientific Knowledge* London: Routledge & Paul, 1963.

Prestige, G. L. *God in Patristic Thought*. London: SPCK, 1964.

Price, Daniel J. "Issues Related to Human Nature: Discovering a Dynamic Concept of the Person in Both Psychology and Theology." *American Science Affiliation*, from *Perspectives on Science and Christian Faith* 45 (1993) 170–80. http://www.asa3.org/ASA/PSCF/1993/PSCF9-93Price.html.

———. *Karl Barth's Anthropology in Light of Modern Thought*. Grand Rapids: Eerdmans, 2002.

Priest, Eric, ed. *Reason and Wonder: Why Science and Faith Need Each Other*. London: SPCK, 2016.

Prigogine, Ilya, and Isabelle Stengers. *Order Out of Chaos: Man's New Dialogue with Nature*. New York: Bantam, 1984.

Provan, Iain W. *Discovering Genesis*. London: SPCK, 2015.

———. *The Reformation and the Right Reading of Scripture*. Waco, TX: Baylor University Press, forthcoming fall 2017.

———. *Seriously Dangerous Religion: What the Old Testament Really Says and Why It Matters*. Waco, TX: Baylor University Press, 2014.

Puhalo, Lazar. *The Evidence of Things Not Seen: A Series of Lectures on Orthodoxy and Modern Physics*. 2nd ed. Dewdney, BC: Synaxis, 2005.

Putnam, Hilary. *Mathematics, Matter and Method: Philosophical Papers*. Vol. 1. Cambridge: Cambridge University Press, 1975.

Ramm, Bernard L. *The Christian View of Science and Scripture*. Grand Rapids: Eerdmans, 1954.

Rana, Fazale, and Hugh Ross. *Origins of Life*. Colorado Springs: NavPress, 2004.

———. *Who Was Adam?* Colorado Springs: NavPress, 2005.

Ratzinger, J. C. *Introduction to Christianity*. Translated by J. R. Foster. San Francisco: Ignatius, 2004.

Ratzsch, Delvin Lee. *Science & Its Limits: The Natural Sciences in Christian Perspective*. 2nd ed. Downers Grove, IL: InterVarsity, 2000.

Reno, R. R. "The Radical Orthodoxy Project." *First Things*, February 2000. https://www.firstthings.com/article/2000/02/the-radical-orthodoxy-project.

Rhodes, Ron. *The Ten Things You Should Know about the Creation vs. Evolution Debate*. Eugene, OR: Harvest House, 2004.

Ridler, Anne, ed. *The Image of the City, and Other Essays*. London: Oxford University Press, 1958.
Romero-Baró, José M. "God's Mark on Nature. A Trinitarian Approach." *Science and Religion: Global Perspectives*, a program of the Metanexus Institute, Philadelphia, June 4–8, 2005.
Ross, Allen. *Creation and Blessing*. Grand Rapids: Baker, 1988.
Ross, Hugh. *Beyond the Cosmos*. 2nd ed. Colorado Springs: NavPress, 1999.
———. *Creation and Time*. Colorado Springs: NavPress, 1994.
———. *Creation as Science*. Colorado Springs: NavPress, 2006.
———. *The Creator and the Cosmos: How the Latest Scientific Discoveries of the Century Reveal God*. Colorado Springs: NavPress, 2001.
———. *The Fingerprint of God*. New Kensington, PA: Whitaker House, 2000.
———. *The Genesis Question*. Colorado Springs: NavPress, 1998.
———. *A Matter of Days*. Colorado Springs: NavPress, 2004.
Russell, Bertrand. *The History of Western Philosophy*. New York: Simon & Schuster, 1973.
Russell, Colin Archibald. *Cross-Currents: Interactions between Science and Faith*. Grand Rapids: Eerdmans, 1985.
Russell, Robert John. "Is the Triune God the Basis for Physical Time." *CTBS Bulletin* 11 (1991) 7–19.
Rüst, Peter. "Early Humans, Adam, and Inspiration." *Perspectives on Science and Christian Faith* 59 (2007) 182–93.
Rutledge, Jonathan. "Philosophical Arminianism: Epistemic Conditionals of Creaturely Freedom." Paper presented at the Logos Institute, University of St Andrews, Scotland, November 24, 2016, soon to be published in the *Journal of Faith and Philosophy*.
Sailhamer, John. *Genesis*. In *Genesis, Exodus, Leviticus, Numbers*. Expositor's Bible Commentary 2. Grand Rapids: Zondervan, 1990.
———. *Genesis Unbound*. Sisters, OR: Multnomah, 1996.
Sarna, Nahum.*Understanding Genesis*. New York: Schocken, 1976.
Schmemann, Alexander. *For the Life of the World: Sacraments and Orthodoxy*. Rev. ed. Crestwood, NY: St. Vladimir's Seminary Press, 1973.
Scholder, Klaus. *The Birth of Modern Critical Theology: Origins and Problems of Biblical Criticism in the Seventeenth Century*. Salem, OR: Trinity, 1990.
Schwöbel, Christoph, ed. *Trinitarian Theology Today*. Edinburgh: T. & T. Clark, 1995.
Schwöbel, Christoph, and Colin Gunton, eds. *Persons Divine and Human*. For the Research Institute in Systematic Theology. Edinburgh: T. & T. Clark, 1991.
Scotus, John Duns. *Ordinatio*, II.d.3, pt. 1. In *Five Texts on the Mediaeval Problem of Universals: Porphyry, Boethius, Abelard, Duns Scotus, Ockham*, edited and translated by Paul V. Spade, 57–113. Indianapolis: Hackett, 1994.
Shapin, Steven. *The Scientific Revolution*. Chicago: University of Chicago Press, 1996.
Shults, F. LeRon. *Christianity and Science*. Grand Rapids: Eerdmans, 2008.
Simmons, Ernest I. "Toward a Kenotic Pneumatology: Quantum Field Theory and the Theology of the Cross." *CTNS Bulletin* 19 (1999) 11–16.
Smith, James K. A. *Introducing Radical Orthodoxy: Mapping a Post-Secular Theology*. Grand Rapids: Baker Academic, 2004.
Snow, C. P. *The Two Cultures*. Canto Classics. Cambridge: Cambridge University Press, 1998.

Spencer, Archie J. *The Analogy of Faith: The Quest for God's Speakability.* Downers Grove, IL: IVP Academic, 2015.

Stafleu, M. D. *Time and Again: A Systematic Analysis of the Foundations of Physics.* Toronto: Wedge, 1980.

Stump, Jim. "Randall Zachman on Calvin's Support of Science." *BioLogos,* October 30, 2015. http://biologos.org/blogs/jim-stump-faith-and-science-seeking-understanding/randall-zachman-on-calvins-support-of-science.

Sullivan, Harry S. *The Interpersonal Theory of Psychiatry.* Vols. 1 and 2 of *The Collected Works of Harry Stack Sullivan.* New York: Norton, 1953, 1956.

Switzer, David K. *Dynamics of Grief.* Nashville: Abingdon, 1970.

Szerszynski, Bronislaw. *Nature, Technology and the Sacred.* Chichester: Wiley-Blackwell, 2005.

Tanner, Kathryn. *God and Creation in Christian Theology: Tyranny or Empowerment?* Oxford: Blackwell, 1988.

Teel, Paul. "Christian Theology and the Modern Science of Nature: A Critical Analysis of Michael Beresford Foster's Mind Articles." Thesis submitted in partial fulfillment of MA requirements, University of Victoria, 2006. https://dspace.library.uvic.ca:8443/handle/1828/2152.

Thiel, John E. *Non-foundationalism.* Minneapolis: Fortress, 1994.

Thomas, Lewis. *The Lives of a Cell: Notes of a Biology Watcher.* New York: Viking, 1974.

Thompson Curtis L., and Joyce M. Cuff. *God and Nature: A Theologian and a Scientist Conversing on the Divine Promise of Possibility.* New York: Continuum, 2012.

Torrance, Alan. *Persons in Communion: An Essay on Trinitarian Description and Human Participation with Special Reference to Volume One of Karl Barth's "Church Dogmatics."* Edinburgh: T. & T. Clark, 1996.

Torrance, Thomas F. *The Christian Doctrine of God: One Being Three Persons.* Edinburgh: T. & T. Clark, 1996.

———. *The Christian Frame of Mind: Reason, Order and Openness in Theology and Natural Science.* Eugene, OR: Wipf & Stock, 2010.

———. "Christian Faith and Physical Science in the Thought of James Clerk Maxwell." In *Transformance and Convergence in the Frame of Knowledge,* 215–42. Grand Rapids: Eerdmans, 1984.

———. Faith and Physics Memorial Lectures, Gordon College Media Center, Wenham, MA, February 27, 1983.

———. *The Ground and Grammar of Theology.* Charlottesville: University of Virginia Press, 1980.

———. "Intuitive and Abstractive Knowledge: From Duns Scotus to Calvin." In *De Doctrina Duns Scoti, Congressus Scotisticus Internationalis,* edited by C. Balic, 291–305. Studia Scholastico-Scotistica 5. Rome: Societas Internationalis Scotistica, 1968.

———. "The Problem of Natural Theology in the Thought of Karl Barth." *Religious Studies* 6 (1970) 121–35.

———. *Reality and Evangelical Theology.* Philadelphia: Westminster, 1982.

———. *Reality and Scientific Theology.* Margaret Harris Lectures, Dundee, 1970. Theology and Science at the Frontiers of Knowledge 1. Edinburgh: Scottish University Press, 1985.

———. *Space, Time and Incarnation.* Edinburgh: T. & T. Clark, 2005.

———. *Theological and Natural Science.* Eugene, OR: Wipf & Stock, 2002.

———. "Theological Realism." In *The Philosophical Frontiers of Christian Theology: Essays Presented to D. M. McKinnon*, edited by B. Hebblethwaite and S. Sutherland, 169–96. Cambridge: Cambridge University Press, 1982.

———. *Theological Science*. Edinburgh: T. & T. Clark, 1996.

Turretin, Frances. *Institutes of Elenctic Theology*. Edited by James T. Dennison. Translated by George Musgrave Giger. Phillipsburg, NJ: P & R, 1992.

Van den Broek, Roelof. *Pseudo-Cyril of Jerusalem on the Life and the Passion of Christ: A Coptic Apocryphon, Supplements to Vigiliae Christianae*. Leiden: Brill, 2013.

Volf, Miroslav. *After Our Likeness: The Church as the Image of the Trinity*. Grand Rapids: Eerdmans, 1998.

———. *The Dramatis Personae: The Person in Christ*. Vol. 3 of *Theo-Drama: Theological Dramatic Theory*. Translated by G. Harrison. San Francisco: Ignatius, 1992.

———. *The Theology of Karl Barth*. Translated by E. T. Oakes. San Francisco: Ignatius, 1951, 1992.

Walsh, Brian J., and J. Richard Middleton. *The Transforming Vision: Shaping a Christian World View*. Downers Grove, IL: InterVarsity, 2009.

Waltke, Bruce, and Cathi J. Fredericks. *Genesis: A Commentary*. Grand Rapids: Zondervan, 2001.

Walton, John. *Genesis*. NIV Application Commentary. Grand Rapids: Zondervan, 2001.

———. *The Lost World of Genesis One: Ancient Cosmology and the Origins Debate*. Downers Grove, IL: IVP Academic, 2009.

Ward, Keith. *The Big Questions in Science and Religion*. West Conshohocken, PA: Templeton, 2008.

Warfield, Benjamin Breckinridge. *The Inspiration and Authority of the Bible*. Edited by Samuel G. Craig. Philadelphia: Presbyterian and Reformed, 1948.

Warfield, Benjamin Breckinridge, and Mark A. Noll. *Evolution, Scripture, and Science: Selected Writings*. Grand Rapids: Baker, 2000.

Webster, John. *Barth's Ethics of Reconciliation*. Cambridge: Cambridge University Press, 1995.

———. *Barth's Moral Theology: Human Action in Barth's Thought*. Edinburgh: T. & T. Clark, 1998.

———, ed. *The Cambridge Companion to Karl Barth*. Cambridge: Cambridge University Press, 2000.

———. "The Christian in Revolt: Some Reflections on the Christian Life." In *Reckoning with Karl Barth: Essays in Commemoration of the Centenary of Karl Barth's Birth*, edited by Nigel Biggar, 119–44. London: Mowbray, 1988.

———. "Eschatology, Anthropology and Postmodernity." *International Journal of Systematic Theology* 2 (2000) 124–39.

———. "Rescuing the Subject: Barth and Postmodern Anthropology." In *Karl Barth: A Future for Postmodern Theology?*, edited by G. Thompson and C. Mostert, 49–69. Adelaide, Australia: Openbook, 2000.

Welker, Michael. "God's Eternity, God's Temporality, and Trinitarian Theology." *Theology Today* 55 (1998) 317–28.

Wen, Clement Yung. "The Monergistic Theme of Participation in the Anthropological Soteriology of John Calvin: A Dialogue with Maximus the Confessor." Master of Christian Studies thesis, Regent College, 2011.

Wenham, Gordon. *Genesis 1–15*. Word Bible Commentary. Waxo, TX: Word, 1987.

Westermann, Claus. *Genesis 1–11*. London: *SPCK*, 1984, 1994.

Whitney, William B. *Problem and Promise in Colin E. Gunton's Doctrine of Creation.* Leiden: Brill, 2013.

Wilcox, David L. *God and Evolution: A Faith-Based Understanding.* Valley Forge, PA: Judson, 2004.

Wilkinson, David. "One World: Science and Christianity in Respectful Dialogue." January 20, 2011. http://biologos.org/blogs/archive/one-world-science-and-christianity-in-respectful-dialogue-part-1#sthash.s9X3lEtB.dpuf.

Wilkinson, Loren. "Cheeses, Chartreuse, Owls and a Synchrotron: Some Thoughts from France on Science and Taste." *Crux* 42 (2006) 9–10.

———. "The New Story of Creation: A Trinitarian Perspective." *Journal of the Faculty of Religious Studies, McGill* 23 (1995) 137–52.

Williams, Charles. "The Concept of Co-inherence in the Writings of Charles Williams." http://web.sbu.edu/friedsam/inklings/coinheretance.htm.

———. *Descent of the Dove: A Short History of the Holy Spirit in the Church.* Vancouver: Regent College Publishing, 1987.

———. *Figure of Beatrice: A Study of Dante.* London: Faber & Faber, 1943.

Witvliet, John. "The Doctrine of the Trinity and the Theology and Practice of Christian Worship in the Reformed Tradition." PhD diss., University of Notre Dame, 1997.

Wolterstorff, Nicholas. *Educating for Shalom: Essays on Christian Higher Education.* Edited by C. W. Joldersma and C.C. Stronks. Grand Rapids: Eerdmans, 2004.

Wright, N. T. *The New Testament and the People of God.* London: SPCK, 1992.

———. "Wouldn't You Love to Know? Towards a Christian View of Reality." Lecture presented as part of the Grasping the Nettle project, sponsored by the John Templeton fund, Glasgow, September 1, 2016.

Wybrow, Cameron. *Creation, Nature, and Political Order in the Philosophy of Michael Foster (1903–1959): The Classic Mind Articles and Others, with Modern Critical Essays.* Lewiston, NY: Mellen, 1992.

Yarchin, William. *History of Biblical Interpretation: A Reader.* Grand Rapids: Baker, 2011.

Yong, Amos. "From Quantum Mechanics to the Eucharistic Meal: John Polkinghorne's 'Bottom-up' Vision of Science and Theology." *Metanexus*, September 1, 2011. http://www.metanexus.net/book-review/quantum-mechanics-eucharistic-meal-john-polkinghornes-bottom-vision-science-and-theology.

———. *The Spirit of Creation: Modern Science and Divine Action in the Pentecostal-Charismatic Imagination.* Grand Rapids: Eerdmans, 2011.

Yong, Amos, and James K. A. Smith, eds. *Science and the Spirit: A Pentecostal Engagement with the Sciences.* Bloomington, IN: Indiana University Press, 2010.

Young, E. J. *Studies in Genesis One.* Grand Rapids: Baker, 1964.

Zachmann, Randall. "Free Scientific Inquiry and Faith—A Lesson from History." James Gregory Public Lectures on Science, Religion and Human Flourishing, University of St Andrews, September 28, 2015.

Zizioulas, John D. *Being In Communion: Studies in Personhood and the Church.* Contemporary Greek Theologians 4. Crestwood, NY: St. Vladimir's Seminary Press, 1997.

———. "The Doctrine of the Holy Trinity: The Significance of the Cappadocian Contribution." In *Trinitarian Theology Today: Essays on Divine Being and Act,* edited by Christoph Schwöbel, 44–60. Edinburgh: T. & T. Clark, 1995.

Name/Subject Index

Achtemeier, Mark T., 16, 52, 54, 61, 106, 108, 109, 124, 139, 159, 162
Agency, 12, 18, 32, 47, 57, 62, 84, 85, 87, 127, 136, 140, 142-62, 164, 165, 167, 173, 205
Alexander, Denis, 21, 38
Anthropology, 32, 35, 82, 101, 134, 137, 150-52, 168-202
Apophaticism, 40-43, 167, 220
Analogy of being (*analogia entis*), 179, 186, 189-92
Analogy of relations (*analogia relationis*), 4, 166, 168, 186, 193
Analogy of faith (*analogia fidé, adventus*) 179, 188-91
Apologetics, 7, 67, 89
Aquinas, Thomas, 24, 43, 47, 48, 52, 56, 108, 145, 165, 167, 212, 213, 217
Anselm of Canterbury, 54, 97, 101, 212
Aristotle, Aristotelianism, 40, 41, 48, 63-65, 69, 71, 91, 104, 109, 160, 192
Arts, 5, 6, 8, 18, 82, 89, 172, 174, 175, 178, 179, 183, 194, 206, 208, 209
Aufbau Principle, 130
Augustine of Hippo, 12, 40, 54, 56, 70, 87, 101, 102, 104, 133, 161, 178, 186, 190, 191, 192, 193, 194,199, 208, 211, 212, 214, 216, 217
Athanasius, 27, 28, 30, 139, 143, 160
Atkins, Peter, 9

Barbour, Ian, 20, 22, 25, 53, 119

Barth, Karl, 12, 23, 33, 35, 39, 43, 50, 54, 55, 64, 75, 97, 101, 105, 106, 108, 119, 126, 132, 134, 136-39, 143, 145-56, 160, 162, 163, 175, 178, 186, 189, 190-95, 199, 208, 211-17
Beauty, 7, 12, 18, 59, 86, 90, 96, 140, 168, 170, 174-76, 179-83, 191, 195, 198, 205, 206, 219-21
Big Bang Theory, 135, 138, 155, 160, 164
BioLogos, 1
Bhaskar, Roy, 112, 119
Bonaventure, 12, 165
Boyle, Robert, 64, 91
Bridging Concepts, 127
Bruno, Giordano, 41, 91, 141
Butterfly Effect, 133
Buxton, Graham, 39, 54, 55, 56, 157, 166, 167, 188

Calvin, John, Calvinism, 32, 33, 64, 70, 71, 72, 73, 74, 77, 81, 137, 148, 178, 184, 186, 193, 208, 217
Canlis, Julie, 32, 33, 34
Cappadocian Fathers, 4, 26, 28, 40, 49, 77, 125, 130, 167, 219
  Basil the Great, 28, 40
  Gregory of Nyssa, 28, 40, 219
  Gregory of Nazianzus, 26, 28
Capra, Fritjof, 77, 78
Carnap, Rudolph, 114
Chrysostom, John, 40
Circumincessio/Circuminsessio, 26, 29, 30, 31, 126

Name/Subject Index

Coe, Douglas E., 22
Collins, Francis, 1, 2, 22, 38
Colyer, Elmer, 52, 53, 158
Compatibilism, Asymmetric, 23, 146–52, 156, 159, 163, 167, 209, 210, 215, 216, 217
Complexification, 18, 164
Conciliar Theology, 23, 24, 58, 120, 206, 207, 208, 210, 211, 217
Conflict Model/Warfare Model, 2, 8, 9, 20, 23, 39, 54, 66, 88
Copernicus, 7, 41, 63, 67, 69, 72, 83, 91, 118, 141
Cosmology
 Copernican, 83, 89, 104, 118
 Newtonian, 79, 85, 87, 88, 92, 104, 131, 159, 160, 201, 215
 Ptolemaic, 63, 69, 104
Council of Chalcedon, Chalcedonian definition, 4, 48, 50
Creation, Doctrine of, 2, 7, 38, 42, 43, 45, 47, 50, 51, 52, 55, 56, 57, 59, 61, 62, 63, 65, 66, 68, 70, 72–76, 81, 82, 84, 85, 86, 87, 89, 90, 91, 93, 95, 96, 101, 105, 109, 110, 111, 117, 120, 123–27, 132–33, 134–47, 159–65, 177, 188–91, 197, 198, 213, 214, 216–22
Creation *ex nihilo*, 45, 47, 105, 138, 159, 160, 161, 163, 188, 197
Creation *ex vetere*, 163, 197, 198
Creation *continua*, 58, 197
Creationism, Young Earth, 24
Creed, Nicene/Niceno-Constantinopolitan, 109, 110, 158
Critical Realism, 8, 17, 18, 25, 43, 54, 61, 89, 96, 101–21, 122, 123, 124, 204, 205, 213
Cuff, Joyce M., 39, 57, 58
Culture, 2, 4, 5, 6, 8, 9, 14, 19, 25, 30, 39, 60, 61, 62, 63, 65, 69, 70, 71, 75, 76, 77, 82, 88, 99, 100, 101, 106, 140, 180, 193, 194
Cultural mandate, 7, 82, 89, 90, 171, 173, 177, 178, 211
Cupitt, Don, 118
Cyril of Alexandria, 35, 50, 148–49, 208, 215

Danaher, William, 119
Darwin, Charles/Darwinism, 10, 20, 44, 47, 71, 88, 89, 92, 93, 155, 156, 168
Darwinism, Universal, 10, 44
Davis, Edward, 112
Davis, Martin, 97, 98, 107
Dawkins, Richard, 9, 10, 44, 97
Death of Christ, Cross of Christ, 33, 144, 147, 154, 158, 166, 168, 198,
Deism, 8, 9, 58, 63, 64, 84–87, 92, 145, 152
Descartes, Rene, 86, 87, 91, 92, 97–99, 116
Design, Intelligent, 226, 229
Dualism, 4, 5, 7, 8, 9, 21, 23, 54, 75, 88, 92, 98–101, 104, 109, 110, 138, 173, 197, 212, 213, 215, 217, 218, 222

Eastern Orthodox Church, 3, 39, 49, 134, 206
Eckhart, Meister, 40
Edwards, Denis, 57
Edwards, Jonathan, 30, 64, 87, 118, 126, 145, 174, 183, 208, 219
Einstein, Albert, 13, 77, 78, 84, 104, 105, 110, 115, 123, 131, 159, 201, 214, 215
Empirical, Empiricism, 7, 8, 11, 12, 17, 19, 20, 22, 25, 40–45, 58, 62–69, 75, 78, 88, 98, 101–2, 106, 108–14, 117, 118, 120, 123, 124, 140, 141, 153, 156, 162, 165, 174, 181, 182, 214, 220
Enculturation, 69, 89
Enlightenment, the, 5, 9, 23, 54, 87, 89, 92, 97, 185, 199, 205, 217
Enns, Peter, 38
Epicureanism, 8, 9, 63, 90–92
Epistemology, 95–121
EPR (Einstein-Podolsky-Rosen) Effect, 131
Ethics, 1, 10, 91, 170, 180, 193, 194, 219

Fairbairn, Ronald, 186

Name/Subject Index 243

Faith/Reason, Understanding, 1, 5, 6, 7–9, 11, 14, 17, 20, 21, 23, 27, 41, 42, 48, 50, 53, 54, 58, 59, 60, 61, 63, 68, 88, 89, 91, 97, 101–3, 107, 111, 113, 120, 121, 124, 141, 167, 170, 179, 185, 189, 191, 192, 193, 195, 202, 205–8, 210, 212, 217
Falsificationism, 65, 113–16, 220
Fecundity, 18, 140, 164–65, 205
Fideism, 10, 97, 217
Flew, Anthony, 115
Florovsky, Georges, 40
Fundamentalism, 8, 9, 22, 40, 41, 89

Galileo, 41, 63, 67, 69, 72, 141
General Relativity, Theory of, 110, 131, 215
Gilkey, Langdon, 25, 38, 39
God
  Creator, 10, 11, 12, 15, 19, 21, 26, 32, 34, 57, 59, 63, 66, 68, 73, 84, 87, 88, 94, 96, 99, 107, 113, 120, 127, 133, 138, 140, 141, 152–58, 160, 166, 168, 170, 173, 174, 175, 178, 180, 182, 190, 195–207
  Energies of, 40, 41, 129, 157, 220
  Essence of, 10, 15, 26, 27, 28, 30, 32, 33, 40, 48, 50, 51
  Freedom of, 135–40
  Goodness of, 140
  Hiddenness of, 110, 167–68
  Immensity of, 141
  Providence of, 12, 19, 60, 127, 138, 146, 147, 152, 154, 155, 158, 163, 164
  Redeemer, 10, 11, 15, 34, 59, 196, 206
Gould, Stephen Jay, 20, 21, 105
Grand Unified Theory, 131
Gunton, Colin, 38, 39, 55, 78, 79, 125, 127, 133, 157, 166, 187

Habets, Myk, 13, 53, 105
Haeckel, Ernst, 133
Hanby, Michael, 38, 39, 42, 43, 44–52, 65, 85, 86, 87, 92, 93, 195
Hefner, Philip, 25, 39
Heisenberg, Werner, 77, 80, 81, 128

Heisenberg Uncertainty Principle, 81, 116, 128
Hick, John, 114
Hilary of Poitiers, 28
History of Ideas, 16, 48, 53, 60–94
Hodge, Charles, 21
Holy Spirit, 3, 25, 56–57, 104, 111, 126, 127, 134, 160, 162, 171, 179, 182, 190, 191, 200, 201, 204, 206
Homousios(n), 22, 76, 78, 98, 106, 109, 162, 200, 201
Human Genome Project, 22
Huxley, Julian, 19
Hypostasis, hypostases, *hypostaseis*, 3, 4, 27, 28, 29, 48, 49, 50, 51, 60, 103, 126, 185
Hypostatic Union, 22, 34, 35, 48, 49, 148, 150, 172, 185, 208, 225

Image of God, *imago Dei*, image-bearing, 134, 135, 136, 140, 148, 168, 169–202
Incarnation, 2, 4, 5, 13, 15, 16, 22, 23, 25, 26, 30–35, 38, 42, 43, 45–47, 50–52, 55, 62, 65–67, 75, 78, 87, 91, 93, 98, 105, 107–9, 120–24, 134, 140, 142–44, 147–49, 153–57, 161–63, 165–66, 168, 172–73, 188–89, 192–94, 197–98, 210, 214, 216–18
Incarnandus, 33, 62, 143–44, 154, 161
In-ness, 33, 210
Inculturation, 60
Individualism, 4, 77, 185
Irenaeus of Lyon, 11, 173, 178
Islam, 40

Jastrow, Robert, 14
John of the Cross, 40
John of Damascus, 16, 29, 40, 57, 109
John Philoponus of Alexandria, 29
Jüngel, Eberhart, 150, 189, 191

Kant, Immanuel, 97, 118
Kuyper, Abraham, Kuyperian, 81–82, 197

Lennox, John, 38

Name/Subject Index

Livingstone, David, 21, 38
Logical positivism, 17, 54, 64, 101, 114–15
Long, V. Philips, 38, 71
Longman III, Tremper, 38
Lorenz, Edward, 133
Lossky, Vladimir, 40, 220

MacMurray, John, 112, 185, 186
Madueme, Hans, 24
Maximus the Confessor, 26, 29, 34, 40, 48, 50
Maxwell, James Clerk, 13, 77–80, 104, 131
McFadyen, Alistair, 3
McGilchrist, Iain, 6–8, 19
McGrath, Alister, 8, 9. 10, 14, 38, 52–54, 63, 68–72, 83–85, 88, 105–6, 111–20, 205, 211, 213–15
McIntyre, Alasdair, 97
McKnight, Scot, 71
Methexis, 32, 75, 111, 138, 160, 217
Meyendorrf, John, 40
Milbank, John, 75, 151
Modalism, 15, 27
Modernism/Modernity, 6, 7, 9, 54, 61, 63, 74–75, 86, 88–98, 112, 118, 136, 147, 180, 204, 217
Moltmann, Jürgen, 33, 38, 39, 55, 57, 108, 125, 153–54, 218
Monophysitism, 48
Monotheletism, 48
Music, 6, 65, 174–75, 194, 198
Mutuality Model, 22–23, 234
Mystery, 3, 14, 25, 39, 42, 48, 110, 112, 127, 141, 142, 146, 159, 204, 216, 219

Neidhardt, Jim, 13, 14, 76, 79
Neo-Darwinism, 89, 92
NeoPlatonism, 40, 63, 69, 75, 109, 111, 119, 146
Nesteruk, Alexei, 38
Newton, Isaac, Newtonian, 8, 63, 64, 77, 79, 83–88, 92, 104, 131, 159–60, 201, 215
Noll, Mark, 6, 21–22, 38, 97
Nominalism, 41

Nonrealism, 120–21
Numbers, Ronald, 38
O'Donovan, Oliver, 3, 170, 173
Oord, Thomas Jay, 38
Osborn, Robert, 137
Ousia, 3, 27, 29, 48, 60, 103, 126

Packer, J.I. 30
Padgett, Alan, 10, 22–23, 101, 161
Palamas, Gregory, 40
Panentheism, 33
Pannenberg, Wolfhart, 4, 11, 38, 125
Peacocke, Arthur, 119
Periodic Table, 64, 128–29, 166, 181
Philoponus, 29
Pickstock, Catherine, 75,
Polanyi, Michael, 13, 54, 97, 98, 110–13, 201
Polkinghorne, John, 1, 2, 12, 13, 14, 18, 22, 38, 39, 42, 58–59, 103, 111–12, 116–17, 119, 128, 131–34, 151, 152–57, 163–64, 168, 176, 179, 181–82, 203–4, 209, 211–13, 215–16, 218
Popper, Karl, 64–65, 114–15, 220
Postmodernism/Postmodernity, 9, 19, 61, 75, 89, 93, 96–97, 214
Prestige, G.L. 26–29, 34–35
Provan, Iain, 38, 62, 71, 72, 197
Pseudo-Cyril of Jerusalem, 29
Pseudo-Dionysius, 40
Public Square, 5, 21, 86, 101, 193
Puhalo, Lazar, 38–43, 56, 165, 219, 220

Queen of Sciences, Theology as, 15, 23, 24, 201, 206, 208

Radical Orthodoxy, 7, 22, 75, 82, 89, 96, 97, 151, 207
Rana, Fazale, 236
Reconciliation, 23, 31, 33, 105, 126, 143, 150, 163, 175, 197
Redemption, 10, 23, 33, 34, 81, 82, 105, 126, 134, 136, 150, 163, 197, 208, 221
Relationality, 3, 4, 18, 32, 55, 56, 59, 80, 124, 125, 127, 128–35, 140,

168, 169, 170, 172, 173, 175, 177, 184, 195, 202, 205
Resurrection, of Christ, of humanity, 17, 23, 31, 62, 63, 65, 89, 108, 159, 163, 172, 173, 175, 185, 194, 197, 198
Romanides, John S. 40
Romero-Baró, José M., 39, 56–57, 130
Ross, Hugh, 236
Russell, Bertrand, 66, 114

Sacks, Jonathan, 10
Schlick, Moritz, 113
Scholastic theology/Scholasticism, 40, 41, 43, 91, 125, 161, 220
Schwöbel, Christoph, 127
Science
  Astronomy, 14, 71, 73, 74, 141, 208
  Biology, Evolutionary Biology, 44, 56, 92, 93, 114, 199,
  Chemistry, ix, 1, 56, 119, 127–30, 133, 183, 220
  Physics, Modern, 6, 104
  Physics, Quantum, 41, 98, 99, 113, 127, 181
  Psychology, 71, 156, 186, 199, 205
  Sociology, 186, 199
  Thermodynamics, Second Law, 6
Scientism, 8, 9, 44, 63, 88, 93, 97, 101, 118, 141, 195
Scotus, Duns, 41, 77, 165–66, 201
Smith, James K. A., 7, 22, 82, 89, 96, 97, 206
Snow, C.P., 6, 8, 19
Southgate, Chris, 38
Spencer, Archie, 189, 191, 238
Stewardship of creation, 2, 7, 21, 23, 65, 134, 195, 219, 221

Technology, 88, 115, 180, 195
Theory of Everything, 38, 59, 203–22
Theotokos, 51
Thisness/*haeccitas*, 41, 92, 166
Thompson, Curtis L., 39, 57–58
Torrance, Alan, ix, 4, 38, 125
Torrance, T.F. 11, 24, 52, 53, 60, 79, 98, 106–8, 158–64, 200

Trace, Traces (of God in creation), 4, 5, 12, 16, 17, 26, 27, 32, 35, 37, 55, 56, 59, 61, 82, 96, 109, 123, 124, 127–30, 133, 134, 140–41, 142, 145, 148, 151, 155, 164–68, 169, 171, 183, 191, 203–4
Transcendence, Transcendence and Immanence, 3, 7, 8, 11, 26, 31, 40, 42–43, 46, 57, 68, 85–87, 89, 94, 107, 108, 120, 126–27, 139, 141, 157, 160, 167, 188–89, 191, 205–6
Trinity
  Persons-in-Relation, 3, 12, 32, 78, 103, 125, 130, 132, 184–85
  Psychological Model, 56,
  Persons as Relations, 125
Trinitarianism
  Classical Trinitarianism, 125, 132
  Social Trinitarianism, 125, 130
Tritheism, 27, 28, 29

Verificationism, 17, 113–15
vestigia trinitatis, 12
Vienna Circle, 64, 113
Vocation, 4, 7, 15, 18, 25, 34, 53, 169–71, 173, 178–80, 188, 196–200, 206, 218, 220–22
  Vocation of a Scientist, 200–202, 218–22
Von Balthasar, Hans Urs, 130, 219
Von Fraassen, Bas, 118

Waltke, Bruce, 38, 71
Walton, John, 38, 71
Watts, Rikk, 71
Warfield, B.B. 21
Wilkinson, Loren, 38, 66, 67, 68, 195, 222
William of Occam, 41
Williams, Charles, 27, 30–31
Wiseman, Jennifer, 38
Witvliet, John, 127
Wright, N.T. ix, 9, 38, 71, 82, 92, 121

X-Ray Crystallography, 103, 113

Yong, Amos, 153, 155, 156–57, 158, 159

Zizioulas, John, 3, 4, 30, 49, 59, 125, 134

www.ingramcontent.com/pod-product-compliance
Lightning Source LLC
Chambersburg PA
CBHW031728230426
43669CB00007B/287